GUIDANCE AND COUNSELLING

GUIDANCE AND COUNSELLING

Arul Jothi
M.Sc., M.Ed.
Principal, Arcot Sri Mahalakshmi Women's Teacher Training Institute,
Villapakkam, Vellore Dist.-632521 T.N.

Dr. D.L. Balaji
B.Com., M.A., M.Phil., D.Lit.,
Correspondent, Arcot Sri Mahalakshmi Educational Institutions,
Villapakkam, Vellore Dist.-632521 T.N.

Pratiksha Jugran
Lecturer, Deptt. of Education,
Drona College of Management and Technical Education,
Dehradun

CENTRUM PRESS
NEW DELHI-110002 (INDIA)

CENTRUM PRESS
H.O.: 4360/4, Ansari Road, Daryaganj,
New Delhi-110 002 (India)
Ph.: 23278000, 23261597

B.O.: No. 1015, Ist Main Road, BSK IIIrd Stage
IIIrd Phase, IIIrd Block,
Bangalore - 560 085 (India)
Tel.: 080-41723429
Visit us at: www.centrumpress.com

Guidance and Counselling

First Edition, 2009

PRINTED IN INDIA

Printed at Balaji Offset, Delhi

Contents

Preface (*vii*)

UNIT-I : Guidance **1**
Guidance—Meaning, Definitions, Aims Nature, Principles and Needs • Types of Guidance—Educational Guidance • Vocational Guidance • Personal Guidance • Relationship between Guidance and Counseling

UNIT-II : Counselling **25**
Counselling—Meaning, Definitions, Elements-Characteries—Objectives—Need • Types of Counselling • Directive Counseling • Nondirective Counseling • Eclectic Counseling—Meaning—Characteristics—Steps—Advantages—Limitations • Difference between Counseling and Guidance

UNIT-III : Guidance Movement in India **43**
History of Guidance Movements in India • Problems of Guidance Movement in India • Ways to Improve Guidance Movement in India

UNIT-IV : Qualities of a Counsellor **58**
Differences between Consellor and Teacher

UNIT-V : Group Guidance and Group Counselling **83**
Group Guidance—Meaning—Definition—Objectives—Problems—Significance—Techniques—Uses • Group Counselling—Meaning, Requirements—Uses

UNIT-VI : Theories of Vocational Choice **100**
Louis Ginzberg • Super's ability Related Theory • John Holland • Robert Havighurst • Fairbairn's Structural Theory

UNIT-VII : Non-Testing Devices in Guidance **153**
Non-testing Devices in Guidance • Observation • Cumulative Record • Anecdotal Record • Case Studies • Autobiography • Rating Scales • Sociometry

UNIT-VIII : Testing Devices in Guidance 172

Testing Devices in Guidance—Meaning, Definition, Measurement • Use of Psychological Tests • Intellegence Tests • Aptitude Test • Personality Inventories • Attitude Scales • Achievement Tests • Creativity Tests • Mental Health • Frustration • Conflict

UNIT-IX : Guidance Services in Schools 210

Guidance Services at Different School Levels-Meaning, Significance, Types • Organization of Guidance Services in Schools • Role of Guidance Personnel • Career and Occupational Information—Sources, Gathering, Filling, Dissemination, Career Corner—Career Conference

UNIT-X : Guidence for Exceptional Children 263

Guidance for Exceptional Children—Meaning and Types • Guidance for Gifted, Backward, Mentally retarded, Orthopaedically Handicapped, Visually Impaired, Deaf and Dumb, Juvenile Delinquents

Bibliography 282

Index 286

Preface

Guidance is assistance given to an individual to help him, to adjust to himself, to others and to his own peculiar environment. Guidance helps him to understand himself. It helps him in his acquaintance with the things and the world around him. Finally, it helps the person to seek harmony between his personal needs and ambitions with peculiarities of his own environment. In this way, guidance can be described as a process of assisting an individual with his adjustment problems. Thus, according to Jones, "Guidance is the help given by one person to another in making choices and adjustments and in solving problems". While Skinner says "Guidance is a process of helping young persons learns to adjust to self, to others, and to circumstances". Guidance aims to prepare an individual for his future life. It helps him to acquire essential skills, abilities and capacities for the tasks to be accomplished in future. It also helps the individual in selecting a proper future profession and role in the society and enables him to play his role successfully. Guidance has personal and social significance. It aims to help an individual in the process of his adjustment with himself and his environment. It helps him to develop his strengths and abilities, to achieve utmost personal and social efficiency. It also aims to stop wastage of human power and physical resources by helping the individuals to find their place in society. Thus, we can say that Guidance is the process of helping an individual to help himself and to develop his potentialities to the fullest by utilizing the maximum opportunities provided by the environment.

On the other hand, Counselling is the service offered to the individual, who is undergoing a problem and needs professional help to overcome it. The problem keeps him disturbed, high strung, under tension and unless solved, his development is hampered or stunted. Counselling therefore, is a more specialized service requiring training in personality development and handling exceptional groups of individuals. For example, individuals suffering from sensory handicaps like, visually handicapped, deaf and mute, speech disorders, or from physical handicaps like malfunctioning of glands or vital organs; orthopaedically handicapped; personal-social handicaps like, neurotics, psychotics, depressed isolates or from intellectual retardation or exceptionally high talent and so on. In other words, when the development is not normal because of certain handicaps, the individual needs help to be able to adjust to the environmental pressures and learn to overcome his handicaps or at least accept them squarely. Counselling services are therefore, required for individuals having developmental problems, because of the handicap they suffer in any area of growth like, physical, mental, moral, social and emotional, either because of hereditary factors or environmental conditions. Counselling therefore is offered to only those individuals who are under serious problem and need professional help to overcome it, while guidance is needed by all at any time. Both guidance and counselling assist the individual to know about himself, to adjust himself, with others and the environment and thus lead the individual to become a Wholesome Person.

This book explains how guidance and counselling can make a person realize his/her self. All these factors have been discussed horoughly in this book. Teachers, those who have to guide and counsel their students in matters relating to education, careers and personal problems, may find the book useful.

— *Pratiksha Jugran*

UNIT-I

Guidance

Guidance—Meaning, Definitions, Aims Nature, Principles and Needs

Guidance is assistance given to an individual to help him, to adjust to himself, to others and to his own peculiar environment. Guidance helps him to understand himself. It helps him in his acquaintance with the things and the world around him. Finally, it helps the person to seek harmony between his personal needs and ambitions with peculiarities of his own environment. In this way, guidance can be described as a process of assisting an individual with his adjustment problems. Thus, according to Jones, "Guidance is the help given by one person to another in making choices and adjustments and in solving problems". While Skinner says "Guidance is a process of helping young persons learns to adjust to self, to others, and to circumstances".

Guidance aims to prepare an individual for his future life. It helps him to acquire essential skills, abilities and capacities for the tasks to be accomplished in future. It also helps the individual in selecting a proper future profession and role in the society and enables him to play his role successfully. Guidance has personal and social significance. It aims to help an individual in the process of his adjustment with himself and his environment. It helps him to develop his strengths and abilities, to achieve utmost personal and social efficiency. It also aims to stop wastage of human power and physical resources by helping the individuals to find their place in society.

Thus, we can say that Guidance is the process of helping an individual to help himself and to develop his potentialities to the fullest by utilizing the maximum opportunities provided by the environment.

On the other hand, Counselling is the service offered to the individual, who is undergoing a problem and needs professional help to overcome it. The problem keeps him disturbed, high strung, under tension and unless solved, his development is hampered or stunted. Counselling therefore, is a more specialized service requiring training in personality development and handling exceptional groups of individuals. For example, individuals suffering from sensory handicaps like, visually handicapped, deaf and mute, speech disorders, or from physical handicaps like malfunctioning of glands or vital organs; orthopaedically handicapped; personal-social handicaps like, neurotics, psychotics, depressed isolates or from intellectual retardation or exceptionally high talent and so on. In other words, when the development is not normal because of certain handicaps, the individual needs help to be able to adjust to the environmental pressures and learn to overcome his handicaps or at least accept them squarely.

Counselling services are therefore, required for individuals having developmental problems, because of the handicap they suffer in any area of growth like, physical, mental, moral, social and emotional, either because of hereditary factors or environmental conditions.

Counselling therefore is offered to only those individuals who are under serious problem and need professional help to overcome it, while guidance is needed by all at any time.

Both guidance and counselling assist the individual to know about himself, to adjust himself, with others and the environment and thus lead the individual to become a Wholesome Person.

Philosophy of Guidance

Guidance is universal and the basic principles of the philosophy of guidance are common to all countries with a slight modification to suit the locally accepted beliefs and the specific guidance services offered. The eight principles of the philosophy of guidance are:

1. The dignity of the individual is supreme.
2. Each individual is unique. He or she is different from every other individual.
3. The primary concern of guidance is the individual in his own social setting. The main aim being to help him to become a wholesome person and to gain fullest satisfaction in his life.
4. The attitudes and personal perceptions of the individual are the bases on which he acts.
5. The individual generally acts to enhance his perceived self.
6. The individual has the innate ability to learn and can be helped to make choices that will lead to self-direction, and make him consistent with the social environment.
7. The individual needs a continuous guidance process from early childhood through adulthood.
8. Each individual may, at times, need the information and personalized assistance best given by competent professional personnel.

The Goals to Achieve in Guidance

At present, Guidance has taken an unprecedented lead over all the other helping professions, for it empowers an individual to charter his life successfully, inspite of all odds.

The main goals are :

1. *Exploring-self:* The basic aim is to help an individual increase his understanding and acceptance of self; his physical development, his intelligence, aptitudes, interest, personality traits, attitudes and values, his achievements in scholastic and other spheres, his aspirations and life-style preferences and above all his here-and-now needs which keep him highly motivated to behave positively *or otherwise.*
2. *Determining Values:* The second aim is to help an individual recognize the importance of values, explore

different sets of values, determine personal values and examine them in relation to the norms of society and their importance in planning for success in life.

3. *Setting Goals:* This aim is to help an individual set goal for him self and relate these to the values determined by him so that he recognizes the importance of long-range planning.
4. *Explore the World of Work:* The aim here is to help the individual explore the World of Work in relation to his self-exploration, his value system and goals that he has set for himself to achieve success in life.
5. *Improving Efficiency:* The individual is helped to learn about factors which contribute to increase effectiveness and efficiency and to improve his study habits.
6. *Building Relationship:* The aim is to help the individual to be aware of his relationship with others and to note that it is a reflection of his own feelings about himself.
7. *Accepting responsibility for the future:* The individual is helped to develop skill in social and personal forecasting, acquire attitudes and skills necessary for mastering the future.

To sum up, guidance empowers him to be an integrated individual, actualizing his potential to the fullest.

Why Guidance?

Guidance is needed at every stage of development right from the beginning of life till the end. Everyone needs guidance at one time or the other. If properly guided, every individual will be satisfied in life.

Aim and Meaning of Spiritual Guidance

It is good to know how properly to practice asceticism in spiritual life: asceticism to be practiced in knowledge; spiritual ascent and transformation to be in knowledge; repentance in knowledge, obedience in knowledge, prayer in knowledge, deeds in knowledge, as the Holy Fathers say.

Awareness of where we stand at all times. To know what we strive after and in which direction we move every single moment. Christ to be our touchstone. Many times, in different contexts and studying the process of spiritual maturation from various aspects, we point out that there are three stages (levels) in the spiritual development of a person. The ascetical-hesychastic living Tradition names them as:

- First stage-purification of the heart from passions
- Second stage-illumination of the mind
- Third stage-deification of man's person.

Why is it necessary to repeat already said and even adopted things? Because we forget! Knowledge is preceded by ignorance, which is the greatest sin, as the Holy Fathers say. And, it is followed by forgetfulness! Knowledge is not a mental category in the Church. Knowledge is grace! It is a gift of the Holy Spirit by the prayers of the spiritual father. We acquire knowledge, it is given to us only through practice, through the graceful experience in the practice of obedience during which at first the energy of the mind is purified and then the mind is illumined and deified to its very essence or getfulness happens in the instance of repeated fall, falling away, losing grace, when we return to the life and deeds according to the passions of the old man.

Thus, to each of the above-mentioned stages there is a certain corresponding process of purification, of prayer, of temptations. To each of these three stages there is a corresponding priestly rank, when it comes to canonical ordination. To each of these stages there is also a corresponding mode of organisation of monastic life: Community (cenobium), Skete, Desert. At each of these three stages also occurs certain, specific and different for each level, spiritual relationship of the spiritual child with the spiritual father, which depends, among other things, on the stage in which each of them is. This relationship is dynamic. It passes from one level to another. It transforms.

The spiritual father gives birth (spiritually, by grace) to his spiritual child. And he has to raise him, to educate and bring him up, to set him free. This development is inevitable and takes place only in the Holy Mystery of the personal relationship between them, in the Church. Such a relationship can be unique, deep, sincere, loving. When the spiritual child is in the first stage of spiritual growth, the quality of this relationship depends, first of all, on the openness and the unreserved trust and obedience of the spiritual child to his father, and not as much on the holiness of the spiritual guide. Starting point of this relationship is the degree of darkness of ignorance and captivity by passions of the spiritual child, especially by the main one-vainglory.

It is necessary to reach the level at which the spiritual child experiences purification and opening of the heart (as a spiritual centre of our being) and gushing forth of the mind-and-heart prayer. Then their relationship most frequently becomes communion and exchange, in humility, of the graceful experience between brother and brother, brother and sister, in Christ. St. John the Baptist says: *He must become greater; I must become less.* So it is in the spiritual relationship of the spiritual father with his spiritual child: his supervision and guidance are diminishing more and more, in proportion of Christ's revelation and growth in the heart of the spiritual child.

Hence, the meaning of guidance in spiritual life through the personal relationship spiritual father-spiritual child is a new quality of relationships, growing in Christ, in the image and likeness of God: the Holy Trinity. And it is not a relationship as some understand it and which is most frequently found in the philosophic-religious systems of the Far East, in the form of once for all given idolatrous relationships: guru (master)-disciple.

What is the Starting Position?

Diagnosis of Our Disease: Within us, with various intensity, depending on the circumstances and the degree of inner spiritual maturity, three main passions are operating: self-indulgence, avarice, and vainglory. The main passion that closes our heart and severely obstructs the process of purification and spiritual growth is vainglory-pride, vanity.

Your heart is closed?! Examine yourself! A closed heart is a captured heart; captured by passions. But how do we know that most often because of high self-opinion (conceit), and not because of some other passion, our heart is closed? We recognise this by the form of the attack.

Here is how the process develops from the moment the demonic thought appears till we consent to it in our heart. At first, a thought is offered to us in the form of:

1. *a suggestion*-so the mind can indulge itself in
2. *conversation* with it-after which usually follows
3. *consent to the thought and bringing it down into the heart*-from which a desire for it to be realised is born.
4. *carrying* it *out*-if there is an opportunity for that.

How are you tempted by the passion of self-indulgence? A pleasure-indulgent thought assaults you. Depending on the spiritual stage you are in, you recognise the thought and you do not consent to it or-you struggle against it, then you rebut it or consent to it. If you consent to it, you can confess it, while you have not yet carried it out. Are you by any chance attacked by the passion of avarice? A thought assaults you. Then you rebut it. It assaults you again-you enter into dialogue with it. You have enough time and ways to defeat it, or else to confess it before sinning in deed. So, the usual process of development of a thought-from suggestion to deed-takes place.

Still, let us consider what happens when self-love is in question? If someone only for a moment just slightly steps on our pride, our vanity, high opinion about ourselves-we immediately experience spiritual darkness. In this case there is no thought to defend ourselves from or agree with, as in the previous cases. There is no standard attack! There is no standard defence. For we are captured by pride and the enemy of our salvation, the slanderer, the evil one, has no need to conquer our heart from the outside, by suggestions in form of thoughts.

Make a Distinction!

When we are captured by the passion of vainglory it rules over us, our heart, our thoughts, words, reactions and we have no control whatsoever over ourselves, over what happens in our heart and over how we react in certain situations when our pride is wounded. In other words, sinful feelings and thoughts occasioned by our wounded pride, and due to the captivity, freely invade our heart, without us having an opportunity immediately to check and recognise them. Instantly, without brakes, our feelings about the one that hurt us become negative and we fall with obvious consequences on our spiritual life.

So, the thoughts that assault at such temptations do not move in the usual way, but starting from the position of the conquered space in the hearts, tend to lead us into even greater evil. When at the very moment, after the damage is done, you condemn someone and your love for him turns cold, they lead you to start hating him. If you already hate him, they give you suggestions how to do him evil.

The fall, in a moment of slackening off and consent, can be disastrous from the perspective of the soul's salvation. This is what happens when the passion of vainglory is in question. Whereas, as we have noticed, if the demon wants to activate our passion of self-indulgence or avarice, the usual process from a suggestion to consent and realisation of the thought has to take place.

The diagnosis of the disease is: *pride*. Pride is the most powerful, most imperceptible and subtle of all passions-disease of the fallen mind. There is a remedy. It is given to us when we truly want to be healed. The healing begins with the appearance of the spiritual father to whom, by the choice of our free will, with love and humility, we put ourselves under obedience, we open the wounds of our soul so that they may be appropriately treated.

Characteristics of the fallen mind are: pride, distraction, and darkness. Traits of the mind restored in the likeness of Christ are: humility, concentration in the prayer, illumination. The way of healing, therefore, is to put our fallen mind under obedience to a spiritual father. Since in the state of fall and darkness we cannot make a distinction what is good indeed, what might do us good, and what might do us harm. God arranges our salvation in ways much unfathomable for us. To the ones that sincerely wish to be saved-He fulfils their wish, inspires them, supports them, creating conditions, fortifies them in the good. Still, He does this in a way that He never violates the freedom given to them.

In the first stage of spiritual development, in the stage of purification, we voluntarily and freely enter into obedience. At this level we strive with our will-power to keep at distance every desire, feeling, or thought until they are checked with our spiritual father. And we accept or reject them, following his advice. We check everything with him. That is how the process of healing begins. The spiritual father is the one that thinks and decides on our behalf-carrying all the weight and responsibility for that. This is his voluntary sacrifice out of love, a risk that serves our salvation. Obedience provides the spiritual child with a carefree state of mind, which, for its part, is a precondition for prayerful stillness. This process lasts until our heart opens.

Thus, in the first stage the ascetical struggle consists of:

- Not identifying with thoughts, desires, and feelings and their checking with the spiritual father;
- Proper confession at which we reveal the reactions of our heart when falling into temptation, and we do not judge the others;
- Bodily effort (abstinence from food and all kinds of bodily comfort; fasting, prostrations, regular attendance at the church services, etc.) through which we likewise trample on our self-love and habit of self-indulgence of the fallen nature in us and we set the framework, the foundation, the atmosphere for mourning, by which the gift of tears of repentance, that will lead us to the mind-and-heart prayer, is opened to us.

If we hold to such endeavour persistently, to the last detail-because it is the small things that we stumble on, fall and get darkened-little by little we are healed by the grace of the Holy Spirit, which is given to us through obedience to the spiritual father. On small things we stumble and fall! Even if the spiritual father is not illumined, he certainly will not lead us into sin, although he can make mistakes in giving some usual, daily commandment (*Go!, Come!, Do it this way or the other!... This is alright-that is not!,* etc.). Here lies our wisdom to obey, even though we may not agree with some of his commandments or some of them may not make sense for us. This is why we say that when we are in the first stage it does not matter if our spiritual guide is holy, if he is in the stage of deification or not. What matters is to oppose pride with humility and contrition, in a real personal relationship with our spiritual father.

This healing process is not subject to the logic of this world. It is interpenetration and life in Christ and a living tradition, which is passed on only from a father to a child, directly and personally.

There is no other way! It is a process where in force is the law of love beyond reason-ascetical in the beginning and subsequently graceful love. Here the spiritual father risks being hurt, as he "hurts", heals his spiritual child, while cutting off the passion of his mind. The spiritual father usually keeps silent when trifles are in question. Yet, if there happened to occur identification with a desire, feeling, or thought that is disastrous for the spiritual growth and salvation of his child, the spiritual father must react on time and cut it off. At the same time there is a risk this to be understood as rejection of the person, which is due to the identification. Then the spiritual child, being captured by that thought, desire, or feeling, automatically returns the blow with non-love.

What is the Risk of the Spiritual Father?

First, receiving blows all the time, being hurt by his child: with a thought, gesture, word, deed, on the level of human relationships. It is natural for him to be hurt: the spiritual child will return with non-love and will hurt the spiritual father in proportion to the captivity by and identification with the passion. Second, on spiritual level, at the same time the demon attacks him as well, because he is trying to save one more soul, disentangling it from the nets of the sin. Third, the spiritual father remits sins in the Holy Mystery of Confession. When he, lovingly, covers his spiritual child–lessening his canonical penance (epitimion) or releasing him completely from it-he takes a great risk as well. He takes upon himself the responsibility and the whole weight of the demonic attack falls on him, in the measure of the sin he remitted from. And fourth, when the spiritual father invests with schema and ordains to priesthood-without canonical backing and with real obstacles for it-he again takes all the responsibility upon himself and risks, covering in everything his spiritual child.

The father always faces a demonic attack equivalent to the shortcomings or the sins he covers. Errors can be made: if the spiritual child, when tempted, imprudently falls away from his spiritual parent. Yet, can the parent stop caring even if the child abandons him completely?!

There is a spiritual rule here that few are aware of. In a state of darkness man must not undertake anything; he must not act. It takes a little patience; he must wait. When enlightened, then to make a decision. And yet, on the contrary, it is exactly in this passionate gloom that people most often make vital decisions-and fall-sealing, making impossible, temporarily or for good, the process of healing and spiritual growth.

In the first stage, the stage of purification, the spiritual child cannot come to know Christ, except through his spiritual father. Although intellectually imagines to know something under the delusion of conceit. The mind is captured by pride and vanity and vainglory. The heart is closed for the mind-and-heart prayer. The inner areas within the heart and the graceful fount, in which the mind transforms, are inaccessible for the mind and it needs guidance and purification. Without a spiritual father this first level cannot be passed!

Therefore, those that are still in the stage of purification, and say they have a spiritual father who lives somewhere far away from them-for instance on the Holy Mountain or in Jerusalem, whom they rarely see, and they live day to day as they wish, guided by their own desires, feelings, and thoughts-cannot overcome the first stage of spiritual ascent. They are under misapprehension. They are not getting anywhere. Who guides them?!

In the first stage it is necessary to eat your daily bread with your spiritual father and live together with him every single day. Him to keep an eye on you, to suppress you-you to feel pain; and return the blow, hurt him-him to be patient with you; you to humble yourself before him. This is inevitable! Without this there is no cure, no spiritual life, and no growth. There is no opening of the heart. There is no illumination.

Now, in the second stage-the stage of illumination, when the heart opens and the mind prayerfully descends in it-it is important that we have a spiritual father with illumined mind and gift of the mind-and-heart prayer. Because, he will know how to provide his spiritual child with conditions for prayerful stillness. Unless the needs of the Church demand something else. Then once the heart is opened, the necessity of this is crucial.

Where Does the Relationship 'Spiritual Father-spiritual Child' Stand Here?

If the spiritual father is in the third stage-the stage of deification, then he can guide the spiritual life of his child who is in the second stage-of illumination, and the spiritual child has to obey him. The vows are still binding. If not, if the spiritual father is in the second stage, their personal relationship is in essence a relationship of brothers in Christ, who mutually advise and supervise each other so as not to leave, by any chance, room for the demon, since the perfection of deification has not yet been reached.

A meeting, seeing each other-from time to time. Exchange of experience. Then I can freely say that my by honour spiritual father is on the Holy Mountain, on Sinai or in America; that I meet him once a year, and we occasionally write to each other or, when necessary, consult on the telephone.

Spiritual father of a diocese should be its diocesan, and not somebody else. If the episcope has too many priests to supervise, then he may transfer the spiritual guidance to one or more experienced fathers, who, in any case, will confess to him. All else is not in concord with Orthodox Tradition.

A characteristic for those who reckon to be spiritual fathers, and are still at the first level of spiritual development, is never to discuss the mind-and-heart prayer, since they have no experience in it. Yet, something must be a subject for discussion. Those that are less educated discuss in a judgmental tone on zealot matters, on the calendar, on ecumenism, on the last times and the apocalypse hereas, the highly educated ones tend to publish ethical-philosophical treatises disguised under a theological mask, burdened with many vague words and complex expressions that reach neither the mind nor the heart of the people. And they dare not speak on purely dogmatic issues.

Genuine spiritual life and struggle start from the moment of descent of the mind in the heart. Then responsibility becomes much greater, along with repentance. It encompasses the dimensions of Adam's lament for all mankind. Then it is necessary to persist in the feat of bringing and keeping the mind in the heart. Then, as the Fathers put it, the demon will raise temptations even from the end of the earth to prevent the ascetical unceasing mind-and-heart prayer.

But we, still fallen and too proud, are marking time for years, entrapped, remaining in the initial steps of the first level of spiritual development, often even going backwards. And, with obedience and humility we could have run across the beginning swiftly, in the attempt to fulfil the commandments- on the narrow road to unceasing prayer.

Definitions

Aim: a broad, general statement of educational intent that indicates the overall desired goal of the course / programme.

Learning Outcome: an achievement that may take the form of acquired knowledge, understanding, an intellectual, practical or transferable skill, and which is intrinsically linked to assessment.

Learning outcomes should articulate what the student will have learned or be able to do as a result of undertaking a particular course / programme. The art of producing meaningful learning outcomes lies in producing statements that are intrinsically important to a course/programme, but at the same time sufficiently specific so that they can be readily understood and tested.

The vocabulary used in this area of course design is prone to change, and frequently causes confusion. Previously, the terms "objective" and "learning outcome" have been used, sometimes interchangeably. As courses / programmes are now outcomes-driven, the use of objectives in course descriptors has now been abandoned.

Nature of Guidance Provided

Since this manual mostly covers new legislation, it necessarily lacks the level of detail of manuals devoted to areas of tax law where the principles have been examined and refined over a considerable period. It will take time for examples to surface that will illuminate the meaning of the legislation, and enable our interpretation of it to develop. As more detailed guidance is written in the light of practical experience it may also be the case that some of the general assertions in the manual will need to be qualified as a result. When matters arising on individual companies are under review, appropriate weight has to be given to the particular facts and circumstances. The general advice and comment that is offered in the following pages is not intended to displace full and proper consideration of all of the actual relevant particulars.

Inevitably, with a substantial block of new material, there is the likelihood of the occasional typographical or similar error creeping in. We will eliminate these as we discover them, but if you notice any, please draw them to our attention. Contact details are given at CIRD00510. More substantive suggestions as to how this manual might be improved are also welcomed.

The Principle of Guidance

Sequence: If I were asked which of all the spiritual principles I ranked first, I should feel inclined to say the Principle of Guidance, not in the sense of being more essential that the others—for every portion is equally essential to the completeness of a perfect whole—but in the sense of being first in order of sequence and giving value to all our other powers by placing them in their due relation to one another. "Giving value to our *other* powers", I say, because this also is one of our powers. It is that which, judged from the standpoint of personal self-consciousness, is above us; but which, realised from the point of view of the unity of all Spirit, is part and parcel of ourselves, because it is that Infinite Mind which is of necessity identified with all its manifestations.

Infinite Mind is Internal

Looking to this Infinite Mind as a Superior Intelligence from which we may receive guidance does not therefore imply looking to an external source. On the contrary, it is looking to the innermost spring of our own being, with a confidence in its action which enables us to proceed to the execution of our plans with a firmness and assurance that are in themselves the very guarantee of our success.

Understanding

The action of the spiritual principles in us follows the order which we impose upon them by our thought; therefore the order of realisation will reproduce the order of desire; and if we neglect this first principle of right order and guidance, we shall find ourselves beginning to put forth other great powers, which are at present latent within us, without knowing how to find suitable employment for them. This would be a very perilous condition: for without having before us objects worthy of the powers to which we awaken, we should waste them on petty purposes dictated only by the narrow range of our unilluminated intellect. Therefore the ancient wisdom says, "With all thy getting, get understanding".

The awakening to consciousness of our mysterious interior powers will sooner or later take place, and will result in our using them whether or not we understand the law of their development. The interior powers are natural powers as much as the exterior ones. We can direct their use by a knowledge of their laws; and it is therefore of the highest importance to have some sound principles of guidance in the use of these higher faculties as they begin to manifest themselves.

Will

If, therefore, we would safely and profitably enter upon the possession of the great inheritance of power that is opening out before us, we must before all things seek to realise in ourselves that Superior Intelligence which will become an unfailing principle of guidance if we will only recognise it as such. Everything depends on our recognition. Thoughts are things, and therefore as we *will* our thoughts to be, so we *will the thing* to be. If, then, we *will* to use the Infinite Spirit as a spirit of guidance, we shall find that the fact is as we have willed it, and in doing this we are still making use of our own supreme principle. And this is the true "understanding" which, by placing all the other powers in their correct order, creates one grand unity of power directed to clearly defined and worthy aims, in place of the dispersion of our powers, by which they only neutralise each other and effect nothing.

Truth

This is that Spirit of Truth which shall guide us into all Truth. It is the sincere Desire in us to reach out after Truth. Truth first and Power afterwards is the reasonable order, which we cannot invert without injury to ourselves and others; but if we follow this order we shall always find scope for our powers in developing into present realities the continually growing glory of our vision of the ideal.

From Ideal to Real

The ideal is the true real, but it must be brought into manifestation before it can be shown to be so, and it is in this that the *practical* nature of our mental studies consists. It is the *practical* mystic who is the man of power: the man who, realising the mystical powers within, fits his outward action to this knowledge, and so shows his faith by his works; and assuredly the first step is to make use of that power of infallible guidance which he can call to his aid simply by desiring to be led by it.

What Types of Guidance and Support are Lacking for Students?

Information and computer technology is the focus in companies. They are pushing for it to be taught and utilized in schools. But the respondents identified this as an issue because even though it is a primary tool in business, it is not the primary tool required to develop people to work and function effectively in organizations. The information presented here indicates problems with the introduction of information technology.

It appears that the data from the respondents and the literature reviewed have little chance of controlling technology and its advancement. However, the more aware of the situation we are, the better prepared we can be and the better we can guide and support the workers of tomorrow, our children. This will allow us to control the direction and development of our future in a techno-centric world. Another way to think of this is to recognize that the big problem is how technology has become invisible and the need to make it visible so we can deal with it.

Challenges for Students Using Technology

Many adults have feared that students would become frustrated by the technical demands of the kinds of technologies described above. Experience suggests to the contrary that learning the technical aspects of working with technology is not a major problem for most students. Students face several other kinds of challenges when they use technology to support them in active, inquiry learning, however. These include:

- Understanding their responsibilities as active learners.
- Getting help with individual learning needs.
- Integrating their technology-supported inquiry learning with their larger school experience.

Understanding Their Responsibilities as Active Learners

Authentic Inquiry Tasks provide exciting new challenges for students and can also require a host of advanced intellectual and social learning skills, involving new levels of independence.

Peggy Healy Stearns (1991c) noted that for many of the students participating in the Software Evaluation Project and using Point of View to create multimedia presentations, working in cooperative groups was an innovation in its own right. The social studies teacher needed to help students develop productive working relationships, so that they could cooperatively research the topics and create a presentation to share with their classmates.

Some students need step-by-step guidance when becoming familiar with a new procedure for generating questions, gathering information, or carrying out a cooperative task; others, and most students over time, need a reminder of the "big picture". They need considerable discussion in the early stages of a new activity, less when their investigation is well under way.

Getting Help with Individual Learning Needs

Although the kinds of inquiry learning these programmes foster is appropriate for all students, many students need special support to manage the social and intellectual challenges of posing and exploring their own questions and in sustaining attention and involvement in long-term projects. EDC's Problem Solving in Science project found that students with even mild learning problems may need considerable coaching in computer-based cooperative learning activities.

Integrating Technology Supported Inquiry Learning with the Larger Educational Experience

Many students' first experience with technology-supported inquiry learning is an isolated one—as part of a pilot project, a new programme, or an individual teacher's experimentation. Until school reform makes this a more pervasive learning environment for students, they may experience a discrepancy between their inquiry learning experiences and the emphasis on factual memorization in other classrooms. Students in the Geometric Supposer research project sharply experienced this dissonance and isolation in comments like "I feel so strange. We're the only class..." and "We can t even associate with other kids in the other classes. We're completely different"

(Yerushalmy, Chazan & Gordon 1990, pp. 26-27). When discrepancies in philosophy and approach across classrooms are made explicit, particularly at the middle and high school levels, students are more able to adapt to these discrepancies. Their resulting awareness of the ways they are learning can help them to generalize new inquiry skills to new, appropriate situations.

Types of Guidance—Educational Guidance

Introduction

Educational Guidance, process of helping students to achieve the self-understanding and self-direction necessary to make informed choices and move toward personal goals. Guidance, a uniquely American educational innovation, focuses on the complete development of individual students through a series of services designed to maximize school learning, stimulate career development, and respond to the personal and social concerns that inhibit individual growth. Although guidance activities are usually associated with educational professionals known as counselors, educational guidance is actually a cooperative enterprise involving the participation of teachers, administrators, other educational specialists, and parents.

Development of Educational Guidance

The origins of educational guidance are firmly rooted in the development of vocational guidance services. In 1908 the Vocation Bureau of Boston was established under the direction of the American lawyer and educator Frank Parsons to assist young men in making vocational choices based on their occupational aptitudes and interests. It soon became obvious that individuals needed vocational guidance while still in school so that they could prepare for their chosen careers. By midcentury, counseling services were being provided in the lower grades, and counselors extended their activities beyond vocational advice to problems of social adjustment.

The National Defense Education Act (NDEA) of 1958 more than doubled the number of trained personnel available to provide expanded guidance services in the public schools. The purpose of the act was to identify students with outstanding abilities, to encourage them to seek higher education, and to assist them in following studies best suited to their abilities. NDEA also provided financial incentives—in the form of grants to training institutions and aid to counselors in training—to make educational guidance an integral part of public secondary education.

Procedures

In public schools, guidance programmes are organized as a series of services. One service is academic planning. Counselors assist students with curriculum and individual course selection. Programmes also are designed to help students who have academic difficulties.

Student appraisal is another counseling function. Standardized tests are administered to assist in appropriate academic placement, to assess academic achievement, to identify individual aptitudes, to explore vocational interests, and to examine personal characteristics. Tests are used also to identify gifted students and those with special learning problems.

Other counseling services include career-development programmes to foster awareness of career alternatives, programmes in human relations skills, and training in actual job skills, as well as the acquisition and dissemination of related information. Counselors work with teachers, administrators, and families in coordinated efforts to help resolve specific student problems. If necessary, they can refer students to trained therapists for additional assistance.

In colleges and universities, administrative offices such as student affairs, admissions, financial aid, housing, student health, and placement provide guidance services. College counseling centers assist students with academic, vocational, or personal problems.

Current Trends

In addition to state certification as educationally qualified personnel within schools, many guidance professionals are seeking licensing outside of school settings. Several states currently license counselors. Increased efforts to license and regulate guidance workers also elicit greater demands for professional accountability.

Guidance workers are required to develop specific programmes with measurable goals and systematic evaluation procedures to demonstrate their effectiveness. Programmes have been developed for such special problem areas as abusive families, divorce, and substance abuse, and for specific groups such as minorities and the physically and developmentally disabled. Community-based programmes also emphasize prevention and crisis intervention as primary guidance strategies.

Vocational Guidance

- The world of work is in a state of continuous change
- The disappearance of some careers and the emergence of new or alternative careers.
- Employers need to recruit individuals who are capable of showing their skills and abilities.
- To match the changing values of individuals with new set of career possibilities.
- To assess the needs of the labor market and match them with the needs of the individuals.
- To avoid unemployment

Process of Vocational Guidance

Vocational Guidance helps individuals to acquire knowledge in the following areas:

1. Self awareness.
2. Exploration of the world of work.
3. Mature decision making

1. Self awareness: is the process of gathering information about the interests, abilities and values. It helps one to answer such questions as:
   - What kind of person I am?
   - What type of work do I enjoy doing?

- What are my interests and abilities?
- What kinds of skills do I possess?
- How can I take a decision regarding my future career?
- How can you know yourself?
- Take self-interest inventories that help you to know better your interests, values and skills
- Have a look at your academic background and other achievements what school subjects were you good at and what subjects were difficult for you?
- Have a look at how you spend your leisure time.
- Identify your skills that you are highly motivated to use.
- Write are sum about yourself and identify the theme that points out to who you are
- Write your personal objectives and identify who you want to be and what you want to achieve in your life.

2. World of work exploration: this involves gathering information about the different careers that might fit your interests, values and abilities. It helps you find answers to the following questions:
   - What kind of education or training is required in each?
   - What are the pros and cons of each job you think of?
   - What are the working conditions in the different types of careers?
   - How does a certain career look like?
   - What are the job requirements?
   - What is the financial output?

To be able to answer such questions:

- Know more about these careers.
- Meet people who work in these careers and ask them questions like the followings

- o What are your responsibilities in a typical working day?
- o Did you work in other jobs?
- o What is the required background (education, training, experience)
- o What do you like and dislike in your work?
- o What are the skills and the abilities required in you job?
- o What are the future trends that you see for this type of job?
- o What is the organizational structure within your institution?
- o How does your department fit within this structure?
- o What are your advices to someone who is looking for a training in this field?

3. Mature decision making: is the process of exploring the different alternatives, narrowing down the possibilities and then choosing the right alternative to ensure a mature career decision do the followings:
   - look at the different possibilities and ask your self whether here could be other ways that could help you in solving this problem?
   - Think of your decision, can you take it in another way.
   - Listen to others.
   - Weigh the advantages and disadvantages for the different alternatives when you narrow down your choices.

Personal Guidance

Guidance relating to college transition, campus/community resources, social and cultural enriching activities and general personal concerns can be provided by all EDGE professional staff. Limited counseling is available with the project director. A goal section of the Individualized Development Plan (IDP) will be compiled for each participant. Academic, career and personal counseling is available and encouraged. Any participant can schedule an appointment to see the counselor or advisor as needed.

Counselors help students in the transition from high school to college and assist re-entry and late-entry students in adjusting to the academic environment. The counselors aid students in clarifying goals and setting realistic objectives, as well as helping students with specific personal issues.

Relationship between Guidance and Counseling

Guidance is an act of supervising a person, nurturing someone to do good sort of mentoring someone that wants direction with the occasional advice. Counselling is just talking to the person having a problem and giving them advice. School counselors promote and enhance achievement using a comprehensive approach that ensures every that student receives guidance services. School counselors provide comprehensive counseling programmes that incorporate prevention and intervention with continuous academic, career and personal/development activities that will prepare students for meaningful participation in a diverse, changing world.

These activities include classroom guidance, small groups for skill mastery, individual counseling for students with specific needs and a variety of other proactive and innovative ways to support student performance. Guidance and Counselling includes a variety of group oriented activities designed to enhance students' attitudes and values and refers to an individualized or small group process that assists students with specific personal/social difficulties, or educational and career issues. Counselling services may be developmental, preventative, or crisesoriented.

UNIT-II

Counselling

Counselling—Meaning, Definitions, Elements-Characteries—Objectives—Need

Individual Counselling

A counsellor can meet with you on a one-to-one basis, with you and your partner or with members of your family, to talk through issues that are concerning you.

Group Therapy

A counsellor leads the discussion for a group of people (with or without similar issues of concern) who get together on a regular basis to share their experiences or concerns.

Online and Telephone Counselling

Working with a counsellor online, by telephone, by Email, chat-room or instant messaging is certainly not as good as face-to-face counselling but can be very effective when there are long distances involved. This is especially relevant in India, USA, UK & France.

Self-help Groups

People who are experiencing similar problems, such as loss and grief, trauma, divorce and illness, meet to discuss common issues and problems (with or without a counsellor to lead the discussion).

Meaning Given in Counselling

The following headline caught my eye on CNN some time ago: "Uncontacted tribe sighted in Amazon". I assume by "uncontacted" CNN meant that we have no form of communication with this tribe, we are isolated from them. This got me thinking about the process in counselling where one person (the counsellor) meets with another (the client) and they somehow come into contact. They have a connection because meaning is shared

My idea of counselling starts with the client showing the counsellor what the client's meaning is: How the client sees the world and himself in it. This is what some call a person-centred approach; the counsellor takes the lead from the client and strains to see and feel the client's worldview. Other approaches to counselling also do this. Cognitive Behavioural Therapists (CBT) examine the meanings clients carry around with them in order to understand why they feel and behave in certain circumstances. Gestalt therapy uses a certain picture (which can be viewed as an old lady or a young woman, depending on the perspective) to show that we give different meanings to the same things.

But counselling does not stop at understanding a client's meaning. Many would agree that the purpose of counselling is to achieve awareness and change. But change in what direction? If we can somehow communicate with the Uncontacted Amazon tribe, are they to change in line with our meaning, our perspective, or vice versa? And what if the two are irreconcilable? Logotherapy places great importance on changing the way clients think about things, but how are we to assess whether that change is helpful for the client? The narrative approach, such as that advocated by Michael White, would call this re-authoring a client's story Perhaps we are all uncontacted tribes, isolated from each other until we make the effort to somehow share each other's meaning. But once we have shared these meanings, where do we go from there?

Definition of Counselling

Counselling takes place when a counsellor sees a client in a private and confidential setting to explore a difficulty the client is having, distress they may be experiencing or perhaps their dissatisfaction with life, or loss of a sense of direction and purpose. It is always at the request of the client as no one can properly be 'sent' for counselling.

By listening attentively and patiently the counsellor can begin to perceive the difficulties from the client's point of view and can help them to see things more clearly, possibly from a different perspective. Counselling is a way of enabling choice or change or of reducing confusion. It does not involve giving advice or directing a client to take a particular course of action. Counsellors do not judge or exploit their clients in any way.

In the counselling sessions the client can explore various aspects of their life and feelings, talking about them freely and openly in a way that is rarely possible with friends or family. Bottled up feelings such as anger, anxiety, grief and embarrassment can become very intense and counselling offers an opportunity to explore them, with the possibility of making them easier to understand. The counsellor will encourage the expression of feelings and as a result of their training will be able to accept and reflect the client's problems without becoming burdened by them.

Acceptance and respect for the client are essentials for a counsellor and, as the relationship develops, so too does trust between the counsellor and client, enabling the client to look at many aspects of their life, their relationships and themselves which they may not have considered or been able to face before. The counsellor may help the client to examine in detail the behaviour or situations which are proving troublesome and to find an area where it would be possible to initiate some change as a start. The counsellor may help the client to look at the options open to them and help them to decide the best for them.

Models of Counselling

Although there is considerable consensus about the core content of a counselling course, there are nevertheless distinct methods of counselling. Most courses start from a theoretical base-typically humanistic, psychodynamic, cognitive or behavioural. Before enrolling on a course it is advisable to be aware of its theoretical emphasis and what that means in terms of the learning experience offered and the skills acquired.

Characteristics of Effective Counseling

Effective counseling is a two way street. It takes a cooperative effort by both the person receiving counseling and the counselor. And it takes a commitment to make sometimes difficult changes in behavior or thinking patterns.

What you expect to achieve with your counselor should be clearly defined as you begin your counseling. You and your counselor should discuss realistic time frames for reaching your goals and agree on how you will measure your progress.

It's important that you and your counselor establish a good relationship that allows you to be completely honest about your thoughts and feelings. Often, this requires an elusive "chemistry" between both of you in which you feel comfortable with your counselor's personality, approach and style. If after the first few sessions you don't feel this chemistry, look for another counselor with whom you feel more comfortable.

Once you think you've found the right counselor, how do you tell if your relationship is effective? Here are some signs to look for:

While you are responsible for making changes in your life, an effective counselor can help pinpoint the obstacles in your way. If you have control over these obstacles, a counselor can suggest behavioral changes to help you overcome them. If these obstacles involve factors outside of your control, your counselor can teach you coping mechanisms that will foster your well being in trying circumstances.

An effective counselor can identify negative thinking patterns that may be feeding feelings of sadness, depression or anxiety. By encouraging you to build upon personal strengths and suggesting skills that can overcome self-inflicted feelings of hopelessness, a counselor can help you develop a more positive attitude.

A good counselor can assist you in making positive changes in your relationships with others, helping you recognize behaviors that may be contributing to a troublesome relationship. Your counselor can teach you effective ways of communicating, clearing the way for honest exchanges with people in your life who may be causing you emotional pain.

You can determine whether your work with your counselor is effective if you begin to obtain insights about your own thoughts and behaviors that may have eluded you before. Over time, you should be able to recognize patterns in the way you act, trace their sources and identify stumbling blocks to your happiness that you may have unwittingly created. The end result is personal growth that empowers you to control your life and enjoy positive, life-affirming relationships with others.

Objective

Primary Objectives: To provide a well founded Counselling Service, available to students and staff, in the university by:

- offering one-to-one counselling for personal and educational issues
- offering therapeutic group work
- offering a variety of personal skills training (e.g. examination preparation, assertiveness training) on a workshop basis
- developing awareness amongst staff of issues of concern to students
- contributing to providing training in tutoring and other skills relevant to staff in meeting their responsibilities to students

Secondary Objectives: To contribute to the creation of a positive environment for learning within the University by:

- using the knowledge gained through the nature of counselling to help the University identify and address areas of stress
- participation in policy making and policy implementation in areas directly related to student support

Objectives of Genetic Counselling

The results of a survey published in the Journal of Public Health Medicine [Michie, S. et al. (1998) J. Pub Health Med.

20, 404-408 (Abstract)] suggest that, although purchasers, providers and users of genetic services are in broad agreement about the aims of such services, purchasers differ from providers and users in the relative priorities they assign to these aims. The study used the 'Delphi' technique to survey the attitudes of public health doctors and GPs (purchasers), clinical geneticists and genetic counsellors (providers) and users (outpatients and members of a support organisation). There was broad agreement that the five most important aims were to give information, give support, facilitate decision-making, enable risk assessment, and achieve understanding. However, purchasers assigned relatively higher priorities to facilitation of decision-making and risk assessment, while providers and users ranked giving information and support more highly.

Comment: There are several possible explanations for the difference between purchasers and the other groups, but at least on the surface it appears that those responsible for commissioning genetic services tend to value 'active' outcomes from these services, while those directly involved in the service, either as providers or users, value the more neutral aims of providing information and support. This difference may assume increasing importance as the potential range of genetic services widens.

Need Career Counselling?

What do you want to be when you grow up? Which one of us hasn't faced that question when we were younger? Most of us probably had an answer. Teacher! Fireman! Astronaut! The choices seemed endless then. But the question takes on a whole new significance for students fresh out of Class X or Class XII.

In a world filled with career choices ranging from medicine to mass communications, engineering to event management, marine biology to information technology, the confusion teenagers face over which career to pick is understandable. A large number of students continue to choose a career based merely on the fact that their friends are doing the same thing or because their parents told them to do so. This, however, may not be the best way to go about it.

If you've just taken your Class X/ Class XII board exams, and are trying to decide on a profession, the first thing you need to realise is that every individual is different. Not everyone can be a doctor or an engineer (not everyone wants to be one!)—and that's okay!

Choosing a field of study that is not really suited to your interests or skills could prove disastrous. And that's where career counselling comes in.

What is Career Counselling?

Career counselling helps students discover their true potential and interest in various subjects in order to help them choose the right career. Several institutes, including schools and colleges, today offer career counselling through a series of aptitude and IQ tests. The tests usually have multiple-choice questions, which don't need to be prepared for in any way.

Then comes a face-to-face interview with a career guidance counsellor. The interview provides the student with the opportunity to clear any doubts or queries he/ she may have regarding career options and educational courses. It also allows the counsellor to further judge the aptitude of the student, thus building on the preliminary results of the written tests.

Varsha Rebello, manager and senior counsellor, Career Launcher India, says, "Career counselling is the guidance given to a student on the road he/she should take to achieve his/her goals. The advice and counselling provided is based on three deciding factors — personality, aptitude and interest. The counsellor is trained in administering tests that determine the aptitude and skills of a child, his/her personality traits and subjects of interest."

Types of Counselling

There are three main types of counselling or support. These are:

- **Individual work** with one counsellor and either one client, a couple or some members of a family.
- **Group work** where a counsellor leads or facilitates the group.

- **Self-help groups** where there is no leader. Members attend on an equal basis for mutual support.

A group called a **support group**may have a counsellor as a leader or facilitator, or it may be a self-help group without a leader. Some self-help groups follow the 12 step programme developed by Alcoholics Anonymous.

No one has found an approach to counselling that will work with everyone in every situation. Some will work better for you than others. You need to find a counsellor with beliefs compatible with your own. Self-help groups usually have some common beliefs about the issue they share. The 12 step groups, for example, share common beliefs about the causes of addiction and the steps necessary for recovery.

No matter how much knowledge a counsellor has, if she can't listen to you and understand you she won't be able to help you. In fact, some women believe that the personality of the counsellor is more important than technical skill or training.

A counsellor may have trained in a particular style of counselling but use other types as well. Very few of the training courses for counsellors include training in cultural awareness or working with an interpreter. A counsellor's training may not have challenged her racism or sexism or prejudices about lesbians or women with mental illnesses.

Some counsellors are trained to use the medical model and only look at what is happening within you, your body or your mind. They ignore things that are happening to you and the ways you're affected by other people. For example, you may be very stressed by your family situation in which you're being abused or not getting enough support. You may be told that 'it's just your nerves' and only be given pills to take. You may have been diagnosed as having a mental illness but find that it is treated as purely a physical problem when you also need to talk about traumatic experiences you've had. You need to ask each individual counsellor about her work.

People Who Offer Counselling

Counsellors: People with many different backgrounds work as counsellors. The name is not used to refer to any one type of training or qualification. There are many training courses in counselling skills.

Psychotherapists

Psychotherapists have a variety of qualifications. They have usually been in counselling or psychotherapy themselves and can work on personal change at a deeper level.

Community Health Nurses

They are qualified nurses who have completed extra training in community health which includes some counselling skills.

Family Therapists

They have a variety of qualifications. Members of the Victorian Association of Family Therapists (VAFT) have at least two years additional training in working with individuals and families.

Feminist Counsellors

There is no specific qualification in Victoria in feminist counselling. They have an awareness of the specific experiences and pressures on women. You need to ask each individual what she means by feminist counselling.

Financial Counsellors

They are trained to help sort out finances and renegotiate contracts and other financial obligations.

Social Workers

Social workers have a degree in social work. Some of them do counselling and they use a variety of approaches.

Psychiatrists

They are medical doctors with extra training in psychiatry. They deal with the diagnosis and treatment of mental illness. They can prescribe drugs. Some of them use other approaches as well.

Psychologists

They have university qualifications in psychology. Some with extra training are registered psychologists. They counsel people in a variety of settings using a range of techniques. They do not prescribe drugs.

Psychoanalysts

They can train in several ways which are regulated by the Psychoanalysts Association. Some are medical doctors. They use a specific process to explore buried feelings from childhood. It can involve several sessions per week and take many years.

'Support groups are good later on, particularly with incest the secrecy means that it is incredibly threatening to start doing that in a group it's very exposing. Later on it's great and what you get is understanding and not feeling isolated and validating your own experiences.'

'I was on medication prescribed by a psychiatrist, but another doctor said that it was bad for me and took me off it.'

Directive Counseling

Directive counseling is the process of listening to a member's problem, deciding with the member what should be done, and then encouraging and motivating the person to do it. This type of counseling accomplishes the function of advice; but it may also reassure; give emotional release; and, to a minor extent, clarify thinking. Most everyone likes to give advice, counselors included, and it is easy to do. But is it effective? Does the counselor really understand the member's problem? Does the counselor have the technical knowledge of human behavior and the judgment to make the "right" decision? If the decision is right, will the member follow it?

The answer to these questions is often no, and that is why advice-giving is sometimes an unwise act in counseling. Although advice-giving is of questionable value, some of the other functions achieved by directive counseling are worthwhile. If the counselor is a good listener, then the member should experience some emotional release. As the result of the emotional release, plus ideas that the counselor imparts, the member may also clarify thinking. Both advice and reassurance may be worthwhile if they give the member more courage to take a workable course of action that the member supports.

Nondirective Counseling

Nondirective, or client-centered, counseling is the process of skillfully listening to a counselee, encouraging the person to explain bothersome problems, and helping him or her to understand those problems and determine courses of action. This type of counseling focuses on the member, rather than on the counselor as a judge and advisor; hence, it is "client-centered." This type of counseling is used by professional counselors, but nonprofessionals may use its techniques to work more effectively with service members. The unique advantage of nondirective counseling is its ability to cause the member's reorientation. It stresses changing the person, instead of dealing only with the immediate problem in the usual manner of directive counseling.

The counselor attempts to ask discerning questions, restate ideas, clarify feelings, and attempts to understand why these feelings exist. Professional counselors treat each counselee as a social and organizational equal. They primarily listen and try to help their client discover and follow improved courses of action. They especially "listen between the lines" to learn the full meaning of their client's feelings. They look for assumptions underlying the counselee's statements and for the events the counselee may, at first, have avoided talking about. A person's feelings can be likened to an iceberg. The counselor will usually only see the revealed feelings and emotions. Underlying these surface indications is the true problem that the member is almost always initially reluctant to reveal.

Eclectic Counseling—Meaning—Characteristics—Steps—Advantages—Limitations

Eclectic Counseling refers to a class of counselors who neither attach themselves to any theoretical approach, nor construct independent systems, but select such approaches as are appropriate for the client in every school. This discussion will focus on eclectic counseling. Initially it will be defined more thoroughly and illustrated by reference to a handful of theoretical cases and eclectic responses to them. Subsequently the advantages and potential pitfalls of the eclectic approach will be considered. Then its appropriateness in the contemporary context will be outlined. Finally, a brief concluding section will highlight the salient elements of the eclectic approach to counseling and consider its relevance, practicality and value.

Steps in the Counseling Process

1. Establish a safe, trusting environment
2. *Clarify:* Help the person put their concern into words.
3. Active listening: find out the client's agenda
   a) paraphrase, summarize, reflect, interpret
   b) focus on feelings, not events
4. Transform problem statements into goal statements.
5. Explore possible approaches to goal
6. Help person choose one way towards goal

Develop a Plan (may involve several steps)

7. Make a contract to fulfill the plan (or to take the next step)
8. Summarize what has occurred, clarify, get verification

Evaluate Progress

9. Get feedback and confirmation

Advantages of Self-disclosure

Being genuine. *There is a danger that the counsellor may appear to be too cold or detached—especially when she is inexperienced and is desperately trying to be non-judgmental. If the mother perceives the counsellor as someone who never responds as a human being, but is always a little aloof and too self-controlled she may find the counselling relationship artificial.*

Effective counselling is not based on a mechanical set of skills, but on a genuine relationship of caring and warm support from the counsellor. Sometimes this can be promoted when the counsellor shares something personal. After all, if I did not care for you at all, I would not be likely to share anything personal with you, would I? Again, the ideal blend of spontaneity and control required from the counsellor is hard to achieve and will certainly take most people a long time to achieve.

Sharing experience. *You may have had an experience which has some similarities to that of the mother. In this case you may consider it helpful to share this experience with the mother so that she may perhaps learn that some resolution is at least theoretically possible. As long as you offer this as your own experience, and make it clear that you recognise that the mother's experience is in some ways unique to her, this may be very helpful to the mother. It can help to build up positive expectations and lets her know that she is not alone in her discomfort.*

Sharing feelings. *As the mother talks with you, you will experience feelings of your own. There may be occasions when you will feel it useful to share these feelings with the mother. We are not talking about the usual expressions of sympathy that one friend might offer to another, but rather something much more deliberate, as in this example:*

> *A mother has been telling you about her difficulties with her doctor and health visitor. In the course of doing so, she keeps telling you how sorry she is for taking up your time, for not being able to express herself clearly, for making mountains out of mole hills and so on. You discover yourself responding with strong irritation to this constant stream of apology.*

Having identified your reaction, you may now choose what to do about it. One possibility is to put it to one side and try to ensure that it does not get in the way of your counselling. But another option is to share your feeling with the mother: "I hear you keep apologising to me, and I find that I'm responding by feeling quite irritated. Do you think that the doctor and health visitor might be responding in a similar way?"

By sharing your feelings you focus on an aspect of the mother's behaviour which might be relevant to her difficulty (though it might not) and try to initiate an exploration of it.

This is something which can be very effective, but it is quite dangerous; and if you find yourself doing it a great deal, you ought to ask yourself about your motives.

Modelling a Skill: *If the counsellor shares her feelings openly and without embarrassment, it suggests to the mother that such behaviour is acceptable (to the counsellor at least). This may have two benefits. Firstly, it may encourage the mother to be more open with the counsellor and secondly, it may give her a model to follow in difficult situations.*

A mother contacts you with a query about weaning. As you explore the issues with her it appears that the root of her difficulty lies in the strength of her husband's expectations about breastfeeding. She wants to start weaning the baby onto solids at five months, but he has read that it is 'better' to wait another month. Because he is so certain she doesn't really know how to share her own feelings with him. By sharing openly with the mother, the counsellor may model behaviour which the mother may be able to follow with the husband.

Advantages for Seeing a Counsellor?

There are several advantages to talking to a counsellor:

- You won't have to worry about upsetting them
- They aren't going to judge you
- They will make sure that you are safe by setting appropriate boundaries such as confidentiality, setting clear goals, sharing their decisions about the direction of the counselling
- They will not say what they think you want to hear
- You can make fundamental and far-reaching changes to your life

Limitations of Counselling

Pravin Thevathasan: Counselling is a vitally important aspect of medical practice; many an experienced GP has commented on the fact that a patient's wellbeing may respond more through the art of counselling than through the science of medicine. Perhaps this art is in danger of being downgraded in an ever growing culture of evidence-based practice.

However, experienced counsellors recognise that counselling has its limitations. It is useful in only certain given circumstances. Their view compares to a widely held belief that any sort of counselling is bound to do some good. "If you have been affected by any part of this programme, you may wish to ring this number for some confidential counselling". As long as someone is seeing or listening to a counsellor, it is said, things are bound to get better.

How many counsellors does it take to change a light bulb? Only one, but the light bulb must wish to change. This joke is now a little over-mature but it does contain a grain of truth. There are certain personalities who simply do not have the built in mechanism to learn from the counselling experience. The histrionic person may be delighted to be told that he has been referred to a counsellor after several visits to his local hospital with various instruments attached to his person. He may proceed to wear down many a counsellor with detailed descriptions of his past medical 'career'; but he is unlikely to gain insight from his counselling experience. The dependent person may indeed make great strides during the counselling process. But when the counsellor starts talking of ending the sessions, he becomes distressed. For him, the counsellor has become a sort of human benzodiazepine. The sociopath does not have the built in mechanism to learn from his past experiences. The classic paedophile, for example, has a pathological need to control others and little insight into his problem behaviours. He has a limited desire to change. Counselling by itself may prove a disaster as others around him may feel that "at least something is being done". The less experienced counsellors may not be able to offer an adequate screening process prior to the counselling sessions.

Assuming that counselling is deemed to be of help, ought a Catholic see a Catholic counsellor? If she needs to see a counsellor because of a fear of spiders, it really does not matter. If she wishes to discuss feelings of guilt after an abortion it would surely help her to see someone who understands her spiritual perspective. In this latter case, seeing a non-directive counsellor is unlikely to prove beneficial. There needs to be a moral framework to guide the counselling process. She is rather like a passenger on board a plane who is unlikely to have much confidence in a non-directive pilot-even if the said pilot shows lots of empathy.

One hears of counselling in certain schools. This may be entirely appropriate if, for example, a child has been bullied, but what happens when a young person wishes to see a counsellor because he is confused about his sexuality? If you have a facilitator counselling a group of young people, he is likely to impose his own set of beliefs on them either consciously or unconsciously by means of group dynamics. Although the facilitator's role is supposed to be value free, that in itself introduces a new dogma.

There is no right or wrong. What is good for you may be bad for me. The mature deliberation is never that clear.

The facilitator first creates the appropriate environment for change. His task is to create doubts about previously held perspectives. This may be done by techniques such as role playing, whereby difficult dilemmas are presented. By enhancing a person's self-esteem, it is possible to make him believe that the old rules are unlikely to work now. "An actualised" person evolves into a more flexible and more "affirming" person.

As has already been stated, self-esteem programmes are entirely appropriate in certain circumstances. However, it needs to be said that they are wholly inappropriate in most circumstances and may promote the values of ethical egoism and a general preoccupation with the self. St Gregory wrote of the "rottenness of wretched self gratitude". Of course he probably never had the benefit of attending a self-esteem seminar. Counselling has its uses. Like any other therapeutic intervention, it has side-effects and contra-indications. There is a generally held view that improving a person's self-esteem is bound to promote authentic values. This view needs to be challenged.

Difference between Counseling and Guidance

Guidance and counseling, concept that institutions, especially schools, should promote the efficient and happy lives of individuals by helping them adjust to social realities. The disruption of community and family life by industrial civilization convinced many that guidance experts should be trained to handle problems of individual adjustment. Though the need for attention to the whole individual had been recognized by educators since the time of Socrates, it was only during the 20th cent that researchers actually began to study and accumulate information about guidance.

This development, occurring largely in the United States, was the result of two influences: John Dewey and others insisted that the object of education should be to stimulate the fullest possible growth of the individual and that the unique qualities of personality require individual handling for adequate development; also in the early 20th cent., social and economic conditions stimulated a great increase in school enrollment. These two forces encouraged a reexamination of the curricula and methods of secondary schools, with special reference to the needs of students who did not plan to enter college. The academic curriculum was revised to embrace these alternative cultural and vocational requirements (see vocational education).

Early guidance programmes dealt with the immediate problem of vocational placement. The complexities of the industrial economy and the unrealistic ambitions of many young people made it essential that machinery for bringing together jobs and workers be set up; vocational guidance became that machinery. At the same time, counseling organizations were established to help people understand their potentialities and liabilities and make intelligent personal and vocational decisions. The first vocational counseling service was the Boston Vocational Bureau, established (1908) by Frank Parsons, a pioneer in the field of guidance. His model was soon copied by many schools, municipalities, states, and private organizations.

With the development of aptitude and interest tests, such as the Stanford-Binet Intelligence Test and the Strong Vocational Interest Blank, commercial organizations were formed to analyze people's abilities and furnish career advice. Schools organized testing and placement services, many of them in cooperation with federal and state agencies. Under the provisions of the National Defense Education Act (1958), the federal government provided assistance for guidance and counseling programmes in the public secondary schools and established a testing procedure to identify students with outstanding abilities. The U.S. Dept. of Labor has been an active force in establishing standards and methods of vocational guidance, helping states to form their own vocational guidance and counseling services. The personnel departments of many large corporations have also instituted systems of guidance to promote better utilization of their employees.

Modern high school guidance programmes also include academic counseling for those students planning to attend college. In recent years, school guidance counselors have also been recognized as the primary source for psychological counseling for high school students; this sometimes includes counseling in such areas as drug abuse and teenage pregnancy and referrals to other professionals (e.g., psychologists, social workers, and learning-disability specialists). Virtually all teachers colleges offer major courses in guidance, and graduate schools of education grant advanced degrees in the field.

UNIT-III

Guidance Movement in India

History of Guidance Movements in India

Due to an increasing demand for guidance and counselling services in-schools, colleges and universities, the guidance movement in India has picked up considerable momentum. However, research in this area at the M.Phil. level is hardly satisfactory. It may be seen from Table 3 1.1 that, in all, 35 studies in the area of guidance and counselling were undertaken during 1973-87. Most of these pertain to occupational aspirations, choices and preferences (Archna, 1980; Singh, 1981; Sidhu, 1983; Ahmad, 1987); vocational attitudes, interests and maturity (Kumar, 1979; Takshak, 1984; Misra, 1984; Mangat, 1984; Porus, 1985; Sindhu, 1985; Singh, 1985); study habits (Seetharam, 1977; Singh, 1979; Sharma, 1979); subject choices (Kaur, 1983; Lamba, 1985); and educational aspirations (Verma, 1982; Kaur, 1984) of students at the school level. Two studies deal with the theme of counselling at the school level. One relates to the impact of counselling on neglectees and isolates (Rather, 198 1) and another to the effect of individual counselling on the achievement of bright under-achievers (Khan, 1987). There is only one study on an evaluative nature pertaining to the evaluation of the personnel services of Delhi University (Sathe, 198 1). The studies on psycho-social correlates of job-satisfaction of anganwadi workers (Lekhi, 1986); vocationalization at the +2 stage in India (Samarakoon, 1986); and education, occupation and morale of railway employees (Ganesan, 1987) are also worth mentioning.

A perusal of research studies in the area of guidance and counselling over 1983-87 at M.Phil. level reveals certain serious gaps. There is hardly any study pertaining to the evaluation and follow-up of guidance and counselling activities, and guidance personnel preparation programmes.

Studies on the effectiveness of individual counselling in relation to specific problems of students at the school, college and university levels have been practically neglected. No worthwhile research effort seems to have been made for exploring the guidance and counselling needs of school, college and university students; the educational and vocational needs of ex-ceptional children, handicapped children and children belonging to disadvantaged communities; and the implications of vocationalization at the +2 stage.

Area-wise Distribution of Studies at M.Phil. Level from 1973 to 1987

Area	Number of Studies	Completed during		Total
	1973-77	1978-82	1983-87	
1. Philosophy of Education	13	14	27	
				(20)
2. Sociology of Education	7	24	43	74
				(56)
3. History of Education	1	6	17	24
				(21)
4. Comparative Education	1	4	3	8
				(7)
5. Economics of Education	1	9	9	19
				(16)
6. Learning, Motivation and Personality	10	75	76	161
				(117)
7. Guidance and Counselling	4	13	18	35
				(24)
8. Evaluation, Tests and Examinations	2	15	23	40
				(30)
9. Curriculum, Methods and Textbooks	13	51	64	
				(52)

10. Educational Technology	18	12	21	51 (30)
11. Correlates of Achievement	6	15	43	64 (48)
12. Teacher Education	13	45	79	137 (78)
13. Educational Management and Administration	6	35	51	92 (61)
14. Non-formal Education	8	21	29	(24)
15. Education of the Exceptional	4	7	17	28 (18)
Total	73	294	486	853 (601)

Problems of Guidance Movement in India

Although problems pertaining to evaluation, tests and examinations at different levels of instruction are of vital importance at the national level, yet the number of studies in this area at M.Phil. level is not impressive. Table 31.1 indicates that only 40 studies have been reported during the period 1973-87. Only two studies were undertaken in the first five-year period, 1973-77, and the rest of during the decade 1978-87.

In the studies relating to test development the emphasis has been on tests measuring locus of control (Mohapatra, 1981); socio-economic status (Visvas, 1982); vocational interests (Selvamuthu, 1982); creativity (Shan, 1983); attitudes (Pradhan, 1985); achievement; and norm referenced and criterion referenced tests (Bala, 1985; Singh, 1985; Dash, 1985; Godbole, 1985; Kulkar 1987). Construction of diagnostic tests and preparation of appropriate remedial instructional programmes have also caught the attention of a few researchers (Pingle, 1986; Jagtap, 1986; Borude, 1986; Angal, 1987; Wagh, 1987).

Some significant issues and problems concerning several aspects of evaluation and the examination system have also been explored. These include studies pertaining to re-evaluation at the university stage (Patel, 1978; Singh, 1980); innovations in the examination system at school or university stage

(Bhatnagar, 1978; Bhardwaj, 1979); internal and external systems of evaluation (Gupta, 1978; Gupta, 1981); question banks in different school subjects (Ahmad, 1986); and evaluation procedure at the primary stage (Parda, 1986).

A couple of investigations of an experimental nature pertain to the effects of unit tests on retention, achievement motivation and the test anxiety of school students (Bhadwal, 1979); the effect of continuous evaluation and feedback on achievement (Srivastava, 1982); and the comparative effectiveness of verbal and non-verbal methods of assessment and acceleration on the development of the concept of number among young children (Gupta, 1983).

From a perusal of the studies it is evident that the focus of research in test development has been almost exclusively on secondary school students. At the school level also there is hardly any test which has been constructed specially for use on children living in hill, backward and tribal areas. Studies relating to the problems of mass copying and the use of other unfair means in examinations; the grade system of marking; orientation of paper setters; setting of good question papers and evaluation of answer-books; reliability and validity of external examinations and school, college and university levels, use and effectiveness of unannounced tests; the semester system; farmative evaluation; and evaluation in the context of non-formal and distance education are practically absent.

The role of curriculum, teaching methods and textbooks is well recognized in the total teaching-learning process. Meaningful research in these areas provides a sound basis for developing well-designed curriculum, preparing good textbooks, and evolving effective instructional strategies. But the research in this area received very little attention in the decade 1973-82. It is evident from Table 3 1.1 that the number of studies increased quite speedily in the quinquennium 1983-8 7. In all, 64 studies at M.Phil. level on curriculum, methods and textbooks were conducted during the period 1973-87.

In the context of curriculum research, a number of researchers have analysed the curriculum at school, college and university levels in different subjects in various parts of the country (Gupta, 198 1; Rajdan, 1982; Ibrahim, 1982; Awaneendra, 1982; Selvaraju, 1985; Jothi, 1986; Pandya, 1986; Reddy, 1986; Chetanlal, 1987; Nongrum, 1987). A few studies pertain to curriculum analysis and development of professional courses (Jayalakshmi, 1978; Bhat, 1982; Yadav, 1983; Dora 1984; Puri; 1985; Dandavate, 1986; Behari, 1987).

On the understanding that a curriculum programme is brought into action through appropriate instructional strategy, some researches studying the comparative effectiveness of different techniques and methods have also been undertaken. These studies cover the efficacy of the discussion-cum-demonstration method (Pathania, 1985); the Piagetian model (Senapaty, 1985); the Bruner and Ausubel models (Kaur, 1986); the information processing model (Kaur, 1986); the non-directive model (Sahani, 1986); reception and selection oriented models of concept attainment (Sohani, 1986); the jurisprudential inquiry model (Gangrade, 1987); the inductive thinking model (Hota, 1987); and the advance organiser model (Rajoria, 1987) on the achievement and learning of students in comparison with the efficacy of conventional methods of teaching. The effects of brainstorming on divergent thinking (Sharma, 1980) and development of creativity using synetics (Venkataraman, 1985) have also been studied.

Ways to Improve Guidance Movement in India

Human behavior has bio-psycho-socio-cultural base. Behavior development is primarily based on genetic maturation, learning, and socialization pattern. Child is active and interactive with his environment during various developmental phases, which makes dynamic understanding of large number of issues centered around mental health of child a very difficult task. It is not surprising that very little work has been done in this area of mental health of children in the world, more so in India. Varied expressions of the same may be "Child is the discovery of the century," "Biggest discovery of the century is our knowledge of extent of our ignorance," and "I knew various theories of child mental development, now I know many children with the distinct problem of their own."

India presents a unique case in terms of its large population and 50% of them are children and adolescents; characterized by heterogeneity in respect to physical, economical, social, and cultural conditions. India's population of 1050 millions makes 16% of the world population, 68% of which is living in the villages.

India is secular with various languages, cultures, and religions. It has 179 languages, 544 dialects, and 1942 mother tongues; with 148 mediums of instruction at school level. This kind of complex and multifaceted country makes formulation of national policies, programing, and planning very difficult.

The Nation's children are our supremely important assets. Their nature and solitude are our responsibility. Children's programmes should find a prominent part in our national plans for development of human resources, so that our children grow up to become competitive citizens. Equal opportunities of development to all children during the period of growth should be our aim, for this would serve our larger purpose of reducing inequality and ensuring social justice.

It shall be the policy of the state to provide adequate services to children, both before and after birth, and through the period of growth to ensure their full physical, social, and mental development. States shall progressively increase the scope of such services, so that, within a reasonable time, all children in the country enjoy optimum condition for their balanced growth.

India is a country of children, adolescents, and young adults. It is not only the mental health needs of this 60% of the young population that we are addressing to, but also future generation's mental health. Prevention is better than cure. It is well known that adult psychopathology and mental health problems are only an extension of child mental health problems and continuum in psychopathology. It is not surprising that mentally disturbed parents produce mentally disturbed children, who in turn, will again grow into mentally disturbed adult.

According to the World Mental Health Rights of Mentally ill (1998)-depression, suicide, alcoholism, and psychosis comprise of 75% of mental illnesses and hence they need special attention. Adult influence on child mental health is considerable. For the child this adult can be the protector, provider, legal guardian, custodian, or caretaker.

A good quality-of-life for every child includes good housing, health services, financial stability, family environment, social network, practical coping skills, etc. Ninety percent of the children in India have a very poor quality-of-life.

Child and adolescent mental health, which is future of our country, is given inadequate attention. As overall development of any country is dependent on positive mental development of its children, it is definitely the challenge of the day to cope up with poverty, malnutrition, illiteracy, poor health, and hygiene that is crippling millions of children in India.

Changing structure of the family, modernization, westernization, industrialization, globalization, and urbanization have negatively influenced child mental health. Incidences of mental health problems are on increase (278% increase in pedophilia). Depression and suicide have increased three to four folds in large number of states in India. Post-traumatic mental disorders have shown phenomenal rise. During this decade far more children have been killed and disabled than soldiers. Mental health problems in children affected with riots, bomb blasts, and natural catastrophes are perpetually ever increasing in number. Alcohol and other drug abuse in children have increased ten fold. The recent data indicate the overall prevalence of mental and behavioral disorders among children was 12.8%. This amounts to 66 million children needing special care, attention, and guidance.

In India, child mental health services have been neglected for the last 57 years. National Mental Health policy makers (2003) have practically nothing on their agenda as far as child mental health policy and planning are concerned. It is a sorry state of affair. In last 67 years from 1937 when first child guidance clinic (CGC) was introduced till 2003, NIPCCD study located only 164 CGCs-roughly only two CGCs a year and that too only in metro and mega cities. All these child guidance movements and mental health activities and services have been initiated and sustained by efforts from NGOs.

If we target one CGC per one lakh population we will need 10050 CGCs in the entire country. We need to be innovative so that mental health services for children are possible both in rural as well as urban sectors. For this, question of child mental health should be treated as entirely a special subject and there should be separate units and personnel working with and for the children. An autonomous body with an interdisciplinary perspective has to be created, which should be responsible for the development of child mental health services in an organized manner. Decentralization of child mental health services is a must. Health of people should be in the hands of people. An innovative programme and plan should consider important sociocultural dimension and dynamics during implementation.

Following basics in child mental health should not be compromised to make it effective and successful:

- Affordability
- Availability
- Accessibility
- Acceptability
- Appropriate technology

The multidisciplinary and multiple services should be at one center. It is a well-known fact that India does not have enough specialists to manage mental and behavioral disorders. Nevertheless, efforts should be made to have one such team in each district. Centrally placed team should be able to manage all the peripheral CGCs in the district with the help of one community based team that finally reaches the people at their doorstep. With roughly 500 districts in India we will need 1000 multidisciplinary teams. Initially, all those who have been in the child guidance movement and child mental health services should be invited to participate in training programme for the trainers at district level and at periphery.

Experts in the field of child mental health services should be invited to innovate services and training programme for this neglected area. Child mental health issues of our country need to be addressed with intensity and urgency. This should incorporate cross-cultural, multilingual, and multiregional requirements. Child mental health programme should cover prevention, early identification, intervention, rehabilitation, and integration. It is vital that child mental health programme should have local contexts with due regards for local culture and religion.

The amount spent on mental health in India remains only 0.83% of the total budget. Within this limited budget the share of our children is further marginalized. There is no specific allocation for child mental health services in tenth five-year plan. Government contribution to improve the state of affairs is negligible. Grants are reducing every year in spite of increase in cost and population. NGO's work is hindered by need to get licenses for voluntary work.

India has been signatory to all the resolutions including the latest passed on 1 January 1996, which states that every child will have equal opportunities, protection of right, and full participation (The Persons with Disabilities act, 1995). After five decades of independence we have resolved to help the Indian child but only "if within the economic capacity" of the state and central government. Child has never been given the minimum essential in last five decades. It is not surprising that under the "minimum need programme" during last ten years, outlays and expenditure under the 'Mental Health Sector' has been very insignificant and underutilized. This also portrays a negative picture of the needs in this sector and hinders expansion of financial needs of the same by the future planning bodies.

The schism of 'NO FUND' or unutilized or underutilization of fund is typical of India in area of child mental health. It is not surprising to know that none of the states have achieved the national norms of population to be served by community health center (CHC) in last 50 years.

In spite of the dream to achieve "Health for All" by 2000, present emphasis is not on 'REACHING THE UNREACHED'.

Government has not sanctioned a single subcenter in last 14 years (since 1990). Present emphasis is on consolidation of existing services and no expansion. The policy makers have resolved to have qualitative and not quantitative improvement in mental health services and/or general health services in India. It is a stark contrast to have a target and to not do anything to achieve the target.

Facilities should be provided for special treatment, education, and care of children who are physically handicapped, emotionally disturbed, or mentally challenged.

Ten percent of the child population is in need of special care and treatment. Only one in 100 get some. It is high time we reach out to the rest 99% of the child population that is being unattended by any agency. Children with borderline intellectual functioning and various learning, speech, visual, and hearing difficulties are conservatively estimated to be 20% of the total child population. These 114 million children have no facilities even in the urban areas.

In spite of three-fold increase in grants, release for the children in need of special care, who are the beneficiaries, has come down to half. It means more funds for more staff members and service providers and less for the target group that needs these services. To be precise, 90% of expenses go to the staff and only 10% expenditure is on the child. Ideal planning should consider 70% of the expenditure on the child.

Special groups like blind, deaf, mentally challenged, cerebral palsy and multiple handicaps have very specific requirements. It is also important to know that large number of NGOs run various developmental clinics, CGCs, and school mental health clinics to cater to the specific needs of each disability sector. They should be utilized as a central nodal point for further expansion of considerable child mental health services.

Development clinics not only will fulfill requirements of annual examination and evaluation of each and every child in India but also help in early detection and prevention of a large number of disabilities. 'Catch them young, as young as you can', helps in early intervention strategies.

The existing child guidance movement should be a nodal center for further expansion of child mental health services. Following the example of the present team that is working in the CC, a similar multidisciplinary team should also be setup at community level to reach out the unreached in the community.

School mental health programme should get maximum attention and help, as large majority of the children can be reached this way. Thirty percent of the school-going population is in need of mental health care. It is vital that the service model and mental health service delivery system should get top priority to school mental health.

Child population is not homogeneous. Large number of children have no home, no school, and no family. They can be in orphanages, destitute homes, beggars' homes, juvenile homes, rescue homes, and remand homes. They can even be street children. All these groups some how have their own self-help group, one of the motto of such group is "each one teach one" to become self-sufficient. Some of them run their own CGC.

Prostitutes, victims of abuse, traffic, and violence form a special group of children who need entirely different kind of expertise, service, and care.

India is unique. India has largest population of married children below the age of 14 years, which is 14.28% of the total population. This accounts for 43.7 million children in India. These children are unique in their problems as they are minors who are supposed to look after new born and young children. This is a large group that needs to be addressed not only in child guidance but also in group therapy sessions in the community. Family therapy and psychoeducational therapy may be effectively used to help these groups of child population.

It is essential to plan the strategies for such wide, diverse population and create linkages and integrate services in settings where children are already available. Universal education and school for every child would be an excellent ground to integrate mental health services. The schools would then act as safety nets to promote mental health in children and provide timely intervention when required.

Biggest challenge is in developing Human Resources who work in the area of child mental health. From grass-root level, local proximal worker to a large number of paramedical and medical experts need to be committed and devoted. A sustained involvement in this field will need lot of innovation. We will have to give license to hands that care. It is a distant dream in India to have a child development programme, which makes the child a healthy person, partner, and parent. Mental health professionals in child development have lot more to do before one can think of ideal care for children by 21 century clinician.

Rural Primary Education: Solution of our Problems

India, a nation with billion of population, amazed various other countries by the quality of some of the human resources that the Indian education system has produced. The *Vedas, Puranas, Ayurveda, Yoga,* Kautilya's *Arthasahtra* are only some of the milestones that the traditional Indian knowledge system boasts of. There are evidences of imparting formal education in ancient India under the *Gurukul* system. But it is the English language and the reformation movements of the 19th century that had the most liberating effect in pre-independent India. Thus, the Britishers, although rightly criticized for devastating the Indian economy, can also be credited for bringing a revolution in the Indian education system.

Indian education can be divided into primary education, secondary education, senior secondary education and higher education. But in today's scenario there is instant need to improve condition of primary education in country, especially in rural area. Primary education is the only thing which makes a base for whole life. If children got access to better primary school then there parents as well as there surroundings start thinking for there future rater then to just leave on fate. According to the 2001 census, the total literacy rate in India is 65.38%. The female literacy rate is only 54.16%. The gap between rural and urban literacy rate is also very significant in India. This is evident from the fact that only 59.4% of rural populations are literate as against 80.3% urban population according to the 2001 census. Now due to illiteracy it results in poverty, unemployment, migration of villagers to city which some time cause unsocial problem.

Presently India is running many programmes like **Sarva Shiksha Abhiyan** in order to increase literacy rate in villages but till now no markable success is achieved. There are basically deep rotted problem related with it. Economies of rural area are in shattered state. Villagers need there children to do some work in village itself or to assist elders at home in agriculture or so. So, they are quite reluctant in sending there children to school, and if they send that is just for mid day meal or other such thing.

They require short term benefit, but our present education system not able to doing so. That's why there is large number of drop outs from schools. According to 7 all India education survey, 2002 a little over one third of all children who enroll in grade one reach grade eight.

Expansion

So, overcoming these problems, it needs a expansion of schools in different parts of country. According to 7 all India education survey, 2002 in India, only 53% of population has primary schools, and on an average an upper primary school is 3 Km away in 22% of areas in habitation.

It requires creating a good infrastructure in even in small villages. Presently most of our schools are running in prebritishers building which are quite tainted. Expansion of schools help in to join larger number of population of India which is otherwise have to travel long distance to attend them. Improvement in infrastructure helps a child to expose to large cross section of education.

He then has better asses to outer world through library, and can cultivate its other abilities which help to boost its confidence. Presently there is no concept of computer center and of library in villages. Even if in smallest villages with schooling they have assess to such facility then they become more knowledgeable about present scenario of surrounding and they constantly get motivated to do something beneficial for themselves as well as for there villages.

Excellence

This is the far most important thing to do, at primary level. If in rural area they have better access to initial education then only a large chunk of population of rural area can think of to get expertise in some field, or if some children are intelligent enough then it can go to higher studies which are otherwise a dream for them. Excellence has to impart at two levels, first in terms of teacher and second in terms of curriculum.

Quality of teacher here means how well they are exposed to present education scenario. This is not expected to them that they are some kind of rocket engineer or so. They just are able to motivate children in right direction. These teachers should be of there respective villages, so that they are more linked to children. These teachers can get guidance and knowledge about present happening through some other near by cities schools. These teachers have to help village children to cultivate there qualities as well guide them about there qualities more incentives can be given to these teachers not only in terms of money but by gave them chance to attend some kind of workshop. They should motivate student's right from beginning about sources of earning, which in turn create interest among children that education can make them able to learn.

In terms of curriculum, it should give more stress on vocational education which can gave them a taste of earning, which help them to keep attracted towards schooling. Of course this doesn't mean that they shouldn't provide any kind of formal education. Vocational training just help that children get to the school just by the thinking that they can earn if they relate to school, because most of the villagers think for short term benefit. After 7 or 8 grade students which are intelligent enough can be provide chances and should allow to understand that they have to move forward to it's or so ,so that they can help there villages in many terms.

Inclusion

Basic thing is that benefit of higher education can be seen only when most of the population have a taste of primary education, so then they can be aware of there abilities and have an idea that education can reform there lives. Another thing is that drop out should be reduced. Rural students have to provide better exposure to education scenario. They should provide opportunity to show case there talent in different competitions which gave them chance to visit different places and make a healthy environment in village to get attach with school. Talent doesn't mean just well in studies but may be in sports etc., so to make students confident about themselves. Presently they are just interested in mid day meal and such incentives but if they can see benefit of education then we have better productivity from these children. Once some children can get selected to good higher institute, or start earning something due to some expertise, then this will create a wave in particular villages for education. This requires a large amount of patience and dedicated teachers.

But all these require a long term strategy and a nice local level management which can look over proper schooling. It also requires a wholehearted support from upper level management and proper allocation of resources. It is essential to fill the gap between urban and rural education divide otherwise which vision of becoming a developed country remains a vision only.

UNIT-IV

Qualities of a Counsellor

Consellor—Qualities—Functions—Professional Ethics

School Counseling History

The history of school counseling varies on how countries and schools provide academic, career, college readiness, and personal/social skills and competencies to K-9 children and adolescents based on economic and social capital resources in a school counseling programme.

In the United States, the school counseling profession began with the vocational guidance movement at the beginning of the 20th century, now known as career development. Jesse B. Davis was the first to provide a systematic school guidance programme.

In 1907, he became the principal of a high school and encouraged the school English teachers to use compositions and lessons to relate career interests, develop character, and avoid behavioral problems. Many others during this time did the same. For example, in 1908, Frank Parsons, "Father of Vocational Guidance" established the Bureau of Vocational Guidance to assist young people in making the transition from school to work.

From the 1920s to the 1930s in the United States, school counseling and guidance grew because of the rise of progressive education in schools. This movement emphasized personal, social, moral development. Many schools reacted to this movement as anti-educational, saying that schools should teach only the fundamentals of education. This, combined with the economic hardship of the Great Depression, led to a decline in school counseling and guidance. In the 1940s, the U.S. used psychologists and counselors to select, recruit, and train military personnel. This propelled the counseling movement in schools by providing ways to test students and meet their needs. Schools accepted these military tests openly. Also, Carl Rogers' emphasis on helping relationships during this time influenced the profession of school counseling.

In the 1950s the government established the Guidance and Personnel Services Section in the Division of State and Local School Systems. In 1957, the Soviet Union launched Sputnik I. Out of concern that the Russians were beating the U.S. in the space race, which had military implications, and that there were not enough scientists and mathematicians, the American government passed the National Defense Education Act, which spurred a huge growth in vocational guidance through large amounts of funding. In the 1960s, the profession of school counseling grew as new legislation and professional developments were established to refine and further the profession and improve education (Schmidt, 2003).

The 1960s was also a time of great federal funding in the United States for land grant colleges and universities interested in establishing and growing what are now known as Counselor Education programmes. School counseling began to shift from a focus exclusively on career development to a focus on student personal and social issues paralleling the rise of social justice and civil rights movements in the United States. It was also in the late 60s and early 1970s that Prof. Norm Gysbers began the work to shift from seeing school counselors as solitary professionals into a more strategic and systemic goal of having a comprehensive developmental school counseling programme for all students K-12 (ASCA, 2005). His and his colleagues' work and research evidence showing strong correlations between fully implemented school counseling programmes and student academic success was critical to beginning to show an evidence base for the profession especially at the high school level based on their work in the state of Missouri (Lapan, Gysbers, & Sun, 1997).

But school counseling in the 1980s and early 1990s in the United States was not seen as a player in educational reform efforts buffeting the educational community (Stone & Dahir, 2006). The danger was the profession becoming irrelevant as the standards-based educational movement gained strength in the 1990s with little evidence of systemic effectiveness for school counselors. In response, Campbell & Dahir (1997) consulted widely with school counselors at the elementary, middle, and high school levels and created the ASCA National Standards for School Counseling with three core domains (Academic, Career, Personal/Social), nine standards, and specific competencies and indicators for K-12 students (ASCA, 2005). A year later, the first systemic meta-analysis of school counseling was published and gave the profession a wake-up call in terms of the need to focus on outcome research and the small set of methodologically accurate school counseling outcome research studies in academic, career, and personal/social domains (Whiston & Sexton, 1998).

Also in the late 1990s, a former mathematics teacher, school counselor, and administrator, Pat Martin, was hired by The Education Trust to start work on a project to focus the school counseling profession on helping to close the achievement gap overwhelming hindering the life successes of children and adolescents of color, poor and working class children and adolescents, bilingual children and adolescents and children and adolescents with disabilities. Martin was able to develop focus groups of K-12 students, parents, guardians, teachers, building leaders, and superintendents, and then interviewed professors of school counseling in Counselor Education programmes. She hired a retired school counselor educator from Oregon State University, Dr. Reese House, and they worked to create what emerged in 2003 as the National Center for Transforming School Counseling at The Education Trust.

Their foci included both changing how school counseling was taught at the graduate level and by changing the practices of K-12 school counselors in districts throughout the USA in order to teach school counselors how to prevent and intervene to help close achievement and opportunity gaps for all students. In the focus groups, they found what Hart & Jacobi (1992) had indicated was accurate—that too many school counselors were working as gatekeepers for the status quo instead of advocates. Too many school counselors were using inequitable practices and unwilling to challenge inequitable school policies, which kept students from nondominant backgrounds getting the coursework and academic, career, and college readiness skills needed to successfully graduate from high school and pursue rigorous post-secondary options including college. They funded six $500,000 grants for six different Counselor Education/School Counseling programmes, with a special focus on both rural and urban settings, to completely transform their school counseling programmes to include a focus on teaching school counselor candidates advocacy, leadership, teaming and collaboration, equity assessment using data, and culturally competent programme counseling and coordination beginning in 1998 (Indiana State University, University of Georgia, University of West Georgia, University of California-Northridge, University of North Florida, and Lewis & Clark University) and then over 25 other Counselor Education/School Counseling programmes joined as companion institutions in the following decade. By 2008, NCTSC consultants had worked in over 100 US school districts and many major cities and rural areas to transform the work of school counselors to close achievement and opportunity gaps and challenge inappropriate policies and procedures through using data and assessing equity.

In 2002, the American School Counselor Association released the ASCA National Model framework for school counseling programmes, written by Dr. Trish Hatch and Dr. Judy Bowers, comprising some of the top school counseling components in the field into one model—the work of Drs. Norm Gysbers, Curly & Sharon Johnson, Robert Myrick, Carol Dahir & Cheri Campbell's ASCA National Standards, and the skill-based focus for closing gaps from the Education Trust's Pat Martin and Reese House into one document.

In 2003, the Center for School Counseling Outcome Research (Dimmitt, Carey, & Hatch, 2007) was developed as a clearinghouse for evidence-based practice with regular research briefs disseminated and original research projects developed and implemented with founding director Dr. Jay Carey. One of the research fellows, Dr. Tim Poynton, developed the EZAnalyze software programme for all school counselors to use as free-ware to assist in using data-based interventions and decision-making.

In 2004, the ASCA Code of Ethics was substantially revised to focus on issues of equity, closing gaps, and ensuring all students received access to a K-12 school counseling programmme.

Also in 2004, Pat Martin left the Education Trust and moved to the College Board. She later hired School Counselor Educator Dr. Vivian Lee and they developed an equity-focused entity on school counselors and college counseling, the National Office for School Counselor Advocacy (NOSCA). NOSCA has developed research scholarships for research on college counseling by K-12 school counselors and how it is taught in School Counselor Education programmes.

In 2008, The first NOSCA study was released by Jay Carey and colleagues focusing on innovations in selected College Board "Inspiration Award" schools where school counselors collaborated inside and outside their schools for high college-going rates and strong college-going cultures in schools with large numbers of students of nondominant backgrounds (College Board, 2008).

Also in 2008, the American School Counselor Association released School Counseling Competencies focused on assisting school counseling programmes to effectively implement school counseling programmes based on the ASCA Model.

The history of the school counseling profession internationally shifts as more parents, guardians, teachers, building and district leaders, and government officials support the changes in roles, expectations, and skills of current and future school counselor candidates and as the evidence base and equity-building skills of school counselors develop school counseling programmes delivering academic, career, college, and personal/social competencies for every child and adolescent.

On January 1, 2006, The United States' Congress officially declared February 6-10 as National School Counseling Week (for materials and ideas to celebrate NSCW, contact ASCA.

School Counselor Roles, School Counseling Programme Framework, and Ethics

Professional School Counselors ideally implement a data-driven, evidence-based (Dimmitt, Carey, & Hatch, 2007) comprehensive school counseling programme that promotes and enhances student achievement, career and college readiness, and personal and social competencies at the elementary, middle, and high school levels (ASCA, 2005). A fully-implemented school counseling programme ideally delivers academic, career, college readiness, and personal/social competencies to every student K-12—just as the district's mathematics programme is for 100% of the students. Professional School Counselors, in most U.S. states, usually have a Master's degree in school counseling from a Counselor Education graduate programme.

They are employed in elementary, middle, and high schools and in district supervisory, counselor education faculty positions (usually with an earned Ph.D. in Counselor Education) and post-secondary settings doing academic, career, college readiness, and personal/social counseling, consultation, and programme coordination. Their work is varied, with attention focused on developmental stages of student growth, including the needs, tasks, and student interests related to those stages (Schmidt, 2003).

Professional School Counselors meet the needs of student in three basic domains: academic development, career development, and personal/social development (Dahir & Campbell, 1997; ASCA, 2005) with an increasing emphasis on college readiness (Carey et al, 2008). Knowledge, understanding and skill in these domains are developed through classroom instruction, appraisal, consultation, counseling, coordination, and collaboration. For example, in appraisal, school counselors may use a variety of personality and career assessment methods (such as the Self-Directed Search (SDS) or Career Key (based on the Holland Codes) to help students explore career and college needs and interests.

Delivery methods include academic, career, college and personal/social planning for every student; developmental classroom lessons for all students; and individual and group counseling for some students who need more intensive assistance beyond classroom lessons or planning/advising sessions. Classroom lessons and the school counseling curriculum are designed to be preventive in nature and include academic, career, college, and personal/social skills and competencies including self-management and self-monitoring skills (Stone & Dahir, 2006).

The Responsive Services component of the Professional School Counselor's role provides individual and/or small group counseling for students. For example, if a student's behavior is interfering with his or her achievement, the Professional school counselor will observe that student in a class, provide consultation to teachers and other personnel to develop (with the student) a plan to address the behavioral issue(s), and then work together (collaboration) to implement the plan. They also help by providing consultation services to family members such as college readiness, career development, parenting skills, study skills, child and adolescent development, and help with school-home transitions.

Additionally, professional school counselors may lead classroom lessons on a variety of topics within the three domains such as personal/social issues relative to student needs, or establish groups to address common issues among students, such as divorce or death. The topics of character education, diversity and multiculturalism (Portman, 2009), and school safety are important areas of focus for school counselors. Often counselors will coordinate outside groups that wish to help with student needs such as academics, or coordinate a state programme that teaches about child abuse or drugs, through on-stage drama (Schmidt, 2003)

The ASCA National Model (2005) operationalizes much of the above into four main areas of focus: Foundation (a written school counseling programme mission statement, a beliefs and philosophy statement, and a focus on the ASCA standards and competencies and how they are implemented for every student; Delivery System (how lessons and individual and group counseling are delivered); Management System (use of calendars, time, building leader-school counselor role agreements, creation of action plans); and Accountability System (use of a SC programme audit, results reports, and School Counselor Evaluations based on 13 key competencies. The model is implemented using key skills from the Education Trust's Transforming School Counseling Initiative: Advocacy, Leadership, Teaming and Collaboration, and Systemic Change.

School Counselors are also expected to follow a professional code of ethics in many countries. In the United States, they are primarily the American School Counselor Association Code of Ethics and the American Counseling Association Code of Ethics.

Elementary School Counseling

Elementary professional school counselors following best practices provide developmental school counseling curriculum lessons (Stone & Dahir, 2006) on academic, career, college readiness, and personal and social competencies, advising and academic/career/college readiness planning to all students, and individual and group counseling for some students and their families to meet the developmental needs of young children K-6 (ASCA, 2005).

Increased emphasis is starting to be placed on college readiness counseling at the elementary school level as more school counseling programmes move to evidence-based work with data and specific results (Dimmitt, Carey, & Hatch, 2007). Research has shown that school counseling programmes help to close achievement and opportunity gaps in terms of which students have access to school counseling programmes and early college readiness activities and which students do not (College Board, 2008). To facilitate the school counseling process, school counselors use a variety of theories and techniques including developmental, cognitive-behavioral, person-centered (Rogerian) listening and influencing skills, systemic, family, multicultural (Holcomb-McCoy & Chen-Hayes, 2007; Portman, 2009), narrative, and play therapy. Sink & Stroh (2003) released a research study showing the effectiveness of elementary school counseling programmes in Washington state.

Middle School Counseling

In middle school counseling, professional school counselors following best practices provide developmental school counseling curriculum lessons (Stone & Dahir, 2006) on academic, career, college readiness, and personal and social competencies, advising and academic/career/college readiness planning to all students and individual and group counseling for some students and their families to meet the developmental needs of late childhood and early adolescence according to sources such as the ASCA National Model (ASCA, 2005).

Increasing emphasis has been placed on college readiness counseling at the middle school level as more school counseling programmes move to evidenced-base work with data and specific results (Dimmitt, Carey, & Hatch, 2007) that show how school counseling programmes help to close achievement and opportunity gaps in terms of which students have access to school counseling programmes and early college readiness activities and which students do not (College Board, 2008).

Middle School College Readiness curricula have been developed by The College Board that can be used to assist students and their families in this process. To facilitate the school counseling process, school counselors use a variety of theories and techniques including developmental, cognitive-behavioral, person-centered (Rogerian) listening and influencing skills, systemic, family, multicultural (Holcomb-McCoy & Chen-Hayes, 2007; Portman, 2009), narrative, and play therapy. Transitional issues to ensure successful transitions to high school are a key area including career exploration and assessment with seventh and eighth grade students. Sink, Akos, Turnbull, & Mvududu released a study in 2008 confirming the effectiveness of middle school comprehensive school counseling programmes in Washington state (Sink, Akos, Turnbull, & Mvududu, 2008).

High School Counseling

In high school, professional school counselors following best practices provide developmental school counseling curriculum lessons (Stone & Dahir, 2006) on academic, career, college readiness, and personal and social competencies, advising and academic/career/college readiness planning to all students and individual and group counseling for some students to meet the developmental needs of adolescents according to sources such as the ASCA National Model (ASCA, 2005).

Increasing emphasis is being placed on college readiness counseling at the early high school level as more school counseling programmes move to evidence-based work with data and specific results (Dimmitt, Carey, & Hatch, 2007) that show how school counseling programmes help to close achievement and opportunity gaps ensuring all students have access to school counseling programmes and early college readiness activities (Carey et al, 2008). High School College Readiness curricula have been developed by The College Board to assist this process.

To facilitate school counseling, school counselors use varied theories and techniques including developmental, cognitive-behavioral, person-centered (Rogerian) listening and influencing skills, systemic, family, multicultural (Holcomb-McCoy & Chen-Hayes, 2007; Portman, 2009), narrative, and play therapy. Transitional issues to ensure successful transitions to college, other post-secondary educational options, and careers are a key area. The high school counselor helps students and their families prepare for rigorous post-secondary education and/or training options (e.g. college, trade school) by engaging students and their families in finding accurate and meaningful information on entrance requirements, financial aid, recommendation letters, test-preparation and so forth. Professional School Counselors at the high school level spend much of their time helping students and their families monitor their progress toward graduation and being adequately prepared for post-secondary options including college. Some students now turn to private college admissions counselors specialized in college admissions but the ethics of so doing is open to great debate in terms of who has access to this funding and there is little research-based evidence of effectiveness on the part of these outside parties.

The fees for these college admissions counselors can be as high as $30,000.

A framework for Professional School Counselor responsibilities and roles is outlined in the ASCA (American School Counselor Association) National Model (2005). Lapan, Gysbers, & Sun's (1997) study showed correlational evidence of the effectiveness of fully implemented school counseling programmes on high school students' academic success. Carey et al's 2008 study showed specific best practices from school counselors raising college-going rates within a strong college-going environment in multiple USA-based high schools with large numbers of students of nondominant cultural identities.

Education and Certification/credentialing of School Counselors

The education of school counselors (school counsellors) around the world varies greatly based on the laws and cultures of specific countries and the historical influences of their respective educational and credentialing systems and professional identities related to who delivers academic, career, college readiness, and personal/social information, advising, curriculum, and counseling and related services..

In the United States, a professional School Counselor is a certified educator with a master's degree in school counseling (usually housed in a Counselor Education graduate programme) with specific school counseling graduate training including unique qualifications and skills to address all students' academic, career, college readiness and personal/social needs through the use of school counseling programmes that deliver specific measurable competencies. About half of all Counselor Education programmes that offer school counseling are accredited by the Council on the Accreditation of Counseling and Related Educational Programmes (CACREP) and all but one are currently in the United States with one in Canada and one programme under accreditation review in Mexico as of 2008 and maintains a current list of accredited programmes and programmes in the accreditation process on their website. CACREP has identified in 2008 an interest in accrediting more programmes outside of the United States.

According to CACREP, an accredited school counseling programme offers specific coursework in Professional Identity and Ethics, Human Development, Counseling Theories, Group Work, Career Counseling, Multicultural/Diversity Counseling, Assessment, Research and Programme Evaluation, and Clinical Coursework in a 100-hour practicum under the supervision of both a school counseling faculty member and a certified school counselor site supervisor (master's degree in school counseling or higher, and appropriate certification) and a 600-hour internship under the supervision of both a school counseling faculty member and a certified school counselor site supervisor (master's degree in school counseling or higher, and appropriate certification) (CACREP, 2001).

CACREP released the revision of the Standards for 2009 in 2008, and made a major change moving toward performance-based accreditation including evidence of school counselor candidate learning. In addition, in the 2009 standards, CACREP greatly tightened and enhanced the school counseling standards with specific evidence needed of how school counseling students receive education in foundations; counseling prevention and intervention; diversity and advocacy; assessment; research and evaluation; academic development; collaboration and consultation; and leadership in K-12 school counseling contexts. (CACREP, 2009).

Certification practices for school counselors vary around the world. School Counselors in the United States may opt for national certification through two different boards. The National Board for Professional Teaching Standards (NBPTS) requires a two-to-three year process of performance based assessment, and demonstrate (in writing) content knowledge in human growth/development, diverse populations, school counseling programmes, theories, data, and change and collaboration. As of February, 2005, 30 states offer financial incentives for this certification.

Also based in the USA, The National Board for Certified Counselors (NBCC) requires passing the National Certified School Counselor Examination (NCSC), which includes 40 multiple choice questions and seven simulated cases which assess school counselors' abilities to make critical decisions on the spot. Additionally, a master's degree and three years of supervised experience are required. NBPTS also requires three years of experience, however a master's degree is not required, but only state certification (41 of 50 require a master's degree). At least four states offer financial incentives for the NCSC certification (McLeod, 2005). Both certifications have benefits and costs that a school counselor would want to consider for national certification. NBCC has credentials counselors in the United States and internationally.

Job Growth and Earnings for School Counselors

The rate of job growth and earnings for school counselors depends greatly on the country that one is employed in and whether the school is funded publicly or privately. School Counselors working in international schools or "American" schools around the world may find similar work environments and expectations to current best practices in the United States. Outside of those schools, expectations (and pay) vary greatly based on the level of school counselor or school counselor roles, identity, expectations, and legal and certification requirements and expectations.

In the United States, according to the Occupational Outlook Handbook (OOH) the median salary for school counselors in the United States in May 2004 was $45,570. The middle 50 percent earned between $34,530 and $58,400. Also, school counselors could earn additional money working summer jobs as counselors for schools or community agencies, and among all counseling fields, are currently (2004) paid the highest salary. Overall employment for counselors is faster than average, and school counselors should find a favorable job market because demand is higher than the graduation rates of school counseling programmes. In the United States, rural areas and urban areas traditionally have been under-served by school counselors in public schools due to both funding shortages and often a lack of best practice models. With the advent of No Child Left Behind legislation in the USA and a mandate for school counselors to be working with data and showing evidence-based practice, school counselors who are able to show and share their results in assisting to close gaps are in the best position to argue for increased school counseling resources and positions for their programmes (ASCA, 2005). For more international specifics, see external links.

International School Counseling Issues

How school counseling services are provided in K-12 schools varies on public versus private schools and divergent financial and social capital resources in various countries and communities. Worldwide, there are large achievement, opportunity, funding, and attainment gaps for who has access to a quality K-12 education and can pursue additional educational resources including college. In some countries, school counseling, frequently career education/development/ counseling, is provided by educational specialists (for example, Botswana, Finland, Israel, Malta, Nigeria, Romania, Turkey, United States). In other cases, school counseling is provided by classroom teachers who either have such duties added to their typical teaching load or teach only a limited load that also includes school counseling activities (for example-China, India, Japan, Mexico, South Korea, Taiwan, Zambia). .

In Korea, school counselors must teach a subject besides counseling, and not all school counselors are appointed to counseling positions. Even though Korean law has required school counselors in all middle and high schools.

There are groups in Africa, the Americas, Asia, and Europe that have provided international counseling conferences but none have had an exclusive school counseling focus. The IAEVG focus is primarily on career development and has some international school counseling foci in publications and conferences .

Attitudes and Qualities of a Counsellor

To be considered a capable counsellor there are a number of qualities you must possess, along with a few attitudes you should develop. It is a counsellor's responsibility to make the client feel at ease with the counselling process. Building rapport and creating a counselling relationship that uses trust as a solid foundation, is a key requirement and counsellors must also be able to demonstrate genuine, caring attributes.

The Bare Essentials

A counsellor must be able to show a positive, unconditional regard for the wellbeing of a client, if a successfully progressive counselling relationship is to be formed. It is the basis from which a client can explore their thoughts, feelings and experiences, and develop an understanding and acceptance of their emotions. Without this unconditional support a client will feel inhibited and unable to express their true personality, difficulties and emotions.

Whilst maintaining a professional focus a counsellor must be able to show a genuine openness, within the counselling relationship. A client must feel comfortable, safe and confident that confidentiality will be maintained at all times, and also that the counsellor is committed to helping, encouraging and supporting.

Empathic understanding, and the ability to see things from the client's perspective is also important, as is the counsellor's ability to demonstrate an investment of their time and full attention.

How to Show Warmth and Understanding?

Showing empathy and genuineness encourages a client to relax and trust. It also encourages client self-disclosure. Maintaining warmth and understanding, without being judgmental, provides the client with a comfortable foundation within the counselling relationship. A counsellor should also show their own personality and ensure there is a friendly atmosphere and attitude, in order for the counselling relationship to grow.

Conveying warmth through body language–using posture, maintaining eye contact and personal space–encourages a client to trust. Counsellors should also be aware of the way they speak–the tone of voice, speed of speech and delivery–as the words used should be in agreement with the way their body language provides reassurance.

Warmth should be handled with care however, as a client who exhibits feelings of unease, distance and mistrust may feel initially threatened by sympathetic behaviour.

Demonstrating Positive Regard

Valuing and respecting a client is of vital importance in a counselling relationship. Demonstrating a positive acceptance of the client is the key to encouraging interaction and disclosure. Unconditional positive regard creates an opportunity to explore change, and provides a client with acceptance and genuine caring.

A counsellor must not judge in any way. This may be difficult in some situations, but is the basis of a counselling relationship built on trust. Accepting a client shows the individual that you value them and are there to support them through the counselling process, regardless of their weaknesses, negativity or unfavourable qualities.

Important Values of Counselling

At all times counsellors must show a commitment to:

1. Human Rights and dignity.
2. Supporting and alleviating personal distress.
3. Appreciating the differences in culture and human experience, and remaining non-judgmental.
4. Providing adequate counselling services whilst ensuring the integrity of the client/counsellor relationship.
5. Maintaining client confidentiality and ethical principles.

Personal Qualities of an Effective Counsellor

All the counsellors are not alike. They differ in various ways. Their personal characteristics, as well as, their personality differ quite substantially. A number of research organisations have tried to ascertain the personal qualities of a **counsellor**, which are essential to bring about therapeutical transformation in another person (i.e. the client). Three researchers namely Carkuff, Truax & Carl Rogers came up with the under mentioned characteristics, which are as follows:

a) *Empathy:* The empathic behaviour is the ability of a **counsellor** to stand in the shoes of the client i.e. to see the things from the point of view of the client. The quality of empathy is a must for the counselling process to succeed. Empathy calls for 'forgetting oneself so that the **counsellor** surrenders himself completely towards the client. The process of empathisation is never total or complete, which leaves a lot to be desired, for the counselling process to succeed. Several empathy enhancing activities helps in enhancing the quality of empathy in a **counsellor**.

b) *Genuineness:* Rogers as well as Truax considered genuineness, as a very important part of counselling. The employees of various public services are well trained to meet the public at large, in a very cordial and friendly manner. "Genuineness" is synonymous with good or honest intentions. A genuine interest in the client is a must for the counselling process to succeed.

c) *Warmth:* Personal warmth or being warm is a controversial issue. There is a hairline difference between being warm or being dubbed as 'sickliness'. The quality of being warm refers to a situation, where a person shows interest in other individual/group. 'Cold' individuals rarely become good counsellors. A word of caution here, a too warm **counsellor** may lead towards the development of over-dependence on the part of the client. The ideal feeling of being warm is the one which demonstrates that the **counsellor** is non-judgmental and is honestly interested in his/her client. Care should be taken to see that the **counsellor** does not try to dominate the process of counselling.

d) *Concreteness:* It can be termed as a type of skill. It is an ability to listen, to what is being said by the client, instead of what is being implied. Concreteness in counselling is essential, if the counselling process has to succeed. A **counsellor** possessing the skill of 'concreteness' does not go for details (regarding psychological explanations) of what the client is speaking about, but instead tries to understand what the client is trying to express. Any quick, preconceived or initial judgment about what the client is saying will not be particularly helpful. In fact, it will be counterproductive. The concept of concreteness almost integrates all the important elements of the counselling process. A concrete **counsellor**, invariably, listens to and accepts what the client is saying and does not quickly make his judgments.

e) *Unconditional Positive Regard:* Rogers came up with a term called, 'unconditional positive regard' to refer to 'necessary and sufficient conditions for therapeutic change' in the counselling relationship. Rogers emphasized that the counsellor's positive feeling for the client must never be conditional in nature. He further suggested that the **counsellor** should feel warmly disposed towards the client, irrespective of the client's feelings or emotions, which is almost impractical or unreal. This is impossible. Further, it is important that a **counsellor** is broad minded and initially non-judgmental. Also positive general disposition towards the client is a must for the counselling process to succeed.

f) *A Tragic Sense:* In order to get involved with a client's problem a 'tragic sense of life' must be developed. All human beings have some limitations. A tragic sense helps the **counsellor** to remain humble. It also inducts a sense of humanity in him. Counsellors are not people with better brains, but are the people who readily listen to the problems of their clients.

g) *A Sense of Humour:* A sense of humour comes quite handy, in rescuing most of the sensitive or delicate situations. It does not means that a **counsellor** should resort to a comedian's tactics. It also does not mean that a **counsellor** should start taking the conversation during counselling session lightly. But, it means to help a client to regain the sight of the larger picture of a problem. It helps in calming down the tense atmosphere, that builds up because the clients generally blow the things out of proportion. Even subjects dubbed as 'taboos', can be easily confronted with the help of a sense of humour.

h) *Self-awareness:* It means to being aware of oneself i.e. to be aware of one's own limitations and strengths. It means to explore oneself. It is a realistic attempt of comparing oneself with other people. It means to explore one's own life situations.

A MAN is literally what he thinks, his character being the complete sum of all his thoughts.

The Concept of Roles and Functions in Counselling

The terms role and function have been used almost synonymously in the literature and in most counselling discussions. It is only recently that writers are beginning to look at the terms separately with a view to highlighting their specifications. Role, according to Shertzer and Stone (1981), is viewed as a set of complementary expectations that result In behaviour. This view looks rather loose usage that writers have suggested a more prescriptive and definitive approach.

From a perceptual approach to role definition, Shertzer and Stone (1980) stated that to identify the role of school counsellors, an examination of their perceptions by those they serve i.e. the students, teachers, principals and parents should be carried out. Using a specification and expectation approach, Ipaye (1986), stated that a role is a part of function assumed by someone, a specific set of responsibilities assumed by a professional worker, or s set of perceived duties or such a professional in a given setting or organisation. Durojaiye (1976) simply Refined a role as a part one plays in any given position, social situation or social relationship. From these views, it seems that a role may be perceived as a concrete set of expected behaviours.

What then is a function? Ipaye (1986) stated that a function refers to the activities assigned to a role. According to Wrenn (1973), the distinction between a role and a function may be conceptualised as one of purpose (role) and process (function) or as one of ends (role) and means (**functions**). In this paper, therefore it is assummed that in carrying out a role, an individual 'is also carrying out a set of activities (**functions**).

Who should determine counsellors' roles and **functions**? If a role is a set of expected behaviours, it is expected that, apart from counsellors themselves, employers or consumers would have an input in defining counselling roles through their various expectations. Thus, would expect that in Nigeria, employers of counsellors such as the Ministries of Education, Schools Boards, and private school governing is may be involved in defining counsellors' roles because they are responsible for hiring counsellors for specific set of well defined tasks.

They should state their (counsellors') expected roles very clearly as well as determine what their consumers (i.e. students, teachers and parents) should expect from their employee-the **counsellor**. On the other hand, if **functions** are seen as the activities in which professionals are engaged in performing their roles, then judgement of the **functions** to be performed remains the prerogative of the professionals as long as they fulfil appropriate culture and institution-bound expectations of the role.

This writer believes that the professional body of counsellors (e.g. CAN) should play a major role in defining **counsellor** functioning because it ensure that counsellors are trained to exercise judgement in determining how best to utilise their skills and qualifications as well as to conform to the varying settings where their specific **functions** match the existing situations. It is expected that the **functions** of counsellors would differ from setting to setting, i.e. the function of a

counsellor in a school would differ from that of an industrial **counsellor**; and that within a given setting, e.g. in the schools, individual counsellors may function differently according to the school's characteristics. Thus, it is also expected that the approaches and procedures employed by counsellors in the same setting may differ to suit individual client needs and the collective institutional needs.

The questions of what should be counsellors' identities (their roles) and how they should best do it (their **functions**) have continually surfaced in most counselling circles seeking solution: As obscure as answers to these questions may seem, it is clear that counsellors' roles and **functions** go hand in hand and that counsellors themselves should have some responsibility in defining their roles and specifying the services or **functions** they provide such that it is different from, and cannot be mistaken for, those provided by other professionals. However, this does not presume that all **counsellor** will work in the same way under all conditions. Afterall, **counsellor** themselves are not the same: they differ in their personalities motivations and levels of experience. Any documentation of **counsellor** functioning thus serves as general guidelines for professions practice with the proviso that it is flexible enough to allow for each counsellor's individuality, the job setting and his/her level of experience.

Confidentiality and Professional Ethics in Counselling

Have you ever found yourself involved in an ethical dilemma? Even if you are not a counsellor or mental health professional, it is most likely that at some stage of your life, you have been directly or indirectly involved in a situation in which ethical conduct was to be considered.

The growth and standardisation of service industries, as well as the increasing awareness and obligation imposed by Privacy legislation, has led to the development of codes of conduct designed to protect both sides of the professional relationship-particularly the interests of clients. In counselling, ethical conduct is not only expected, but in many cases, is required by legislation.

So how does ethical conduct apply to the counselling relationship? Basically, ethics in counselling is comprised of two areas: confidentiality and professional ethics.

Confidentiality

"For counselling to be maximally effective, the client must feel secure in the knowledge that what they tell the counsellor is to be treated with a high degree of confidentiality. In an ideal world a client would be offered total confidentiality so that they would feel free to openly explore with the counsellor the darkest recesses of their mind, and to discuss the most intimate details of their thoughts." (Geldard & Geldard, 1998)

It is recommended that counsellors discuss confidentiality issues with clients before the counselling relationship is established. In most cases, the counsellor will tell the client that their relationship will be relatively confidential. Relative confidentiality is required in order to improve the quality of the service, as on many occasions, the counsellor may have to: discuss session details with supervisors, exchange valuable information with other professionals, or maintain notes and formal records of every session that has occurred. Furthermore, there are legal issues involving confidentiality: if a court order is issued, the counsellor must release personal records in order to comply with legislation. This can be a very sensitive matter, especially when the counsellor acquires knowledge that a client is dangerous and may put other lives at risk. These dilemmas are faced by many counsellors working in prisons, or with aggressive and potentially dangerous clients.

"While I worked for Drug Arm as a Project Officer for a programme called HART (Home Assessment Response Team), my role was to visit people in their own homes, who were affected by substance misuse challenges. Sometimes their home was within the confines of Community Correction Centres. Because confidentiality was stretched sometimes at certain stages of their imprisonment, I would strongly recommend to my clients that it would be preferable for them not to mention names or dates so that I would not have that unnecessary information (and evidence) to cause them harm should there ever be the need to have my duty to report or disclose some evidence of a particular situation, challenged."

(Kathleen Casagrande-Professional Counsellor)

Due to such situations, some counsellors even affirm that promising absolute confidentiality is unethical. The following are common aspects of a counselling relationship which prevent counsellors from providing absolute confidentiality to their clients:

- Keeping records of sessions and client's personal data;
- Release of information to Supervisors;
- Protection of third persons from endangering situations;
- Court orders or similar law enforcement issues which require information disclosure.

Professional Ethics

Because counselling is not a regulated profession in many countries (including Australia), the use of a professional code of ethics is a method of guiding the quality of the services provided by counsellors, the quality of training provided to counsellors, and protecting clients. These codes provide conduct guidelines for professionals and are an effective way to provide practice standards to many counsellors lacking experience or knowledge of the industry. It also serves the purpose of structuring the counselling industry, providing common professional descriptions, definitions and service boundaries according to each type of counsellor.

The Australian Counselling Association is one industry association in Australia that provides ethical guidelines and a code of conduct for counsellors. The ACA's Code of Ethics and Code of Practice are part of the Code of Conduct.

Complying with ethical guidelines is one of the most important aspects of being a professional counsellor. Creating awareness in both counsellor and clients of the boundaries of the services provided will lead to a better development of the profession, and overall improvement of industry standards. Counsellors are responsible for keeping up-to-date with professional codes of ethics, confidentiality guidelines, and other relevant information.

Differences between Consellor and Teacher

Counsellors, like coaches, create a space in which clients can talk about their issues. The key difference is that counselling deals primarily with helping people overcome problems whereas coaching is concerned with enhancing performance. Counselling generally tends to focus on the past in its search for reasons why we behave the way we do.

The goal is to assist people in understanding the root cause of long-standing issues. Counsellors might use 'why' questions such as "Why do you keep doing that?" whereas coaches more often ask 'what' questions such as "What would you like to do instead?"

In comparing coaching and counselling, the former might be seen as solution focused and action orientated, while counselling is more meaning based. Coaching addresses aspirations, objectives and tasks, while counselling focuses more on feelings. Coaching tends to be more structured while counselling can have a more free-form approach. Coaching puts greater emphasis on gaining clarity about what people want and how to achieve it, whereas counselling aims to help people to understand themselves better.

The word 'mentoring' originates from Greek mythology, where it is said that Odysseus entrusted his home and the education of his son to his friend Mentor.

"Tell him all you know," said Odysseus, hence the common understanding of mentoring as passing on experience and knowledge.

Widely used in professions, mentoring provides a mechanism by which experienced managers can pass on their wisdom – helping to shape their protege's values and beliefs in a positive way. This is in contrast to coaching and counselling, where the emphasis is on getting the person to come up with their own solutions, mentors often give advice and guidance.

Training is defined in the Collins English Dictionary as the "process of bringing a person to an agreed standard of proficiency by practice and instruction."

Training is about passing on information, skills and knowledge. Training helps people to develop cognitive skills and capabilities. While often directive "Do it this way" training is also delivered in a coaching, facilitative style. However this does not make it coaching.

The primary difference between the two is that training imparts information and coaching draws existing knowledge and understanding out of the person concerned.

UNIT-V

Group Guidance and Group Counselling

Group Guidance—Meaning—Definition—Objectives—Problems—Significance—Techniques—Uses

Group guidance and group counselling are effective means of responding to the varying needs of students.

Group guidance or group work in the classroom is typically used to address developmental needs and to implement preventative programmes. It is informational and instructional in nature.

Group counselling addresses specific, individual needs. It is an efficient and effective way of supporting and helping students to deal with problems and issues in educational, career and personal/social areas. It is healing and therapeutic in nature. Ethically, group counselling requires the counsellor to have specific training.

Aims of group guidance and counselling include:

- to provide a means of sharing information on topics such as career information and study skills
- to help students develop skills for programmes such as conflict management, peer helping, and peer tutoring
- to help students develop knowledge and learn personal management and social skills such coping with feelings, dealing with peer pressure, goal-setting, problem-solving, and communication skills

Using Diagonals for Guidance, Energy and Meaning

If you study my gallery on photographic composition (Gallery Nine), you will notice that many of my examples stress the importance of diagonal flow as a key element of composition. I consider diagonal flow so important that I am adding this gallery, devoted entirely to this critical component of photographic composition.

Diagonals not only can guide the viewer's eye through an image—they can also energize it and change what might otherwise be a static image into a dynamic one. I often read that diagonals make pictures "more interesting to the eye," but I like to go beyond mere interest and instead use diagonals to help tell a story, organize subject matter for coherence, and build rhythms that can create emotional response.

There many different ways to create diagonal flow. We can find subjects that already may have diagonals in them. Or we can create diagonal flow ourselves by tilting the camera (as long as no horizon is involved) so that a subject flows from corner to corner instead of from side to side. Corner to corner flow creates a line of power and thrust that emphatically emphasizes our point. We can also isolate and link repeating diagonals, sweep them from corner to corner, or use them elsewhere within the frame. We can even make use of diagonals created by the interplay of light and shadow, or arrange flows of specific colors in diagonal fashion.

I begin this gallery with a group of images using diagonals that I made in Vietnam at the end of 2007 and the beginning of 2008. I hope to add additional examples of diagonal flow from images made on future trips as well.

I present this gallery in "blog" style. A large thumbnail is displayed for each image, along with a detailed caption explaining how I intended to express my ideas. If you click on the large thumbnail, you can see it in its full size, as well as leave comments and read the comments of others. I hope you will be able to participate in the dialogue. I welcome your comments, suggestions, ideas, and questions, and will be delighted to respond.

Group Guidance: Concepts, Need and Significance

Group guidance encompasses those activities of **guidance** which are carried on in a. **group** situation to assist its members to have experiences desirable or even necessary for making appropriate decisions in the prevailing contexts. In a more specific tenn, **group guidance** is guiding the individual in a. **group** situations. For example, orientation programmes **and** for new entrants, in a school, career talks by a career counsellor in classroom situations **of Guiclance** are some of the common examples. You may be organizing and producing a number of **group guidance** situations to your students with respect to academic, career or other **guidance**.

A number of questions may **be** bothering you, like:

Why Group Guidance?

Why not impart **guidance** to students individually? What is the need of it? What benefit does it provide to the students?

In those schools, which promote **group guidance**, school students are in a position to avail the following benefits through participation in them:

1. Information that will help them in adjusting to their various areas of experience including:
   a) Educational progress
   b) Occupational opportunities and vocational preparation
   c) Leisure time activities
   d) Social and civic conditions.
2. Experience in cooperative living leading to the development of
   a) Initiative
   b) Good sportsmanship
   c) Self and social understanding
   d) Consideration of others.
3. Development of individual's abilities and interests through:
   a) Participation in **group** projects

b) Organization of student initiated activities

c) Special services and programmes in and out of the schools.

Advantages of Group Guidance

i) It is suitable for certain kinds of **guidance** activities like information about careers or orienting new entrants about the school. Here individual **guidance** will be a mere waste of time and other resources involved in undertaking the activity.

ii) It establishes a relationship between students and **guidance** worker which creates avenues for other **guidance** services. For example, new entrants to 11th standard or +2 stream want to help in selection of subjects from the school counsellor after a talk was delivered 'on "How to plan your career effectively?'.

iii) It pravides orientation to unfamiliar situation on new experiences. For example, the new batch of 10+2 level felt at ease when a counsellor told them about the school, the various facilities available in the school, the rules and regulations and the expectation from them.

iv) It paves the way for individual counselling. **Group guidance** saves time and effort on part of the counsellor as well as the students. Further it reduces monotony. Imagine how boring it is to repeat the class talk on time management separately for each student in a class of 40.

v) It focusses collective attention on common problems. A **group** situation helps individual more readily to find a solution for a problem than he could if he works on it alone.

Further he develops an awareness that the problems **are** not peculiar to the individual but **are** shared by others too. Therefore he discusses the problem in a permissive atmosphere and the emotional tension gets a release. The suggestion made during **group** discussion are thus more acceptable to him.

vi) It provides the individual with a chance for real **group** life and learn how to deal with people. In **group** situation students are more exposed to a variety of **group** experiences in the schools life which helps them to modify their behaviour in a socially acceptable ways. They also learn to respect others point of views.

vii) It also help a counsellor to multiply contacts with the students.

viii) The informal and free atmosphere of the **group** rliscussion provides a good opportunity to the counsellor to observe student as helshe reacts in a **group** situation and to learn about hiinher which otherwise is not feasible. In an individual counselling session, artificiality in behaviour may occur. Further the counsellor may not be able to note the interaction pattern of the student. Thus **group guidance** is very much required in certain situations.

Problems in Organizing Group Guidance

Group guidance activities serve useful purposes specially saving in time and effort. While organizing these activities, some problems that a counsellor may face are mentioned below:

A rigid type of administration is often a major cause of trouble. Generally, when the counsllol-asks for time in the time table for conducting these **guidance** activities, helshe may get a discouraging reply, the tiine table is already full. No periods are free. So the counsellor is left with no other choice than to take the substitute management period. Lack of cooperation on part of the administration as well as the staff members may also creace problems in organizing such activities. Teacher may feel this as an addition burdon. Lack **of** adequate funds is another problem.

These problems can be overcome if tackled with a bit of planning, patience and boldness. **E.g.** the problem of time table, .which does not have a period for **guidance** activities, one may take **Group Guidance Techniques and** work experience/S.U.P.W. classes. Further, co-curricular activity classes can be taken in rotation **Procedures of Guidance** every week. Career quizzes can be arranged with no difficulty if the entire plan has been discussed with management.

Further, the use of **guidance** in teaching and reducing the problem of truancy and indiscipline, underachievement can be conveyed to the teachers. Once they find a positive correlation between the two, they will be most willing to help. As far as the inadequacy of funds is considered, the management needs to be convinced about the minimum requirement.

Guidance Techniques that Work

In the previous chapters, suggestions for identifying gifted students, providing career counseling, providing academic **guidance**, and dealing with specific psychological adjustment problems were presented. Many **techniques** and strategies are useful across all kinds of counseling with gifted students. In a way, many **techniques** presented here are actually just the manifestations of positive, helpful attitudes toward gifted and talented students. These suggestions for counseling gifted students are based on the experiences of counselors at the **Guidance** Laboratory for Gifted and Talented at the University of Nebraska and the Counseling Labo-ratory for Talent Development at The University of Iowa. They are grouped into two categories: designing **guidance** services for the gifted and talented, and counseling **techniques**.

Designing Guidance Services

Although it is probably not necessary that gifted students have a separate, specialized counseling service, it may be useful for the counselor to have a different system for keeping records and providing services to gifted students. Having a system of records and a plan for counseling gifted students ensures that gifted students' needs will not be overlooked in the course of trying to provide a wide variety of services to a diverse student **group**. Sometimes a school already has an individualized approach to **guidance** that emphasizes the talent development of each student; a system like this can be easily modified to provide for the special needs of gifted students. Some suggestions for structuring **guidance** services to gifted and talented students follow.

1. The file of every gifted and talented student should contain the transcripts of that student's coursework; a clear description of the student's special talents; a description of all results from ability tests that have been administered to that student by the counselor, school psychologist, or a private psychologist; any interest, personality, or values inventory results that may exist for that student; are cord of summer school attendance and attendance at special camps and institutes for the gifted and talented; a description of out-of-class accomplishments, particularly awards, recognitions, and outstanding products; and a goal-setting sheet similar to the one described in chapter 5 on Career Planning in which a student has outlined two or three goals and his or her plans for attaining those goals.
2. If an assessment programme does not already cxist in the school, the counselor may wish to develop his or her own psychological assessment system for gifted students. Psychological assessment may consist of additional tests of intellectual abilities and aptitudes that the counselor is qualified to give; vocational interest tests; personality tests with which the counselor is familiar and competent; and values inventories.
3. The counselor should keep a library of materials likely to be of particular interest to gifted and talented students. Career education materials should include biographies such as those listed in the Resources section for gifted girls, materials for career counseling, as well as career education and college planning materials specially designed for gifted students. I referred to many of these materials in chapter 6 on counseling gifted girls, chapter 5 on career counseling, and chapter 4 on college planning. Also'in the counselor's library should be a copy (or multiple copies) of favorite books for bibliotherapy.
4. Counselors can design a **guidance** plan for each gifted student that focuses on the development of talent. Each

academic year the counselor should meet with the student alone several times, and at least once with parents to plan for the academic year ahead. Individual sessions with the gifted student alone can be devoted to developmental counseling focusing on the student's adjustment and achievement of his or her own goals. Sessions with parents can evaluate the overall impact of curriculum and special activities on the student's development, and also can be informational sessions about future opportunities and goals.

5. For the counselor with a large case load of gifted and talented students, **group guidance** is not only an efficient way of providing registration, but also an opportunity for gifted students to interact with one another in planning for the future and discussing current issues in their lives. **Group guidance** with the gifted and talented can be organized around topics covered in this handbook. **Group** sessions might include a workshop on adjustment and self-esteem; a workshop on sex roles, relationships, and giftedness; a career planning workshop; and a college planning seminar.

6. The counselor should work closely with the gifted coordinator and with teachers of gifted students in developing a consultative relationship. The gifted education coordinator and other teachers need to be aware of the counselor's special expertise. In addition, the counselor can learn from the gifted educator and teachers more about the characteristics and needs of his or her gifted clients. Too often consulting remains on an informal basis and busy schedules overwhelm the good intentions of all parties to meet. Therefore the counselor might want to set up, at the beginning of each year, at least one formal meeting with the teachers of the gifted and perhaps the gifted student representative in order to develop a plan to meet the needs of gifted students.

Techniques for Counseling the Gifted and Talented

Most of the **techniques** for counseling gifted and talented students are simply the **techniques** all good counselors use: listening skills, persuasion skills, and behavior change skills. The following **techniques** are really attitudes and behaviors that can help the counselor to be more effective with intellectually able students and students with specific extraordinary talents (Kerr, 1990).

1. Counseling with gifted students must be child-centered, as Holling worth (1926) first demonstrated. The more remarkable the gifts of the bright student, the greater is the investment that individuals have in the decisions that student makes. In the life of every gifted student there are teachers, parents, administrators, and friends with strong opinions about that child. In addition, there is often a great deal of information available in the records from former teachers and counselors. Despite the involvement of parents and teachers and despite the documents and records that exist, the counselor's first duty is to receive the gifted child's description of the problem or concerns in the child's own words. The child must be the focus of the counseling and therapy process. Sometimes in our rush to develop a child's talent we forget the child's own feelings and beliefs about his or her gifts. Only by understanding the child's giftedness from within the child's frame of reference can the counselor help to develop the child's gifts to their full potential.
2. In understanding the psychology of the (gifted child, intellectual abilities as well as personality characteristics must be taken into account. Many counselors of oifted students have observed that 0ifts seem to have a life of their own. For example, verbal precocity is a hunger for reading, writing, and expression that the individual cannot ignore. Mathematical precocity has an insistence of its own, demanding that the student go further and deeper into an understanding of math. Almost every talent carries with it its own

drive and appetite for actualization. Therefore, to attempt to counsel the child without guiding the gift is to misunderstand the nature of the gifted child. It is often said that the gifted child is a child first, and then gifted. However, this statement may be misleading. A 'aifted child cannot be understood apart from his or her gifts.

3. A counselor's attitude toward a gifted student should be positive, constructive, and comfortable. As Hollin' worth (1926) noted long ago, professionals who work with gifted students often feel threatened or are overly admiring. Neither of these attitudes is helpful. The counselor who feels threatened by the gifted child may feel tempted to test the child's knowledge, as if to make the child prove that he or she is gifted. The counselor who is threatened may avoid 'ifted students, not wanting students to know about his or her lack of experience. The counselor who is overly admiring may be equally harmful. The awestruck counselor may feel overwhelmed by the verbally brilliant student's conversational abilities, allowing the counseling session to be sidetracked. Instead of being fri-htened or dazzled, probably the best attitude to strive for is one of friendly helpfulness and positive challenge. A counselor can be an empathic listener as well as a mentor who expects excellence from the student.

4. A counselor should always show curiosity rather than ignorance or indifference. For better or worse, many gifted students base their opinions of others on their perceptions of others' intellectual interests and abilities. In order for counselors to be effective and influential with their lifted students, it is necessary that their students perceive them as intelligent people with lively interests in the kinds of intellectual endeavors in which the students are interested. This does not mean that the counselor has to be an expert on such things as Fermat's theorem, Dylan Thomas's poetry, or the language of dolphins. Instead, it means that when

students discuss these kinds of subjects the counselor should show a lively curiosity and willingness to learn about the topics that are exciting to the students. The basic **techniques** of good attending behaviors are exactly those that enable the counselor to show curiosity and interest. When a student remarks that she or he is interested in developing software for playing Dungeons and Dragons, the counselor can simply respond with, ""That sounds fascinating! Tell me more about it." Or "What is it about developing software for games that excites you'?" The counselor will learn a lot of interesting facts in these kinds of conversations, and gifted students will perceive the counselor as credible and persuasive.

5. The counseling process with gifted students often points up the necessity for change not only in the student but in the family, the school, and society. Many problems gifted students present to the counselor are not really their own problems but rather problems of the system in which they are trying to learn and grow. To help a gifted child to cope with the boredom of being in the regular classroom, the counselor must do more than help the student with coping skills. Instead, the counselor must act as an advocate for that student, helping the student to achieve a more challenging curriculum. To help the student who is experiencing extraordinary stress from academic pressure, the counselor must work with parents and students together to create a healthier attitude toward achievement.

Often, if the counselor is to do a good job as a helper to gifted students, he or she must become involved in action for change in the school system and in society. Many counselors who are experienced in working with gifted students enjoy the opportunity to meet other counselors of the gifted at state and national professional organizations that work for the betterment of gifted students. Counselors also can help empower gifted students to bring about changes themselves. By teaching their gifted students communication and persuasion skills, counselors may be able to help them to influence teachers and administrators to provide the kind of education they need.

Summary

At the beginning of this book, I said that those counselors who decide to guide gifted students are taking on a challenging but rewarding task. I have reviewed the challenges to the counselor in providing for the psychological adjustment, career planning, and academic **guidance** of the gifted student. The rewards of counseling the gifted student are much more difficult to describe; in fact they must be experienced. Perhaps the best way to describe the experience of counseling gifted students is to liken it to cutting diamonds. Like the jeweler who cuts precious gems, the counselor to the gifted gently guides and shapes the student's abilities and interests so that the brilliance might shine through.

Group Counselling—Meaning, Requirements—Uses

Effective Group Counseling

There is a natural tendency for people to gather in groups for mutually beneficial purposes. Through groups, individuals accomplish goals and relate to others in innovative and productive ways (McClure, 1990). People would not survive, let alone thrive, without involvement in groups. This reliance and interdependence is seen in all types of groups from those that are primarily task-oriented to those that are basically therapeutic.

In order to be effective, group leaders must be aware of the power and potency of groups. They must plan ahead and they must be sensitive to the stage of development of the group. Equipped with this knowledge they can utilize appropriate skills to help their groups develop fully (Gladding, 1994). Proper preparation and strategic intervention increase the chance of running a counseling group smoothly and effectively.

Beginning Counseling Groups

A crucial element in starting counseling groups is making decisions beforehand. Pregroup planning is the first step in the process. Leaders design groups so that they will yield productive and pragmatic results for participants. Among the most important considerations are those associated with objectives, membership, rules, time, place, and dynamics.

Objectives of Group Counseling

Group counseling involves individuals who are having difficulties they wish to resolve that are of a personal, educational, social, or vocational nature (Corey & Corey, 1992). These groups are primarily run in educational institutions or agencies.

They deal with specific, nonpathological problems that members are aware of prior to joining and which do not involve major personality changes. For instance, group counseling may focus on how members achieve such goals as relating better to their families, becoming organized, or relaxing in the presence of supervisors at work.

Group Membership

Group membership is either homogeneous or heterogeneous. Homogeneous groups are composed of individuals who are similar, such as adolescent boys, single parents or individuals working with grief and loss issues. Heterogeneous groups are made up of people who differ in background, such as adults of various ages with varied careers. While homogeneous groups can concentrate on resolving one issue, their members may be limited experientially. In contrast, heterogeneous groups offer diverse but multifocused membership.

Effective group leaders screen potential members before accepting them. Screening allows leaders to select members and members to select leaders and groups. The ideal group size of eight to 12 allows members an opportunity to express themselves without forming into subgroups. In order to help dispel and overcome misconceptions about groups, leaders can utilize pregroup interviews to identify fears related to upcoming groups. Through feedback and explanation, misunderstandings can be immediately clarified and corrected (Childers & Couch, 1989).

Rules in Counseling Groups

Counseling groups run best when the rules governing them are few and clear. If there are more than a dozen rules, many members will tend to forget some of them. Likewise, if the rules are vague, some members will inevitably violate the letter or spirit of them. In counseling groups, rules should follow the ethical standards of professional organizations, such as the Association for Specialists in Group Work. Members should agree to keep each others' confidentiality, not attack each other verbally or physically, to actively participate in the group process, and to speak one at a time.

Time and Place of Groups

Although counseling groups vary, members need a specific, consistent time and place to meet. Most groups meet for one and one half to two hours each week for 12 to 16 sessions. The meeting room should be quiet and inviting and away from other activities. Groups work best when chairs are arranged in circles where everyone feels a sense of equality with one another and the flow of communication is enhanced (Gladding, 1994).

Group Dynamics

Group member interactions appear simple but they are not. They are complex social processes that occur within groups and that affect actions and outcomes (Lewin, 1948). Group dynamics occur in all groups, and involve the interactions of group members and leaders over time, including the roles the members and the leaders take. Individuals have an impact on groups just as groups influence members. The number of group interactions increases exponentially as the size of groups grows. Therefore, keeping track of communication patterns in counseling groups is a demanding job.

The complexity of interaction is magnified by the fact that messages are sent within counseling groups on a verbal as well as a nonverbal level. The nature of this communication is crucial to comprehending what is happening within groups. For example, a member who physically or emotionally distances from a group influences how the group operates as clearly as if he or she makes a statement. As groups develop, members frequently switch roles and patterns of interaction.

Group Stages

In addition to preplanning, effective group counseling leaders recognize that groups go through five stages: dependency, conflict, cohesion, interdependence, and termination. The stages are often called "forming, storming, norming, performing, and adjourning (Tuckman & Jensen, 1977). Recognizing group stages gives counselors an opportunity to devise or utilize appropriate leadership interventions.

The first group stage is "dependency" or forming. At this time, group members are unsure of themselves and look to their leaders or others for direction. This process gives members an opportunity to explore who they are in the group and to begin establishing trust. The second stage in group counseling is "conflict," or storming. It may be overt or covert. The type and amount of conflict that is generated relates to how much jockeying for position goes on in the group.

Stage three focuses on "cohesion," or norming, which can be defined as a spirit of "we-ness." In it, members become closer psychologically and are more relaxed. Everyone feels included in the group and productive sharing begins to occur. In the fourth stage, performing, the main work of the group is begun. Interdependence develops. Group members are able to assume a wide variety of constructive roles and work on personal issues. The level of comfort in the group increases too. This is a prime time of problem solving. It occupies about 50% of a typical group's time. The final stage, adjourning deals with termination. Issues of loss in separating from the group are raised. Celebrating the accomplishment of goals is also a primary focus within this stage.

Group Counseling Skills

As with other groups, leaders of effective counseling groups need to employ a variety of interpersonal skills (Corey & Corey, 1992). Among the most important of these are:

a) active listening, where leaders are sensitive to the language, tone, and nonverbal gestures surrounding members' messages;
b) linking, where leaders help members recognize their similarities;
c) blocking, where leaders keep unfocused members from disrupting the group by either redirecting them or preventing them from monopolizing conversations; and
d) summarizing, where leaders help members become aware of what has occurred and how the group and its members have changed.

Empathy, personal warmth, courage, flexibility, inquiry, encouragement, and the ability to confront are vital skills too. Counseling group leaders must wear many hats in helping their groups make progress. The more skills within the counselors' repertoires the more effective they will ultimately become.

Conclusion

Conducting effective group counseling relies on the preparation of group leaders and their abilities to plan and conduct groups. Extra time in preparation is crucial to the life of the group. This process includes screening of members, selecting a manageable number of group participants, establishing a regular place and time for the conducting of the group, and setting rules. In running groups leaders must then recognize and utilize group stages and employ appropriate counseling skills in a timely fashion. Successful group counseling is dependent on many factors. Ultimately, the secrets of conducting effective counseling groups are in learning how groups operate and then personally investing in them.

The Use of Exercises in Group

Career Counseling: As will be noted in the examples provided throughout this book and specifically with the GCC model in chapter three, exercises are integral to most GCC sessions. Structured exercises help participants to access information and data on the world of work as well as provide the benefits of improved career decision-making.

As **group** counseling emerged in the 1960s, Carl Rogers and others did not advocate the use of exercises. However, currently most **group** leaders view the use of exercises as invaluable aids to the leader, the members, and the **group** process itself (Corey et al., 1982; Dyer & Vriend, 1980; Yalom, 1995). Indeed there are several distinct advantages to the use of exercises in **group** counseling (Jacobs et al., 1994, p. 163), which will often (a) generate fruitful discussion and **group** participation, (b) focus or shift the focus of the **group**, (c) provide an opportunity for experiential learning, (d) provide the leader with use fulinformation about the **group** members, (e) increase the comfort level of the **group**, and (f) provide a source of fun and relaxation.

UNIT-VI

Theories of Vocational Choice

The result of making a career decision. It is a generic term for any broad decision that orients an individual toward a particular job, occupational, or career goal. Such a choice may be fleeting or permanent, and may be only an intention or may be put into action.

Some theories of career development—such as Holland's (1997) theory of vocational choice—focus on vocational choice as a central construct. Other theories may refer to the construct by other names, such as "career decision-making" or "career choice" or "occupational choice." What these theories have in common is the believe that the choice process involves some degree of selection of one option from a set of alternative courses. The theories vary in the degree to which such choice need be rational, freely made, or even consciously made.

Vocational psychologists have considered the question of what might constitute a minimum theory of vocational choice, although none have referred to the issue as such. In philosophy of science, theorists frequently attempt to determine what might constitute "minimum" theories of various areas, stripping away potentially unnecessary theoretical structures so as to ultimately arrive at the bare nubbins of an absolutely bare minimum account of the construct of interest. Gati's various accounts of various possible decision-making methods probably comes nearest to the mark here; some of his proposed methods are in a sense more minimal than others. Other theorists, such as

Holland, have proposed theories in which basic career decisions may be made with some basic mechanism, with the nature of such choices elaborated through a set of additional mechanisms.

At minimum, a theory of vocational choice would presumably require only three elements: (1) a cognitive structure within which more than one possible course of future career progression may be represented, such that particular features of such options may be represented, without necessarily being common features across each option; (2) a cognitive function through which a choice amongst such options may be made, through some means, possibly based on the particular features of the various options; and (3) a cognitive structure capable of retaining and preserving information about the choice made, such that such information could be made available for future application and guidance of behavior. However, just because philosophically such a theory might be a minimum description of vocational choice does not mean that this is what we actually do in practice. In all likelihood, more complexity is required to adequately capture the process.

Louis Ginzberg

Biographical Background

Ginzberg was born into a religious family whose piety and erudition was well known. The family traced its lineage back to the legendary Gaon of Vilna. In his own mind, Ginzberg emulated the Vilna Gaon's intermingling of 'academic knowledge' in Torah studies under the label 'historical Judaism'. In his book *"Students, Scholars and Saints"*, Ginzberg quotes the Vilna Gaon instructing, "Do not regard the views of the Shulchan Aruch as binding if you think that they are not in agreement with those of the Talmud."

He writes in his memoirs that he felt saddened that he had grieved his father. Ginzberg recognized that his pious father was disappointed that his son chose to become a scholar in lieu of a gaon. Ginzberg first arrived in America in 1899, unsure where he belonged or what he should pursue. Almost immediately, he accepted a position at Hebrew Union College and subsequently wrote articles for the Jewish Encyclopedia. Still, he had not found his niche.

Judaism Studied in a Historical Context

In 1903, he began teaching at the Jewish Theological Seminary of America in New York City, where he taught until his death. Throughout his life, all of his works were infused with the belief that Judaism and Jewish history could not be understood properly without a firm grasp of Halakhah. Instead of just studying Halakha, Louis Ginzberg wrote responsa, formal responses to questions of Jewish law.

Many of Ginzberg's Orthodox Jewish peers had deep reservations about his choice to work at JTS. JTS explicitly encouraged its faculty and students to study rabbinical literature within its social and historical context; this was sometimes known as Wissenschaft, or the "scientific study of Judaism". As a result of this, many Orthodox Jews viewed his work as unacceptable.

On account of his impressive scholarship in Jewish studies, Ginzberg was one of sixty scholars honored with a doctorate by Harvard University in celebration of its tercentenary. Ginzberg's knowledge warranted him the expert to defend Judaism both in national and international affairs. In 1906, he defended the Jewish community against anti-Semitic accusations that Jews ritually slaughtered gentiles. In 1913, Louis Marshall requested that Ginzberg refute a blood libel charge in Kiev based on Jewish sources.

Legacy at JTS

Ginzberg began teaching Talmud at the Jewish Theological Seminary from its reorganization in 1902 until his death in 1953. For fifty years he trained two generations of future Conservative rabbis. Ginzberg impacted upon almost every single rabbi of the Conservative Movement in a personal way. For some, Louis Ginzberg serves as a role model even today. Today's leading Conservative posek in Israel, Rabbi David Golinkin, has written profusely on his mentor Louis Ginzberg. Golinkin has recently published a collection of responsa containing 93 questions answered by Ginzberg.

In the opening address, Ginzberg spoke of the need to keep Conservative Jewry under the rubric of Halakhah. The conception that in religious matters anyone, however ignorant, can judge for himself, is the direct denial of the old Jewish maxim, 'The ignorant cannot be pious' (Avot 2:5)... The majority vote of a Board of Directors of a synagogue is, after all, a negligible quantity when it is in opposition to the vote of historical Judaism with its myriad of Saints and thousands of Sages...The sorting, distributing, selecting, harmonizing and completing can only be done by experienced hands. Ginzberg's initiative to base halakhic decisions on law committees and not laymen is the method employed by the Conservative movement today.

In 1918, at the Sixth Annual Convention, Ginzberg, as the acting president, declared that United Synagogue of Conservative Judaism stood for 'historical Judaism' and thus elaborates:

> *"Now let us understand the exact meaning of the expression historical Judaism...Looking at Judaism from a historical point of view, we become convinced that there is no one aspect deep enough to exhaust the content of such a complex phenomenon as Judaism...Accordingly, Torah-less Judaism... would be an entirely new thing and not the continuation of something given...*

Responsa on Wine during Prohibition

One of his responsa concerns the use of wine in the Jewish community during Prohibition. On January 16, 1920, the United States Government enforced the Eighteenth Amendment to the United States Constitution which declared that "the manufacture, sale, or transportation of intoxicating liquors within... the United States... for beverage purposes is hereby prohibited." One of the three stipulated exceptions to the prohibition was for sacramental use. The Christian Church was able to successfully regulate the use of ceremonial wine. The clergy could easily monitor the nominal amount of wine that each worshipper drank especially because it was usually drunk only in Church and only on Sundays.

This was not the case for the Jews. Jews needed a greater quantity of wine per person. Furthermore, the wine was drunk in the privacy of the home on Shabbat, Jewish holidays, weddings and ritual circumcisions. This alone would have made the regulation of ceremonial wine complicated. It was not difficult for crooks to rig illegal 'wine synagogues' to trick the government to receive their wine which would then be bootlegged.

The Reform Movement in 1920 proclaimed that grape juice be used instead of wine further to eliminate future complaints. Shortly afterwards, on January 24, 1922, the Conservative movement publicized the 71-page responsa written by Ginzberg tackling the halakhic aspects of drinking grape juice instead of wine in light of the historical circumstances. Besides Ginzberg's well-grounded decision to permit grape juice, he includes meta-halakhic reasoning:

> *"...The decision of the author of Magen Abraham that the commandment is honored best by the use of old wine is rejected. Even this authority would admit that it is better to pronounce the Kiddush over new wine than to desecrate the Name and to disgrace the Jewish people, and we well know the damage caused the Jewish people by the trafficking in sacramental wine."*

Five years later, Rabbi Isaac Simha Hurewitz, an Orthodox rabbi from Hartford, Connecticut, challenged Ginzberg's ruling on unfermented wine. The critique did not appear in the newspapers for the masses to read; rather it was only to be found in his commentary, the Yad Levi, on Sefer HaMitzvot. Rabbi Hurewitz did not just challenge Ginzberg's responsa based on legal logic. Part and parcel of Hurewitz's attack is an attempted character assassination on Ginzberg himself:

> *Rabbi Hurewitz prepares a twofold attack. First he attacks the Conservative Movement by calling them Karaites and thus attempts to diminish Ginzberg's status as a legitimate rabbinic authority. Though he does not mention Ginzberg by name, it is obvious that Hurewitz was familiar with both the activities of the Conservative Movement and Ginzberg's responsa. Second, he attacks*

the erudition of Ginzberg. He says that 'Ginzberg does not have a brain' since even a non-Jewish child could tell you that wine is tastier and preferred to grape juice'. Thus, with this ad hominem attack he claims that all of Ginzberg's intellectual arguments are invalid. Rabbi Hurewitz exemplifies the Orthodox stance that recognized Ginzberg as the leader of Conservative Judaism in the 1920's, whether or not Ginzberg would have agreed.

Works

Ginzberg was the author of a number of scholarly Jewish works, including a commentary on *Talmud Yerushalmi* (the Jerusalem Talmud) and his six-volume (plus a one-volume index) *The Legends of the Jews,* which combined hundreds of legends and parables from a lifetime of midrash research.

Legends of the Jews is an original synthesis of a vast amount of aggadah from all of classical rabbinic literature, as well as apocryphal, pseudopigraphical and even early Christian literature, with legends ranging from the creation of the world and the fall of Adam, through a huge collection of legends on Moses, and ending with the story of Esther and the Jews in Persia. Ginzberg had an encyclopedic knowledge of all rabbinic literature, and his masterwork included a massive array of aggadot. However he did not create an anthology which showed these aggadot distinctly. Rather, he paraphrased them and rewrote them into one continuous narrative that covered four volumes, followed by two volumes of footnotes that give specific sources. See Jewish folklore and Aggadah.

Apart from *Legends of the Jews*, perhaps his best known scholarly work was his *Geonica* (1909), an account of the Babylonian Geonim containing lengthy extracts from their responsa, as discovered in the form of fragments in the Cairo Genizah. This work was continued by him in the similar collection entitled *Ginze Schechter* (1929).

Professor Ginzberg wrote 406 articles and several monograph-length entries for the *Jewish Encyclopedia* (Levy 2002), some later collected in his *Legend and Lore.* He was an important halakhic authority of the Conservative movement in

North America; for a period of ten years (1917-1927), he was virtually *The* halakhic authority of this movement. He was also founder and president of the American Academy of Jewish Research.

Super's ability Related Theory

One half of D. Super's (D. Super, M. Savickas, & C. Super, 1996) theoretical propositions that relate to abilities have been operationalized into a psychometric instrument, the Ability Explorer (T. Harrington & J. Harrington, 1996). Interpretations illustrate how D. Super's career development theoretical concepts can be implemented in career counseling.

This is an article about abilities and their importance and use in career counseling. In spring of 2002, career professionals had an opportunity to examine the role that abilities play in career development with the U.S. Department of Labor's release of its aptitude/ability measures as part of the O*NET occupational information system (U.S. Department of Labor, Employment and Training Administration, 2000). O*NET replaced the Dictionary of Occupational Titles (U.S. Department of Labor, 1991). However, the main focus in this article is the Ability Explorer (AE; Harrington & Harrington, 1996), a psychometric device for career counseling purposes that operationalizes 7 of the 14 propositions constituting Super's career development theory (Super, Savickas, & Super, 1996). Only portions of the theoretical propositions that relate to abilities are addressed. The specific propositions used, with illustrated applications, are listed later in the Interpretation section.

Osipow (1994, p. 219) identified Holland's theory, social learning theory, developmental theory, and work adjustment theory as four of the five foundational career theories. However, vocational scholars thought that all of these theories, except the work adjustment theory, neglected the concept of ability in career development theory (Savickas, 1994). Inspection of the four theory descriptions in Career Choice and Development (Brown, Brooks, & Associates, 1996) also reveals that three of the theories have psychometric devices that play central roles in implementing of the theories: Holland's (1970) Self-Directed Search, social learning theory in the Careers Belief Inventory (Krumboltz, 1988), and work adjustment theory in the Minnesota Satisfaction Questionnaire (Weiss, Dawis, England, & Lofquist, 1967) and in the Minnesota Importance Questionnaire (Weiss, Dawis, & Lofquist, 1975). However, no psychometric instrument was cited that covers Super's comprehensive theory.

The Salience Inventory (Nevill & Super, 1986a) and the Values Inventory (Nevill & Super, 1986b), pertinent to specific issues in Super's theory are mentioned, as well as the C-DAC (an acronym for Career Development Assessment and Counseling; Osborne, Brown, Niles, & Miner, 1997) model. "The C-DAC model uses constructs from life-span, life-space theory to supplement the trait and factor model's attention to abilities and interests" (Super et al., 1996, p. 150). Although the C-DAC model views dealing with self-concept in a segmental and developmental way, the assessments used to implement the model focused more on late adolescents and young adults (Osborne et al., 1997). However, several of the C-DAC instruments (e.g., the Career Development Inventory and the Adult Career Concerns Inventory) are now out of print.

The intent of this article is to attempt again to convert Super's (Super et al., 1996) popular theory into practice, specifically focusing on abilities and the translation of abilities and self-concept into occupational language to help identify educational and career goals. The reason for the focus on ability is the belief, expressed in Savickas's (1994) observation, that "ability is the integrative construct for much of the rest of psychology" (p. 238). The AE's components focus on development, self-concept, and learning orientations and on using the most common methodology in career practice—the matching of personal characteristics with occupations.

Instrumentation

The AE uses a newer self-report methodology than do models that were developed over a quarter of a century ago (i.e., the Self-Directed Search [SDS], Holland, 1970, and the

Harrington-O'Shea Career Decision-Making System [CDM], Harrington & O'Shea, 1974). For example, SDS respondents self-estimate each of 12 abilities simply designated by name (e.g., clerical ability) on a 7-point rating scale (1 = low, 5 = average, and 7 = high). In a method that was developed later, the CDM defines the meaning of the abilities and asks respondents to select 4, from a list of 14, of their best abilities (e.g., "clerical ability—running business machines, collecting information in person or by telephone, keeping correct records, typing"). The AE uses a new methodology and asks individuals to rate how good they would be at doing something if they were given a chance from a list of 140 items and how well they can do an activity from a list of 112 items. Respondents indicate their ratings from very good, good, little above average, little below average, poor, or very poor. This third generation of self-report methodologies is more comprehensive and more specific and provides richer information to use during interpretation than did the earlier approaches.

The AE assesses 14 major work-related abilities identified in the research literature as used in job performance. The AE includes 9 abilities (i.e., artistic, interpersonal, leadership, manual, musical/dramatic, organizational, persuasive, scientific, and social) in addition to the 5 abilities (i.e., language, numerical, clerical, mechanical, and spatial) that are traditionally measured. Each of the 14 abilities represents the total score of performance self-ratings, ranging from 6 = very good to 1 = very poor on each of 10 micro-skill statements (e.g., selling products) that define the competencies that make up the macro-ability (e.g., persuasive). Questions were drawn from activities that job analysts noted that workers perform. This information was then written into 5th-grade reading-level language. Statistical item analysis data were used to determine whether students above Grade 5 had sufficient exposure to make a judgment of proficiency. (Not yet tried was one of the possible response choices for "activities.") A test bias panel of 12 experts examined the questions to determine whether they were within the common experience of gender, racial, and ethnic groups in order to be included in the AE. The AE also collects self-reported grades in school courses that relate to each of the abilities, as well as a sampling of noncourse experiential activities (e.g., worked in an election) that can foster the development of abilities. Grades and activities are seen as behavioral reinforcers and are presented visually in the interpretive materials for comparative purposes, either supporting or being inconsistent with self-perceptions of self-ratings of abilities.

The AE uses the individual's highest two abilities to suggest specific career groups to explore. The specific job groups are part of an overall list that includes the jobs in which most U.S. workers are employed. The matrix for assigning occupations to abilities was based on the Occupational Aptitude Pattern Structure of the General Aptitude Test Battery (U.S. Department of Labor, 1979), the CDM's 106 concurrent validity studies on the abilities of workers and college and vocational—technical school students (Harrington & O'Shea, 2000), and expert opinion. Research showed AE patterns differentiated between majors (i.e., health sciences, science, engineering, education, liberal arts, and business administration) in six colleges (Harrington & Harrington, 2001). National middle school, high school, and college and adult norms are available. The machine-scored edition is available in two levels, in addition to a hand-scored edition. Both editions are printed in English and Spanish.

Interpretation

The following integration of some of the theoretical concepts into an ability assessment and its interpretation are organized according to seven of Super's theoretical propositions (as given in the list that follows Figure; Super et al., 1996). Figure, which depicts the AE report that is shown to an individual, helps the individual visualize the interpretation process.

1. People differ in their abilities and personalities, needs, values, interests, traits, and self-concepts.

   In Figure, the Ability Areas rating chart illustrates how people differ in their abilities and, because norms are used, how an individual also differs from others on the same ability. The profile shows that people have multipotentiality. Figure contributes to self-awareness by presenting intrapersonal and interpersonal comparisons.

2. Each person is qualified, by virtue of these characteristics, for a number of occupations.

   Depending on the level of development of a person's unique abilities, each person is qualified for a number of occupations. The AE's Individual Report displays a person's results in clusters of career groups. The "Interpreting Your Ability Explorer Results" section in Figure reports the occupations in which a person can use persuasive ability, the highest self-reported ability, in conjunction with the person's other abilities. These occupations include advertising manager, membership director, public relations representative, actor, drama teacher, and radio/TV announcer. The range of occupations is broad enough to accommodate different choices, depending on an individual's interests.

3. Each occupation requires a characteristic pattern of abilities and personality traits, with tolerances wide enough to allow some variety of occupations for each individual as well as some variety of individuals in each occupation.

   Although different occupations require a certain pattern of abilities, each job is broad enough to permit a variety of people in each position. An important component of the Level 2 AE's counselor's report (not shown) is the Ability Configurations section, which gives minimum recommended percentile ranks for various career groups. Most occupational performance requires multiple abilities. Clients often fail to think that although language and persuasive abilities are needed for such competitive positions as advertising manager and public relations work (a 60th percentile and above is required in both areas), the advertising person also generally has artistic and spatial skills as shown in Figure. Thus, the counselor's report is an important resource for counselors who do not have much background in occupational requirements. This theoretical proposition involves a learning component for both client and counselor to gather information related to self-development toward achieving specific goals.

4. Vocational preferences and competencies, the situations in which people live and work, and, hence, their self-concepts change with time and experience, although self-concepts as products of social learning are increasingly stable from late adolescence until late maturity, providing some continuity in choice and adjustment.

   Vocational preferences and competencies are related to self-concepts, which can change over time. Self-esteem and self-concept are associated with self-perceptions of abilities. For example, a high persuasive score in the Ability Areas chart of Figure can have different meanings, depending on such supporting data as school grades and performance in nonschool activities. A reinforcing interpretation to a client is when a self-evaluated ability, indicated by a dark diamond in the chart, is supported by high grades in related course work, indicated by a small circle, along with self-reports of doing a considerable number of related activities very well or well, indicated by an open diamond. A report demands that probing occur with clients whose self-evaluation of an ability is high, but neither their grades nor activities appear in the same score range. The chart notes the person's medium level on activities and that no course work was taken for this high self-reported ability.

   An interpretation of lower self-efficacy beliefs might be indicated by the high grades and activity performance but a considerably lower self-evaluation in leadership ability, as shown in Figure. Another possible interpretation could be that there is low interest in using clerical ability despite being good at it. Regardless, examining the discrepancies between the three areas of abilities, grades, and experiential activities is a major

AE interpretation goal. A client's explanation may clarify a self-concept perception. People who are speaking in declarative sentences and explaining their strengths and weaknesses in relation to goals can be exhibiting self-esteem. A student who consistently performs well in all subjects, as this "all As" student in Figure, can project her self-concept by confidently asserting an interest in a specific area and, for the moment, not use other areas of competence.

5. Development through the life stages can be guided, partly by facilitating the maturing of abilities, interests, and coping resources and partly by aiding in reality testing and in the development of self-concepts.

   The "Interpreting Your Ability Explorer Results" section of Figure lists the activities to help develop each ability and the courses to take that can help improve an ability area. This is important for individuals who have not had the opportunity or experience to benefit from exposure to a particular ability area.

   The counselor's report also provides a detailed summary of the client's two highest abilities; the ability responses indicated as very good and good; the specific activities reported as done very well, well, not well, and not tried; and the grades in courses (with grades indicated as A or B; C, D, or F; and not taken). This information enables the counselor to offer specific suggestions during interpretation. The intent of examining the congruence between self-reports of ability and related activities and course work is to aid in reality testing and the development of self-concepts.

6. The process of career development is essentially that of developing and implementing occupational self-concepts. It is a synthesizing and compromising process in which the self-concept is a product of the interaction of inherited aptitudes, physical makeup, opportunity to observe and play various roles, and evaluations of the extent to which the results of role-playing meet with the approval of supervisors and peers.

Super's career development beliefs are essentially that of developing and implementing self-concepts. Integration of personal preferences and characteristics into a self-identity is a difficult and lifetime task that involves a synthesizing and compromising process.

As shown in the concluding AE activity provides the student or adult with opportunities to further explore his or her results and to do career or educational planning. Each integrative activity is grade or age appropriate and tied directly to the National Career Development Guidelines (National Occupational Information Coordinating Committee, 1996). The assessment experience is only meaningful when people have the opportunity to look closely at their results and then make connections with the world of work and/or future educational planning. They only then begin to see that there is a link between their interests, skills, abilities, and their future success. This activity is also an ideal component for inclusion in a career portfolio.

7. Work satisfactions and life satisfactions depend on the extent to which an individual finds adequate outlets for abilities, needs, values, interests, personality traits, and self-concepts. Satisfactions depend on establishment in a type of work, a work situation, and a way of life in which one can play the kind of role that growth and exploratory experiences have led one to consider congenial and appropriate.

   Satisfaction is also a major concept of the work adjustment theory, and its authors emphasize the belief "that valid theoretical formulations are best developed on the basis of sound empirical study" (Dawis, 1996, p. 77). Separate satisfaction studies do not exist for the AR, but Harrington and O'Shea (2000) offered support for Super's propositions. They conducted large-scale studies of abilities, values, interests, and school subject proficiencies for workers and college and vocational-technical students-in-training. These authors found substantial agreement with job analysts' findings on these same characteristics for people employed in the same occupation. The samples covered one half of the career clusters in which U.S. workers are employed and included professional, managerial, clerical, skilled, and unskilled occupations. Regardless of their unique ability patterns, people may be considered satisfied when they continue to work in the same occupation. This is further supported when students and workers-in-training possess the same patterns as the employed adult workers.

Conclusion

It stands to reason that individual differences appear when more, rather than fewer, abilities are used to describe a person. Career professionals have increasingly relied on self-assessments that assess more abilities than do the existing normative measures that have fewer scales. Many normative measures must be used cautiously with ethnically and racially diverse clients. In fact, some commonly used aptitude tests that were administered only 5 years ago are no longer used in many schools. Protecting classroom learning time has also contributed to limiting the use of time-intensive ability/aptitude testing. However, people, young and old, need to know what their abilities are.

With 63% of high school graduates continuing on to postsecondary education, many do not know or consider their ability level in deciding their goals (Jamieson, Curry, & Martinez, 2001). Scholastic aptitude tests are limited in that they do not measure a broad range of different skills. Interest inventories measure what a person likes, not what a person is good at doing. Having appropriate abilities is important in job performance. Failure to perform after graduating from high school reflects negatively on schools. Students and parents have the right to expect that students have been exposed to the major work-related abilities in schools and that they have had the opportunity to reality test these abilities.

Interpretation is a key part of administering an instrument. Interpretation can be a difficult situation, because not all clients listen to, or care about, what the counselor has to say. Information can be threatening because it may reveal that a dream job is not possible. Information can also be misunderstood. Information can affect a person's self-esteem. However, information can also result in good communication and be both powerful and informative. The effectiveness of any information rests in the way the provider communicates with the respondent.

John Holland

This typology theory was developed to organize the voluminous data about people in different jobs and the data about different work environments, to suggest how people make career choices and to explain how job satisfaction and vocational achievement occur. Holland suggested that "people can function and develop best and find job satisfaction in work environments that are compatible with their personalities"; (ICDM, 1991, p. 4-4). Holland based his theory of personality types on several assumptions. People tend to choose a career that is reflective of their of their personality. Because people tend to be attracted to certain jobs, the environment then reflects this personality.

He classified these personality types and work environments into six types which he labeled realistic, investigative, artistic, social, enterprising, and conventional (often referred to by the acronym RIASEC). He suggests that the closer the match of personality to job, the greater the satisfaction. All types are part of each of us. However, one type is usually evidenced most strongly. We may even resemble up to three of the types. Holland developed a hexagon model that illustrates some key concepts: consistency, differentiation, identity, and congruence.

A very brief overview of the six personality types, six work-related activities, and sample occupations is presented below:

TYPE	ACTIVITIES	OCCUPATIONS
Realistic	Working with things, i.e. tools and machines	Farmer, Carpenter, Mechanical Engineer
Investigative	Working with information, i.e. abstract ideas and theories	Chemist
Artistic	Creating things	Painter, Writer
Social	Helping people	Social Worker, Counselor
Enterprising	Leading others	Sales Representative, Entrepreneur
Conventional	Organizing data	Night Auditor

"Holland's theory places emphasis on the accuracy of self-knowledge and career information necessary for career decision making".—(Zunker, 1994, p.49).

Although the theory appears to be applicable to both male and female workers, there is some question of gender bias in that most females frequently tend to score predominately in three personality types: artistic, social, and conventional. Holland suggests that in our sexist society, females will display a greater interest in female-dominated occupations.

Holland's Theory Discussed

Assumptions behind the theory:

- The selection of an occupation can be a reflection of a person's personality.
- An interest inventory can be a personality inventory. This is because Holland holds that perceived abilities, anticipated success, and expected satisfaction help define interests.
- Vocational stereotypes hold important psychological meaning.
- In our culture, there exist six different personality types against which we evaluate ourselves. Most people are a combination of types, not a pure type.
- There exist six distinct working environments; each is dominated by a specific type.
- People are motivated to seek out hobs that compliment their personalities, thereby maximizing their individual strengths and minimizing their weaknesses.
- Specific career related behaviors, such as success, satisfaction, and job stability, can be reasonably predicted by examining a person's P/E (personality/ environment) fit.

Holland's Typology

- *Realistic* Type, known in other interest surveys as mechanical, practical, technology/outdoors. R types are often pragmatic and like to work with their hands.

- *Investigative* Type, also called scientific or logical. I types are often engineers or scientists and like problem-solving and working alone.
- *Artistic* Type, also referred to as artistic, literary, and expressive. A Types often have jobs in the visual or performing arts, or as writers. They are known for their high degree of creativity often have jobs in the visual or performing arts, or as writers. They are known for their high degree of creativity.
- *Social* Type, also called helping or service-oriented. S Types often have jobs in the health or social fields. They are often altruistic people with an intuitive sense for reading others' feelings.
- *Enterprising* Type, sometimes called persuasive or assertive. They enjoy influencing others. E Types are drawn to positions in management and politics.
- *Conventional* Type, also known as socialized, clerical, computational, or organizational. They enjoy order and are often mathematically inclined. C Types are often found doing highly procedural work such as filing or bookkeeping.

Holland believed that the greater the **congruency** (or compatibility) between a person and their work environment, the greater that individual's chance of success. Also, the greater the **consistency**, or degree of similarity, between the first two letters of the code (as determined by their proximity on Holland's hexagon), the easier it is to make a career choice.

It is easier to decide on a career when there is a high magnitude of difference between the highest and lowest types instead of flatline (like, or dislike, everything about the same). Holland held that if the difference between the scores the first two codes was less than 8, they could be used interchangably. However, if the difference was less greater than 8, then the first code is dominant.

Robert Havighurst

The idea of "developmental task" is generally credited to the work of Robert Havighurst who indicates that the concept was developed through the work in the 1930s and 40s of Frank, Zachary, Prescott, and Tyron. Others elaborated and were influenced by the work of Erik Erikson in the theory of psychosocial development. Havighurst states:

"The developmental-task concept occupies middle ground between two opposed theories of education: the theory of freedom—*that the child will develop best if left as free as possible*, and the theory of constraint—*that the child must learn to become a worthy, responsible adult through restraints imposed by his society*. A developmental task is midway between an individual need and societal demand. It assumes an active learner interacting with an active social environment" (1971, p. vi).

The Developmental Task Concept

From examining the changes in your own life span you can see that critical tasks arise at certain times in our lives. Mastery of these tasks is satisfying and encourages us to go on to new challenges. Difficulty with them slows progress toward future accomplishments and goals. As a mechanism for understanding the changes that occur during the life span.

Robert Havighurst (1952, 1972, 1982) has identified critical developmental tasks that occur throughout the life span. Although our interpretations of these tasks naturally change over the years and with new research findings. Havighurst's developmental tasks offer lasting testimony to the belief that we continue to develop throughout our lives.

Havinghurst (1972) *defines a developmental task as one that arises at a certain period in our lives, the successful achievement of which leads to happiness and success with later tasks; while leads to unhappiness, social disapproval, and difficulty with later tasks.* Havighurst uses lightly different age groupings, but the basic divisions are quite similar to those used in this book. He identifies three sources of developmental tasks (Havighurst, 1972)

- *Tasks that Arise from Physical Maturation:* For example, learning to walk, talk, and behave acceptably with the opposite sex during adolescence; adjusting to menopause during middle age

- *Tasks that from Personal Sources:* For example, those that emerge from the maturing personality and take the form of personal values and aspirations, such as learning the necessary skills for job success.
- *Tasks that have Their Source in the Pressures of Society:* For example, learning to read or learning the role of a responsible citizen.

According to our biopsychosocial model, the first source corresponds to the "bio" part of the model, the second to the "psycho," and the third to the "social" aspect. Havighurst has identified six major age periods:

- infancy and early childhood (0-5 years),
- middle childhood (6-12 years)
- adolescence (13-18 years),
- early adulthood (19-29 years),
- middle adulthood (30-60 years), and
- later maturity (61+).

Table Presents Typical Developmental Tasks for Each of These Periods

The developmental tasks concept has a long and rich tradition. Its acceptance has been partly due to a recognition of sensitive periods in our lives and partly due to the practical nature of Havighurst's tasks. Knowing that a youngster of a certain age is encountering one of the tasks of that period (learning an appropriate sex role) helps adults to understand a child's behavior and establish an environment that helps the child to master the tasks.

Another good example is that of acquiring personal independence, an important task for the middle childhood period. Youngsters test authority during this phase and, if teachers and parents realize that this is a nomal, even necessary phase of development, they react differently than if they see it as a personal challenge (Hetherington and Parke, 1986)

For example, note Havighurst's developmental tasks for middle adulthood, one of which is a parent's need to help children become happy and responsible adults. Adults occasionally find it hard to "let go" of their children. They want to keep their children with them far beyond any reasonable time. For their own good, as well as that of their children. Once they do, they can enter a happy time in their own lives if husbands and wives are not only spouses but friends and partners as well.

Havighurst is not alone in the importance he places on the developmental task concept (Cole, 1986; Goetting, 1986; Cristante & Lucca, 1987; Cangemi and Kowalski, 1987). For example, Goetting (1986) has examined the developmental tasks of .siblings and identified those that last a lifetime, such as companionship and emotional support. Other tasks seem to be related to a particular stage in the life cycle, such as caretaking during childhood and later the care of elderly parents.

Identifying and mastering developmental tasks help us to understand the way change affects our lives. Another way to understand life span changes is to identify those needs that must be satisfied if personal goals are to be achieved. To help you recognize the role that needs play in our lives, let's examine the work of Abraham Maslow and his needs hierarchy.

Developmental Tasks of Infancy and Early Childhood:

- Learning to walk.
- Learning to take solid foods
- Learning to talk
- Learning to control the elimination of body wastes
- Learning sex differences and sexual modesty
- Forming concepts and learning language to describe social and physical reality.
- Getting ready to read

Ages birth to 6-12:

1. Learning physical skills necessary for ordinary games.
2. Building wholesome attitudes toward oneself as a growing organism

3. Learning to get along with age-mates
4. Learning an appropriate masculine or feminine social role
5. Developing fundamental skills in reading, writing, and calculating
6. Developing concepts necessary for everyday living.
7. Developing conscience, morality, and a scale of values
8. Achieving personal independence
9. Developing attitudes toward social groups and institutions

Developmental Tasks of Adolescence:

Ages birth to 12-18

1. Achieving new and more mature relations with age-mates of both sexes
2. Achieving a masculine or feminine social role
3. Accepting one's physique and using the body effectively
4. Achieving emotional independence of parents and other adults
5. Preparing for marriage and family life Preparing for an economic career
6. Acquiring a set of values and an ethical system as a guide to behavior; developing an ideology
7. Desiring and achieving socially responsible behavior

Developmental Tasks of Early Adulthood:

1. Selecting a mate
2. Achieving a masculine or feminine social role
3. Learning to live with a marriage partner
4. Starting a family
5. Rearing children
6. Managing a home
7. Getting started in an occupation
8. Taking on civic responsibility
9. Finding a congenial social group

Super" Vocational Development Stages:

1. Growth B-14 Development of Abilities, Interests, Needs Associated with Self-Concept
2. Exploration 15-24 Tentative Plans, Choices Narrowed not Finalized
3. Establishment 25-44 Stable Career Identity
4. Maintenance 45-64 Small Adjustments
5. Decline 65 + Reduced Productivity and Retirement

Super" Adolescent Attitudes and Competencies (Vocational Maturity):

1. Oriented to Vocational Choice? Knows choices need to be made and emotionally engaged.
2. Information and Planning? Has information and engages in long term planning including educational plans.
3. Consistent Vocational Preferences? Has stable vocational goals and plans.
4. Vocationally Independent? Makes decisions independently
5. Wise Decisions? Decisions fit aptitude, ability, resources

Havighurst's Theory of Personality Development

Another Psychologist that further elaborated on Erickson's view on personality development was Robert. J Havighurst. He asserted that "Erickson's analysis of stages of development could be applied in a different way to shed light on other facets of development. He suggested some development tasks for different age levels, starting from the pre-school and kindergarten age.

Pre-school/kindergarten Age: According to Havighurst, this age ushers in an era of formation of simple concepts of societal and physical reality. It is a familiarity seeking stage with the social surroundings including every day objects. Children are curious at this stage asking questions. The questions if answered expose them to experiences they hitherto do not have. The child would want to relate emotionally with his parents, siblings and other people around mostly through imitation. He would like to distinguish right from wrong and develop a conscience.

The tasks appear to be incompatible with the age whose accomplishment would be difficult. The personality of children at this age is just beginning to take shape, and assuming that children are in a position to undertake these developmental tasks will amount to impossibilities.

However, teachers are expected to serve as desirable role models and expose children to many objects and experiences. They should patiently answer their curious questions.

Elementary Grade: Nine (9) developmental tasks have been identified for this age grade. They include learning physical skills necessary for ordinary games; building wholesome attitudes towards oneself as a growing organism; learning to get along with age mates; learning appropriate masculine or feminine roles; development of fundamental skills in reading, writing and calculations. Others are developing concepts necessary for everyday living; developing conscience, morality and scale of values; achieving personal independence and developing attitudes towards social group and institutions.

Teachers have a stake in ensuring that children emerge from these Herculean development tasks successfully. They must bring to bear all the teaching principles and methods in the teaching/learning situations. They should emphasize socially acceptable behaviors, health and eating values to their students. They should make effort at seeping and integrating curriculum materials and experiences that would lead to the accomplishment of masculine and feminine tasks.

Secondary grades: At the secondary grade, nine (9) developmental tasks have been similarly identified by Havighurst, which are related mostly to adolescents and adult behaviors. The list comprises of:

Achieving new and mature relations with age mates of both sexes;

Achieving masculine or feminine social role;

Accepting one's physique and using the body effectively;

Achieving emotional independence from parents and other adults;

Achieving assurance of economic independence and selecting and preparing for occupation;

Preparing for marriage and family life;

Developing intellectual skills and concepts necessary for civic competence;

Desiring and achieving socially responsible behavior; and

Acquiring a set of values and an ethical system as a guide to behavior.

Havighurst emphasized the importance of timing and teachable moments in addressing issues related to the achievement of the developmental tasks, failing which there would be an adverse repercussion in later aspects of development. These issues have also been discussed under psychology of adolescence.

Factors Affecting Personality Development

Based on the general assumption that personality refers to the peculiar thinking of the individual, his emotions and behaviors in adapting to the world, some psychologists proposed five major factors that make it up. These include emotional stability, extraversion and openness to experience.

The other two are agreeableness and conscientiousness.. Apart from these major factors, however, there are other equally important ones such as how positive or negative and how self assertive a student can be. By positive and negative, they mean how joyous or happy and how angry or sad a student is respectively.

Emotional Stability

The emotional stability of an individual affects his personality by determining whether he is calm or anxious in his approaches. It also tells whether he considers himself as secure to perform or insecure to participate in activities. And whether he is self satisfied with his tasks or is self pitying is also indicated by his emotional stability.

Extraversion

This factor is responsible for indicating whether the student is sociable or retiring and whether he is run-loving or usually somber. It also shows how affectionate or reserved one is in his association with others or during events.

Openness to Experience

The student's imaginative power or his practicability is known by his openness to the relevant experience. It indicates whether he is more interested in variety or in routine and whether he is more independent in his dealings or simply conforming to others instructions and suggestions.

Agreeableness

It matters a lot to determine whether the student is softhearted or ruthless in his dealings with others. Is he a trusting type or generally a suspicious person? We need to know his position when it comes to whether he is helpful or uncooperative in his behavior.

Conscientiousness

Lastly, the factor of conscientiousness affects the personality of an individual by helping to determine whether he is usually organized, careful or careless. It also suggests whether he is a disciplined individual or is normally given to impulsive behavior.

Person-Situation Interaction

In relation to factors that affect the personality of our students, it is noteworthy however that the description of the personality of each of them is not strictly speaking a straight jacket affair. The situation in which the subjects find themselves must get put into consideration before conclusion is drawn to label them according to the traits enumerated in the factors that affect their personality. This is because their interactions may vary from one situation to another. Therefore, it is for the teacher to observe the situations that are more comfortable to their respective students, to provide cognate learning activities for them.

Fairbairn's Structural Theory

Beginning in the early 1940's, W. Ronald D. Fairbairn developed a unique psychoanalytic theory that anticipated and laid the groundwork for some of the most important current theoretical advancements in psychoanalysis. At the heart of Fairbairn's theory was a notion of endopsychic structure based directly on the vicissitudes of human object relatedness —in a way so radically different from other theories of his time that it is only now, a half-century later, that his ideas are finally having their appropriately profound influence on the general spectrum of psychoanalytic thinking.

In an earlier paper (Rubens, 1984), I advanced the position that Fairbairn had not been studied as widely and thoroughly as might be expected due to the extent to which his ideas depart from classical analytic theory. While increasingly many psychoanalysts had been drawn to Fairbairn's insights into the nature of human interactions and their implications for clinical practice, surprisingly few allowed themselves even to realize the extent to which these insights were based on a radically novel understanding of the human psyche —and fewer still could recognize and acknowledge the full implications of his departures.

It was my contention that it was Fairbairn's complete rejection of Freud's structural theory (and the drive model it embodied) that explained this almost phobic avoidance of the deeper implications of Fairbairn's ideas. The theory of structure is the key issue in defining psychoanalysis in general, and in distinguishing between psychoanalytic theories in particular. Thus, to accept Fairbairn's theory in the fullness of its structural divergence from Freud was to abandon Freud in too radical a way for many psychoanalysts. Also, most psychoanalysts had been so habitually attached to speaking in terms of Freud's tripartite division of the psyche into id, ego, and superego that they failed to notice that this structural theory was based on metapsychological assumptions that they themselves no longer in fact adhered to.

In recent years, there has been a growing awareness of the viability—and even necessity—of alternatives to the metapsychological assumptions embodied in Freud's structural theory. This change is expressed in the perspective developed by Greenberg and Mitchell (1983) that there are two, very different basic models on which psychoanalytic theories are based:

> *The most significant tension in the history of psychoanalytic ideas has been the dialectic between the original Freudian model, which takes as its starting point the instinctual drives, and a comprehensive model initiated in the works of Fairbairn and Sullivan, which evolve structure solely from the individual's relations with other people. Accordingly, we designate the original model the* drive/structure model *and the alternative perspective the* relational/structure model. *(p. 20)*

Mitchell (1988, *p.* 18) describes Fairbairn as one of the "purest representatives" of this relational/structure model.

Although a very large percentage of modern psychoanalysts actually have underlying assumptions far more consistent with those of the relational/structure model, there remains a tremendous inertia toward preserving a connection to the drive/structure model —or, at least, utilizing the terminology of that model.

The typical use which has previously been made of Fairbairn's ideas has been to note their relevance to early development and to those conditions most directly deriving from these stages (i.e., schizoid, narcissistic, and borderline states), while maintaining that the later developments can still be satisfactorily described employing the traditional drive/structure model. Even British object-relations theorists such as Winnicott (1965) have attempted to retain their connection to classical theory through just this sort of adherence to the importance of the drive/structure model in later development. Mitchell (1988) provides a brilliant discussion of the shortcomings of this manoeuvre, which he terms "developmental tilt." (*pp.* 136 *ff.*)

Fairbairn himself, while radically departing from Freud's metapsychological assumptions, was nevertheless guilty of employing terms taken too directly from the language of drive theory. He repeatedly utilized terms like "ego" and "libidinal" in crucial positions in his theories, although they bear virtually no similarity to their original meanings in Freud. Even his use of the term "object" is misleading, since it does not begin to convey how extensively it departs from the drive/structure model's concept of object. Although careful to redefine his use of such terms, Fairbairn's use of the language of drive theory did introduce a great deal of confusion into the understanding of his work—and a considerable opportunity for avoiding the full impact of its novelty.

Nevertheless, Fairbairn did succeed in completely abandoning Freud's structural model. Moreover, in a still more radical way, he developed a new structural theory based on a very different notion of the psyche and of the underlying meaning and role of structure within it. It is only in recent years that psychoanalysis has finally begun to incorporate directly the full implications and novelty of Fairbairn's theoretical innovations.

This paper will attempt to explore the actual extent of Fairbairn's departure from traditional notions of psychic structure by a detailed explication of his own theory of endopsychic structure in light of the assumptions out of which it was developed and the clinical implications which derive from it.

The Basic Nature of the Self

Fairbairn viewed people as being object-related by their very nature. For him, the fundamental unit of consideration was that of a self in relation to an other—and the nature of the relationship in between. Personhood, in the external world, essentially and definitionally involves relationship with other people. Internally considered, the self therefore is to be understood as always existing in and defined in terms of the relationships it has, remembers, desires, or creates. In the relational/structure model of Fairbairn, the shape of the self grows and changes from its experience in relationships, while at the same time the nature of the relationships it has are being shaped and changed by that self.

Fairbairn's theory gives appropriately great weight to the significance of intrapsychic functioning. Unlike some interpersonal theories, it is no way guilty of naively reducing the study of the human psyche to a mere examination of external relationships. His relational/structure model provides room for the most extensive and rich of notions of inner world. Furthemore, as will be discussed below, Fairbairn viewed the self not simply as the result of experience, but rather as the precondition for it.

In an irreducible way, the self is the pre-existent starting point for all experience and provides continuity in all that develops later—coloring and shaping all subsequent experience. On the other hand, Fairbairn firmly maintained that it was in relationship to others that the self expresses its selfhood and is shaped in the course of its development. Fairbairn's theory of self is, therefore, "relational" in precisely the way described by Mitchell (1988), in which the interpersonal and the intrapsychic realms create, interpenetrate, and transform each other in a subtle and complex manner.

It is the self in its relationship to the other that constitutes the only meaningful unit of consideration for Fairbairn. This unit of self, other, and the relationship in between becomes the pattern for Fairbairn's understanding of the form of all subsystems within the self.

The Inseparability of Energy and Structure

Central to Freud's conception of the organization of the psyche is the primary existence of an energic, chaotic entity, the id, the fundamental principle of which being the immediate and indiscriminate discharge of its stimulus-related and endogenous excitation, and the subsequent evolution of a highly structured ego, adaptively derived to mediate contact between the psyche's energic underpinnings in the id and the realities of the external world (Freud, 1900, 1923, 1933). In this way, Freud separated the structure for achieving self expression from that energy within the self which strives to be expressed.

Fairbairn adopted as his most fundamental postulate the notion that structure and energy were inseparable: "both structure divorced from energy and energy divorced from structure are meaningless concepts" (Fairbairn, 1952, *p.* 149). The structure *is* that which gives form to the energy, and the energy does not exist without a particular form.

For him, "impulses" (a term he characteristically set off in quotation marks to indicate his discomfort with this notion of energy treated as through it possessed some independent and separate existence) cannot be considered apart from the endopsychic structures which they energize and the object relationships which they enable these structures to establish; and, equally, "instincts" cannot profitably be considered as anything more than forms of energy which constitute the dynamic of such endopsychic structures.

In Fairbairn's system, the structure for achieving self expression is inextricably interrelated with that which strives for expression. The self is simultaneously structure and energy, inseparable and mutually inter-defining.

The Object-Related Nature of the Self

Even in Freud's late description of the id (1933), the reservoir of energy within the psyche was seen as seeking at all times the reduction of tension through the immediate and indiscriminate discharge of its energy. This pattern was termed by Freud the pleasure principle. In it, there is virtually no consideration of the object towards which this discharge takes place. The pleasure principle was seen by Freud as being developmentally prior to operation in accordance with the reality principle—a mode more co-ordinated with the specific nature of the world of external objects and involving delay of gratification, planning, and purposive awareness of cause and effect and of future consequence.

Fairbairn (1952, *pp.* 149*f.*) understood Freud's position to be a direct consequence of his divorcing of energy from structure, for what goal could there be for structureless, directionless energy other than indiscriminate discharge for the purpose of homeostasis. For Fairbairn, having initially postulated the inseparability of energy and structure, it followed that the goal (or aim) of self-expression could no longer be viewed as mere tension reduction (the discharge of energy, ending the "unpleasure" of excitation and thereby definitionally resulting in pleasure) with little or no reference to the object by means of which this discharge is accomplished. Rather he completely inverted Freud's position, maintaining that relationship with the object was itself the goal, and that the pleasure involved was a secondary consequence. Thus he wrote that, "The function of libidinal pleasure is essentially to provide a signpost to the object" (1952, *p.* 33), and that "The real libidinal aim is the establishment of satisfactory relationship with objects".

To Fairbairn, the pleasure principle, rather than being the universal first principle of self expression, "represents a deterioration of behaviour" (1952, *p.* 139). The rightful mode of libidinal expression, at *all* developmental levels, is more closely related to that described by Freud as the reality principle, at least in so far as this expression is seen as always purposively intending towards relationship with objects in some realistic way, rather than towards pleasure itself:

> *Explicit pleasure-seeking has as its essential aim the relieving of the tension of libidinal need for the mere sake of relieving this tension. Such a process does, of course, occur commonly enough; but, since libidinal need is object need, simple tension-relieving implies some failure of object-relationships.*

Central to this theory is the concept that human beings do not naturally operate with the goal of reducing tensions, but rather with the goal of self expression in relationships with other human beings. This view of fundamental human motivation is one of Fairbairn's most important contributions to contemporary relational theory.

Unitary and Dynamic Origin of the Psyche

Fairbairn maintained that the genesis of the human psyche lay in "an original and single dynamic ego-structure present at the beginning" (1952, *p.* 148); or, as he wrote elsewhere, "The pristine personality of the child consists of a unitary dynamic ego" (1954, *p.* 107). The individual elements of these statements are important enough to the theory to merit expansion and explication. It is first necessary to note again that Fairbairn's use of the term "ego" is in no way equivalent to Freud's structural use of the term. Rather, it refers to the entirety of the psychic self. In adopting this connotation of "ego," Fairbairn is closely paralleling Freud's use of the term prior to his writing *The Ego and the Id*. As Strachey (1961) points out, Freud in this period used the term to apply to the whole of a person's self. Nevertheless, it would be better if Fairbairn had substituted "self" for "ego" to distinguish his usage from Freud's. To minimize any possibility for confusion, and to emphasize the differences inherent in Fairbairn's conception, I have utilized "self" rather than "ego" wherever practical.

That Fairbairn refers to this primitive state as a "dynamic ego-structure" or "dynamic ego" follows directly from his postulate of the inseparability of energy and structure. He could not posit, as had Freud, an unstructured supply of energy out of which an adaptive structure would subsequently develop. Rather he insisted on the innate structural integrity of the self: the self was a "singular" and "unitary" whole. Further, this self was the *a priori* condition of life experience: "original" and "pristine", it existed from the very outset and was not in any way dependent upon experience for its existence.

Combining these notions with Fairbairn's idea that psychic energy is object-seeking, the resulting conception of the psyche is that of a self-generated, unitary center of definition and energy, with the potential for, and the drive toward, self-expression outward into the object world, and the potential for experiencing that world, its own self-expression, and the resulting interaction between the two.

The Nature of Endopsychic Structure

The self as it has been described above requires no further structural development. It begins in a condition of wholeness, already capable of and actively involved in the self-defining processes of self-expression and of experience. While this assertion naturally does not imply that the capacities of this primitive self are fully matured, it does insist that they are all present at least in seminal form.

Fairbairn acknowledged that structural differentiation in fact does occur within the psyche—and even that it is unavoidable and universal (1954, *p.* 107). The substructures resulting from such differentiations he saw as modelled after the self as a whole: each is comprised of an element of self in energic, affective relationship with an element of the object world. He termed these resultant substructures of the self "endopsychic structures."

Fairbairn noted (1952, Chapter 4) that certain unavoidable features of early human experience lead universally to the establishment of two such endopsychic structures: the first formed around the experience of the self in intolerably exciting relationship, and the second formed around intolerably rejecting relationship.

He understood that each of these subsystems of the self represents a particular crystallization of what originally was the growing and continually self defining process of the self as a whole. Whereas the original self is in ongoing and essentially unbounded relationship with the outside world as a whole, such an endopsychic structure is a particularized aspect of that self, in specific relationship with a particular aspect of the object world. Fairbairn eventually came to realize (1952, *p.* 158) that it was the entirety of such a subsystem which constituted the endopsychic structure set up within the self. The first of the two such endopsychic structures referred to in the preceding paragraph will here be termed the Libidinal Self, as Fairbairn never developed an explicit terminology to refer to the entirety of the subsystem composed of what he termed the Libidinal Ego in specific relationship to what he called the Exciting Object. Similarly, the second subsystem will be termed the Antilibidinal Self (following Fairbairn's later terminology for the Internal Saboteur and its Rejecting Object).

The third element in Fairbairn's picture of the structurally differentiated psyche will here be termed the Central Self, consisting of Fairbairn's Central Ego in relationship with the Idealized Object. This entity is what remains of the original self after the other two parts have been separated off. Because of this unique aspect of its origin, as well as for other differences discussed below, the Central Self is not an "endopsychic structure" in the same sense as the other two entities.

The fact that Fairbairn's model of endopsychic structure is tripartite naturally invites comparisons to Freud's structural model —and, of course, certain congruence is to be expected, since both metapsychological models attempt to describe the same clinical phenomena. Nevertheless, Fairbairn repeatedly rejected such comparisons (1952, *pp.* 106 *f.*, 148, etc.).

Freud's ego rather closely corresponds to the "ego" component of Fairbairn's Central Self, in that the ego is the organization of purposive self-expression and experience in relationship with the external world. It was viewed by Freud as a derivative structure, however, and not as the original structure Fairbairn viewed as the source of all other endopsychic structures. It must be agreed, that, as Kernberg (1980, *p.* 81) maintains, the ego psychologists' notion of an undifferentiated ego-id matrix existing prior to the emergence of either individual structure furthers the Freudian model in a direction more consonant with that of Fairbairn.

Nevertheless, the ego-psychological viewpoint still posits the eventual developmental necessity of the progressive structural differentiation of the ego from the id. In so doing, it clearly differs from Fairbairn's understanding of structure. Furthermore, the metapsychological foundations of the ego-psychological view still rest on a drive/structure model —albeit one that recognizes the central importance of relationship in achieving this end— whereas Fairbairn's metapsychology is founded on the need for self-expression in relationship.

The differences become more striking in comparisons drawn with the other two endopsychic structures. The Libidinal Ego, while certainly id-like in many aspects of its functioning, is consistently viewed by Fairbairn as existing in dynamic relationship with the Exciting Object; and the Libidinal Self which is constituted by this relationship is a proper subsystem of the Self, in that it is specifically object-related in a manner foreign to the concept of the id. The Libidinal Self represents a particularized relation of a specific aspect of the self in relationship with a specific aspect of the object world, and not the more generalized, freely displaceable and mutable energic center which the id is conceived as being. The superego is somewhat related to the Rejecting Object of the Antilibidinal Self, although not coterminous with it.

The Rejecting Object does contain the more archaic elements of the superego, although the moral aspects of superego functioning are related more to the relationship with the Idealized Object which occurs in the Central Self and to what Fairbairn discussed as the mechanism of the moral defense. Moreover, the superego concept emphasizes the *object* component of the Antilibidinal Self, and not the Antilibidinal Ego component—it therefore being necessary to include the ego's relationship with the superego to make a more appropriate comparison.

The ego-psychological branch of object relations theory (most ably represented by Jacobson and Kernberg) has attempted, with considerable success, to transform Freud's metapsychology in a direction more consonant with the insights of Fairbairn. Yet it is not possible fully to incorporate Fairbairn's insights without abandoning central tenets of Freud's metapsychology, contrary to the claim to this effect made by Kernberg (1980).

Freud's structural model simply is not the same as Fairbairn's system of Central, Libidinal, and Antilibidinal Selves. Nor do the modifications introduced by Ego Psychology suffice to make Fairbairn's system subsumable under their revised drive/structure model. In the first place, the "self-component" of endopsychic structures is not the equivalent of "what we would now call a self-representation", as Kernberg claims (1980, *p.* 81). One of the most brilliant of Fairbairn's insights lies precisely in his recognition that the self—and not some ideational representation (for who, in that case, would be the one doing the representing?)—has as its primary, innate function active expression in the form of relationship with the object world—and not, until the intervention of some pathological process, with some ideational representation thereof! To alter this conception is to eschew the most essential thrust of Fairbairn's theory.

It is precisely Kernberg's refusal to acknowledge this difference which leads him to cite the criticism put forth by Winnicott & Khan (1953) of Fairbairn's concept of primary identification (which he described as a relationship between the self and object which has not been differentiated from it):

> *If the object is not differentiated it cannot operate as an object. What Fairbairn is referring to then is an infant with needs, but with no "mechanism" by which to implement them, an infant not "seeking" an object, but seeking de-tension, libido seeking satisfaction, instinct tension seeking a return to a state of rest or un-excitement; which brings us back to Freud.*

The self in Fairbairn's theory is a living, growing, self-defining center which he viewed as the point of origin of human psychic process; and, it follows directly from this most basic of principles that it is possible for such a self to have relationships with other human beings, even though they have not yet representationally differentiated as objects separate from the self. Initially this self relates to the world with little basis in experience for self-object differentiation. Nevertheless, it does express itself and experience the world in a manner that is precisely the prototype for all later activities of the self. To assert that this brings Fairbairn's theory back to the pleasure principle of Freud is totally to miss his point.

It is an actual fragment of the self, and not a representation of it, which comprises the essence of an endopsychic structure in Fairbairn's theory. As a subsystem of the self, such a structure is a purposive entity with its own energy. It is not reducible, as Kernberg (1980) suggests it is, to self and object representations energized by "an activation of affects reflecting...drives in the context of internal object relations" (*p.* 80). Such a view *is* quite closely related to Freud's drive/structure model, modified to include the notion of the expression of drive derivatives in object-relational constellations—but is *not* at all the same as Fairbairn's relational/structure model.

The Libidinal and Antilibidinal Selves differ from the original self in only two ways. The first difference is that each is a crystallization of what in the original self was a more freely developing potentiality. Whereas the original self (and later the Central Self, in a more limited way) was free to experience the world and express itself in relationships to that world, the subsidiary selves carry within them a pre-existing template (based on the experiences out of which they were formed) for particularized relationships with specific aspects of the world. As in the case of the Central Self, the Libidinal and Antilibidinal Selves continue to seek experience and self-expression through relationship.

In the case of the Libidinal and Antilibidinal Selves, however, this process is sharply restricted by the fact that the particularized crystallization involved in the formation of each structure tends to permit only that experience and expression which is fundamentally consonant with the specific template involved. Thus, while there is a certain amount of growth within these subsidiary self systems, it is minimal. This limitation on the growth and change of the Libidinal and Antilibidinal Selves is more potently enforced by the factor which is the second way in which they differ from the original self, and later from the Central Self; they were created in an act of repression and at all times continue under the pressure of this repression.

Structure as Pathology

Virtually all psychoanalytic theories have accepted a metaphor for psychic growth which has been borrowed from biology: growth is defined as movement through progressive levels of structural differentiation and complexity. This metaphor is manifest in Freud's notion that psychic growth (and health) involves the differentiation of an ego, structurally separate from the id, and later a superego, precipitated out from the ego. It also stands at the root of the generally accepted belief that the self-object differentiation implies structural differentiation within the psyche—and the unspoken underlying assumption that the process of self and object representation is a structural one.

In what is his most radical departure from the mainstream of psychoanalytic thought, Fairbairn maintained that, far from being the necessary condition for psychic growth, structural differentiation was a defensive and pathological process in human development.

Fairbairn discussed at great length the process by which the psyche of the infant, due to some intolerable inability to cope with the unsatisfying aspects of experience, internalized this experience in such a way ultimately as to eventuate in the establishment of certain endopsychic structures. The creation of such structures involves the splitting of the self and the repression of that part of the self which has been thus split off.

Repression is the key element in the creation of endopsychic structure, because it is the mechanism by which the self becomes split. Experience which is integrable into the self results simply in memory or in the gradual alteration of the nature of the self as a whole. It is only when such experience is unintegrable—hen it is so intolerable as not to permit of consciousness (which after all, is that which is "knowable together", i.e. integrable)—that it must be subjected to repression. When that which is thus in need of repressing is importantly a part of the self, which is to say, when it is relationally so intrinsic to the life of that self that it is part of the definition of that self, then the act of repression must be understood as a splitting of the self. Repression and splitting in this structural sense are merely different perspectives on the identical operation.

A particular aspect of the self, defined by its particular affective and purposive relationship with a particularized object, and reflecting a fundamental aspect of self-definition within the psyche, too intrinsic and powerful to be abandoned and too intolerable and unacceptable to be integrated into the whole —this fully functional, albeit crystallized, subsystem of the self is what becomes an endopsychic structure by virtue of the act of its repression. If it were not repressed, it would continue to exist within the conscious, integrable matrix of the self and there would be no splitting of that self and consequently no formation of endopsychic structure.

Fairbairn came to this understanding in stages. At first, differing from what he viewed as Freud's mistaken notion that what was subject to repression was either intolerably unpleasant memories or intolerably guilty impulses, Fairbairn (1952, *p.*62) developed the idea that it was intolerably "bad" objects that were subject to repression. He later altered this view:

> *It becomes necessary to adopt the view that repression is exercised not only against internalized objects (which incidentally are only meaningful when regarded in the light of endopsychic structures) but also against ego-structures which seek relationships with these internal objects. This view implies that there must be a splitting of the ego to account for repression (1952,* p. *168).*

Although he repeatedly referred separately to the repression of objects and the splitting of the self, it is clear from the above citation that he understood the two to be inextricably bound together in a manner that clearly justifies the use of the notion employed in this paper that it is the entire subsystem of the self (including both the object and what he termed the "ego" —or self—element) that is repressed in the very act which creates its existence as endopsychic structure.

Thus it was that Fairbairn arrived at the notion that existence as a structure within the self means existence as a split-off subsystem of the self, created and maintained by repression, and owing its existence to the self's inability to deal with some important aspect of its experience which it found to be intolerable. He termed the process of establishing such structures "schizoid" because the splitting and repression by which it is constituted invariably diminish the self's capacity for growth and expression, and are, therefore, pathological.

The Libidinal and Antilibidinal Selves, by their very existence, limit the range and depth of the conscious functioning open to the Central Self. Both of these endopsychic structures press continuously for the recreation of experience of the sort which occasioned their creation, which experience always has two determining characteristics: it is equally experienced as intolerably "bad" (which, in Fairbairn's terminology, means unsatisfying), and it is equally experienced as being needed by the self absolutely for survival.

It is in this way that Fairbairn accounted for the clinically ubiquitous phenomenon of the repetition compulsion. There exists, at the very structural foundation of these subsidiary selves, an attachment to some negative aspect of experience which is felt as vital to the definition of the self (at least in the specific particularization thereof involved in each subsystem). The *raison d'etre* of these endopsychic structures is to continue living out these "bad" relationships.

Much as the original self sought to express psychic existence of the whole person, such a subsystem seeks at all times to express itself and have experience in accordance with the template based on the formative intolerable experience which defines its existence. Thus the existence of such an endopsychic structure leads to the seeking of relationships that will be consonant with the specific neurotic paradigms of early experience, to the distortion of current relationships so that they can be experienced in accordance with such paradigms, and to the patterning of activity in the world so as to be expressive of such a relationship—and, in so doing, restricting the freer, more situationally appropriate expression of the self and experience of the world.

It is important to note that this theory is not only more parsimonious than Freud's appeals to explanations based on mastery, masochism, and, finally, a death instinct, but that it also provides a direct explanation for the clinically observed sense of loss that is involved when patients, as the result of a successful psychoanalytic process, begin to relinquish their tenacious adherence to such patterns. The loss is twofold: most obviously, it involves the loss of the object component, which is felt as having made possible the particular internal relationship; and, perhaps more importantly, albeit less obviously, it involves a sense of loss of self, in so far as part of the self had been defined in the crystallization around the particular paradigm.

The fact that the Libidinal and Antilibidinal Selves always exist under repression further contributes to their pathological nature. Although in Fairbairn's view these structures are at least minimally able to grow and evolve through progressive accretion and overlay of later experience (in so far as the experience is fundamentally consonant with the defining paradigm), the isolating effort of the repression results in an inertia that is not readily overcome. Central to the nature of this repression—and the resistance it subsequently offers to growth and change—is the attachment which has just been described. The self chooses to encapsulate and crystallize these aspects of itself and of its relationships rather than to be at risk for their loss. This maintenance of the internal world as a closed system is what Fairbairn (1958) ultimately described as "the greatest of all sources of resistance" (*p.* 380). Furthermore.

> A real relationship with an external object is a relationship in an open system; but, in so far as the inner world assumes the form of a closed system, a relationship with an external object is only possible in terms of transference, viz., on condition that the external object is treated as an object within the closed system of inner reality (*p.* 381).

The splits which create endopsychic structures are, of course, variable in their extent and depth, depending on the nature of the relationships out of which they developed (which involve the specific strengths and weaknesses—constitutional and developmental—of the child, as well as those of the parent, and of the vicissitudes of their interactions). The more profound the splits, the more extensive and the more deeply repressed the subsidiary selves they engender, the greater will be the pathological effect on the Central Self. Just as this Central Self is what remains after the splitting off of the Libidinal and Antilibidinal Selves, so too will the Central Self's ongoing experience and expression be diminished by the tendency of the subsidiary selves to limit and to transform subsequent experience and expression according to the closed systems of their defining paradigms. The more extensive the portion of the self which has been repressed, the less that will be available for open, ongoing interaction with the world.

Not only the quantity of the Central Self's experience and expression is diminished by the extent of the subsidiary selves, but also the quality of its relating to the world is similarly diminished. The more severe the tendency to experience the external world in accordance with the subsidiary selves, the more impoverished and idealized becomes the nature of the objects with which the Central Self relates. It is in this light that the objects of the Central Self become the Idealized Object, rather than the actual objects of external reality —which is to say that all of the complexity and imperfection must be abstracted out and subsumed into the experience of the subsidiary selves. This position is fully in harmony with the clinical observation that all idealizations invariably are based on the denial of some experienced imperfection, inadequacy, or "badness'.

The upshot of Fairbairn's theory is that healthy development is not dependent upon the establishment of endopsychic structures, but rather that such internal structural differentiation is a clearly pathological, albeit unavoidable, schizoid phenomenon which, to varying extents, diminishes the functioning of all human beings. As Fairbairn (1952) concluded,

Psychology may be said to resolve itself into a study of the relationships of the individual to his objects, whilst, in similar terms, psychopathology may be said to resolve itself more specifically into a study of the relationships of the ego to its internalized objects (*p.* 60).

On the other hand, The chief aim of psychoanalytical treatment is to promote a maximum "synthesis" of the structures into which the original ego has been split (Fairbairn, 1958, *p.* 380).

Non-Structuring Internalization

Perhaps the most confused issue in Fairbairn's writings is the question of internalization. This confusion results from the fact that he used that concept of internalization in two distinctly different ways, while never acknowledging the difference existed.

The first sense of internalization is the one which Fairbairn clearly delineated in his theory and which has been discussed in detail in the preceding two sections of this paper. It is that form of internalization which eventuates in the formation of repressed endopsychic structures. For the purpose of clarifying the distinction which Fairbairn did not make explicit, this process will here be called *structuring internalization*.

As noted above, it is only intolerably "bad" experience that gives rise to structuring internalization. It is to just such structuring internalization that Fairbairn is referring in his major theoretical disagreement with Melanie Klein: whereas she had posited the internalization of both good and bad objects. Fairbairn (1952, Chapters 3, 4, and 7) repeatedly disagreed, insisting that it was only *bad* objects that were internalized. "It is difficult to find any adequate motive for the internalization of objects which are satisfying and "good" (Fairbairn, 1952, *p.* 93). Fairbairn's assertion here is that good objects are never *structurally internalized*, which follows directly from the fact that there would be no explanation for the *repression* (which is the essential ingredient of the formation of endopsychic structure) were it not for the intolerable "badness" of the experience with an object.

In apparent contradiction to this strongly propounded position, Fairbairn elsewhere (1952) writes of the internalization of "good" objects. He made it clear, however, that the internalized "good" object is the Idealized Object of the Central Self, which is a system in which none of the components is under structural repression. The apparent contradiction thus is easily resolved by the recognition that "good" objects, while they are internalized are never subjected to structure generating repression. This process, in which there occurs no repression, and therefore no self-splitting and no formation of endopsychic structure, will here be termed *non-structuring internalization*. Thus, it can be true that only "bad" objects are involved in structuring internalization, while it also can be true that "good" objects are internalized, but only in the non-structuring sense.

It is obvious that a human being needs to be able to internalize aspects of his experience in the world in order to grow and thrive. There must be learning that takes place as the result of both positive and negative interactions, and this learning must be integrated into the self in some meaningful way. While Fairbairn did not explicitly write about the nature of growth process, implicitly it is contained in the notion of non-structuring internalization. To understand Fairbairn's position on the nature of the process of non-structuring internalization, it is necessary to extrapolate from certain other of his previously discussed positions.

The most central principle, deriving from the definition of non-structuring internalization, is that such a process cannot lead to repression. Clearly, there is no need for the self to repress segments of its experience which are "good", or even which are "bad" in a tolerable way. Rather, such experience must be integrable into the self in a manner which remains conscious and openly available.

Secondly, it should be clear that such a process cannot lead to the formation of endopsychic structure. Rather, non-structuring internalization must be viewed as resulting in memory, or in the conscious organization of experience. The progressive development of a personal *Weltansicht* —viewed from any of what is an unlimited range of possible perspectives, be it that of Kant's categories of experience, Kohlberg's moral schema of development, or any other dimension of developmental progression— implies learning, memory, organization, and synthesis, but *not* structural differentiation. Even the all important development of self-object differentiation does not, of necessity, imply the structural differentiation *of* the self, but rather the progressive recognition of the separateness of that self *from* the external world with which it interacts, and a progressive organization of the self's awareness of its own nature and potential. In addition, it must be remembered that, for Fairbairn, any fragmentation of the self cannot be viewed as a developmental arrest, but rather must be seen as some pathological miscarriage of development.

A further extrapolation can be made from another disagreement between Fairbairn and Klein. Fairbairn (1952) wrote:

> *As it seems to me, Melanie Klein has never satisfactorily explained how phantasies of incorporating objects orally can give rise to the establishment of internal objects as endopsychic structures —and, unless they are such*

> *structures, they cannot be properly spoken of as internal objects at all, since otherwise they will remain mere figments of phantasy* (p. *154).*

It is clear from this position that non-structuring internalization does not result in the establishment of any "entity" within the self, but rather results in an alteration of the integration of the self, or in the production of a thought, memory or fantasy within the self.

Kernberg (1976) presented a schema for the nature of internalization which is relevant to the present discussion. He wrote:

> *All processes of internalization of object relations refer to the internalization of units of affective state, object-representation, and self-representation. Following Erikson...I considered introjection, identification, and ego identity as a progressive sequence of such internalization processes. In the case of introjection, object-and self-representations are not yet fully differentiated from each other, and their affect is primitive, intense and diffuse. In the case of identification, not only is there a well-established separation between self-and object-representations, but there is an internalization of a role aspect of the relationship, that is, of a socially recognized function that is being actualized in the self-object interaction. The affective state is less intense, less diffuse, and...the spectrum of affect dispositions is broadened and deepened...Ego identity may be thought of as the supraordinate integration of identifications into a dynamic, unified structure* (pp. *75* f.*).*

Although in Fairbairn's theory the notion of structure is radically different and a relational/structure model is employed rather than a drive/structure model, what is being described phenomenologically in both theories is closely related. There is a high degree of correspondence between Fairbairn's non-structuring internalization and Kernberg's concept of ego identity. Both theories recognize that there is a continuity of self experience and expression which is involved in such internalization which results in progressively higher levels of synthesis and integration. The opposite is true with respect to structuring internalization, which like Kernberg's introjection, refers to a level of functioning in which discontinuity and unintegrability result in a pathological form of internalization involving the splitting of the self and the radical formation of structure. Kernberg wrote of this process of introjection and the structures resulting from it that:

> *The persistence of "nonmetabolized" early introjections is the outcome of a pathological fixation of severely disturbed, early object relations, a fixation which is intimately related to the pathological development of splitting(1976,* p. *34).*

Kernberg's intermediate mode of internalization, the important issue of identification, is less obviously but just as certainly related to Fairbairn's non-structuring internalization. Kernberg described normal identification as follows:

> *(1) a partial modification of the total self-concept under the influence of a new self-representation, (2) some degree of integration of both self-and object-representations into autonomous ego functioning in the form of neutralized character traits, and (3) some degree of reorganization of the individual's behavior patterns under the influence of the newly introduced identificatory structure (1976,* p. *78).*

Once again it is crucial to note the emphasis on continuity and integration within the larger unity of the self, as opposed to any sense of structural isolation within that whole. Even in what Kernberg termed pathological identification, it is clear that the correspondence is to non-structuring internalization, although in this case the process takes place largely in relation to either the Libidinal or Antilibidinal Self rather than to the Central Self. This fact accounts for the rigidity and crystallization Kernberg observed to be characteristic of such internalizations.

The final outcome of pathological identification processes is character pathology. The more rigid and neurotic the character traits are, the more they reveal that a past pathogenic internalized object relation (representing a particular conflict) has become "frozen" into a character pattern (1976, *p.* 79).

While such identifications take place under the influence of pathological endopsychic structures and can slowly alter the nature of these structures, they do not eventuate in any further formation of such structures.

Kernberg (1976, 1980) was one of the first important theorists who explored and acknowledged the importance of Fairbairn's theories, and it is clear that he integrated into his theory many valuable aspects of Fairbairn's thought. Most centrally, Kernberg accepted the notion that internalizations, on all levels, have the basic form which Fairbairn suggested—an element of self, an element of object, and the affective, purposive relationship between them.

It is also clear that Kernberg agrees that higher forms of internalization involve less disjunction in the self and more integration and continuity. It remains as a fundamental difference, however, that Kernberg integrates these insights into a drive/structure model, whereas Fairbairn was intentionally departing from such a model. Moreover, Kernberg, as virtually every other psychoanalytic theorist, maintains that the progressively higher levels of internalization involve *increasing* levels of internal structure.

In contradistinction, Fairbairn demonstrated how it is not necessary to view the higher levels of internalization as creating structure *at all*. Rather, he showed that there was a conceptual advantage to differentiating structuring internalization, which is invariably pathological, from non-structuring internalization, which is defined by its continuity with, and potential for, integration into the self as a whole. While Kernberg obviously agrees with Fairbairn's observations concerning the phenomenological differences involved in these different levels of internalization, he does not adopt Fairbairn's conclusions about the nature of structure itself.

Thus, despite the similarities, there are profound differences between them when it comes to crucial issues like the internalization of good experience and the metapsychological understanding of the self in which these questions occur.

The vicissitudes of these forms of internalization and their interrelationships are at the heart of Fairbairn's developmental notion of the movement from infantile to mature dependence, the central issue in which being the move away from primary identification (which, it is interesting to note, is the same issue of self-object differentiation which is central to Kernberg's hierarchy of forms of internalization).

The Growth of the Self

Fairbairn chose to discuss the development of the self in terms of levels of dependency. In so doing, he was emphasizing his contention that all meaningful human activity—from its most primitive to its very highest expression—is at all times involved with relationship, be it with actual people in the external world or with the memory or fantasy of people in the inner world; and that the primary and ultimate goal of this activity, even in the neonate, is self-expression in relationship.

Views of healthy, adult development almost invariably include a positive notion of interdependence with significant others, and particularly the intense closeness and inter-relatedness with loved ones. In such love relationships, it is clearly acknowledged that it is a virtue to be the sort of person who can both 'be depended on' and be able to 'depend on' one's partner. Fairbairn, in labelling the highest level of development mature dependence, was choosing to emphasize the importance of human inter-relatedness and interdependence.

Dependency, in its pejorative sense, was associated by Fairbairn with the concept of infantile dependence. In doing so he was assigning the pathology not to the dependency itself, but rather to its infantile character.

Central to Fairbairn's notion of infantile dependence, and almost synonymous with it, (1952, *p.*42) is his concept of primary identification. In primary identification, the infant relates to an other whom he does not experience as separate or different from himself. It is clear that what is taking place *does* represent a form of relating —complete with a sense of intentionality and expression of the subject involved. Nevertheless, it is equally apparent that the subject is not aware in any differentiated way of the other person as being separate and apart from him. Fairbairn's contention was that the reality of both sides of this situation needs to be accepted: there is a relationship occurring, and self-object differentiation is not present (to a greater or lesser extent).

Although Fairbairn was completely insistent that the infant was object related from birth, he acknowledged that the infantile dependent relatedness of the earliest stages had specifically primitive characteristics: 1) it is unconditional; 2) the quality of need is absolute—if the infant's needs are not met, it will die; 3) the infant is not aware of any sense of option or choice of object—there is no experience of alternative, and the failure of the relationship to meet needs is tantamount to death.

The process of psychological maturation, in Fairbairn's scheme of the movement from infantile to mature dependence, consists of the gradual "abandonment of relationships based on primary identification in favor of relationships with differentiated objects."(1952, *p.*42) The key element in this change is the progressive differentiation of the object from the self: "The more mature a relationship is, the less it is characterized by primary identification." (1952, *p.*34 *n.*)

Fairbairn was clear that this process is a continuous one, ranging through various levels of self-object differentiation. At its most infantile level, there is no sense of separation between self and other—and thus there can be no awareness of any concept of self or other. As the infant has experience in the world, it gradually begins to organize and awareness of self and a concomitant awareness of other.

Although Fairbairn did not speak to the point, his system has obvious implications for the understanding of the highest levels of self-other differentiation. This process does not cease with the establishment of the notion that there is a discontinuity between one's self and others (physically as well as psychologically), but rather involves progressive levels of organization of the meaning of this differentiation and of the nature of the objects being differentiated. Ultimately, it is possible to utilize this schema to explore differences in the most mature levels of emotional development. For example, it is possible to see even moral development as an issue of learning to understand others as differentiated to the point of being ends in themselves (*cf*. Kant, 1785) and having an equally valid claim on shaping and defining their own experience and meaning.

The state of mature dependence implies a recognition of the separateness of individuals, even while they are involved in the most intimate and interdependent of relationships. Separateness thus in no way implies isolation, or even disconnection. Rather, separateness hinges on the recognition of the existence of the selfhood of the other, ultimately conceived of in a form that is not subsumable by one's own selfhood. It is the recognition that the other is a center of experience and intentionality, feeling and will, thought and purposiveness.

In other words, it involves the acknowledgment of the unique individuality of the other in a way that is in no way diminished by the existence of the relationship between the self and that other. It should be clear that perhaps the most salient practical touchstone for this sort of separateness will be the recognition and acceptance of individual responsibility.

Between the stages of infantile dependence and mature dependence, Fairbairn envisioned a stage which he termed quasi-independence. It should be clear, from what has been noted above, that this term is designed, in part, as a negative comment on the traditional emphasis placed on independence in most developmental theories. Nevertheless, it also is designed to convey a sense of the struggle at this level to move out of the state of infantile dependence in a way that is still very much attached to that very state. (For this reason, Fairbairn also referred to this stage as "transitional.")

The state of quasi-independence is ultimately doomed to failure, because it consists of an attempt to change an earlier state without relinquishing the essential tenets of that state. It is that state out of which neuroses, as classically conceived, arise; and thus it is fitting that it be predicated on a situation of conflict between the preservation and abandonment, the expression and inhibition, of an infantile state of affairs.

It is essential to realize that Fairbairn's entire conception of how the self grows is in no way predicated upon the process of structural differentiation. The self's growing awareness of individuation and separateness is based on integrated development of the whole of that self. As the individual achieves progressively higher levels of organization and interpretation of his experience, he functions with an increasing level of self-object differentiation, and moves from operation in an infantile dependent mode towards a progressively more adult mode of mature dependence. This movement represents the growth of the self as a whole, proceeding through the process of non-structuring internalization, and not through the establishment of divisions or structures within the self. This latter process of structuring internalization has been shown to be essential to the development of psychopathology, but not to the healthy development of the self.

Conclusion

It has been shown that Fairbairn's structural model of the psyche is in no way the same as Freud's drive/structure model. Fairbairn's theory is achetypally a relational/structure model. Based on the assumption that the fundamental human motivation is for self-expression in relationship, it is a theory that takes as the fundamental structural building block the constellation of self, other, and relationship between. Substructures of the self naturally are seen as conforming to this same pattern. Furthermore, the theory is predicated on a radically different notion of the nature of structure itself.

Fairbairn's insistence that structure implies pathology and that wholeness and integration imply health is unique among psychoanalytic theories. It presupposes a notion of the self that is in itself a radical departure. For Fairbairn, the self is not reducible to a self-concept, or a self-representation, or a system of reflected appraisals. It is a self-generating center of origin which, while it is shaped and changed in relation to its objects (or, more accurately, its "others") and does in part define itself in terms of those relationships, has an expressive, experiencing existence separate from, and prior to, these relationships.

There is room in Fairbairn's theory to accommodate identifications and representations of self and objects, as there is room to accommodate systems of reflected appraisals. These can be viewed as aspects of the self's experience of itself and its world. The major innovative insight of Fairbairn was that these phenomena do not in any way require structural differentiation of the self. Rather, he made a clear and crucially useful distinction between these non-structuring internalizations, which are far more related to memory and the progressive organization of experience (and which do involve representations of self and object), and the internalizations which involve actual segments of the self (not representations thereof) and that therefore create real structures within the self-crystallized subsystems which function within the self with a dissociated life of their own.

UNIT-VII

Non-Testing Devices in Guidance

Non-testing Devices in Guidance

Primary education forms the basic foundation on which other levels of education rest. It prepares the individuals for the challenges that are usually encountered in life. A weak foundation at primary level could lead to inability of individuals to experience normal development and consequently find it difficult to be independent and self-actualized The relevance of Primary education to human development necessitates proper training of Primary school teachers in order to equip pupils with necessary knowledge and skills needed for survival.

The job of the Primary School teachers is not limited to teaching of different Subjects alone. Teachers are expected to assist students to achieve total development in terms of cognitive, affective and psychomotor domains. This is necessary because education is not limited to the ability to read and write. It covers intellectual physical, moral and spiritual development The rampant cases of indiscipline in Nigeria cannot be divorced from the neglect of affective domain at primary schools as more emphasis is placed on cognitive domain at the expense of other domains.

The consequences of this neglect manifest in forms of corruption high crime rate and indiscipline especially among the Youths. There is therefore the need for the primary school teachers to acquire skills on how they can assist primary school pupils in Nigeria to be good citizens and true leaders of tomorrow. One of the ways by which primary school teachers could assist in promoting morality in primary schools is through the acquisition of knowledge and skills in Guidance and Counselling.

Guidance and Counselling in Primary Schools

Guidance is a term that covers all the means whereby an institution identifies and responds to the individual needs of pupils and thereby helping them to develop their potentials to the maximum. (Ipaye, 1983). Generally there are six guidance services which should be provided at the primary school level. In the absence of professional counsellors, teachers could provide these services as para-counselor. The services are:

a. *Orientation Service:* This involves the introduction of newly admitted pupils to schools and the community. Orientation assists pupils to be familiar with the school environment and to adjust effectively in schools.

b. *Information Service:* It is the provision of useful information to pupils in areas of education, vocation and inter-Persflal relationship. Such information would assist pupils to understand their environment and plan for the future.

c. *Counselling Service:* This is a process by which a counsellor or a teacher assists a pupil on face-to-face encounter to address his/her concerns. It is an enlightened process through which counsellors or teachers help pupils by facilitating positive change through an exercise of growth, development and self-understanding (Makinde, 1983).

d. *Appraisal Service:* This involves gathering organizing and interpreting data about pupils for the purpose of assisting them to understand themselves (Oladele, 1987). It is believed that when pupils understand themselves and are aware of their potentials, they would be able to prepare adequately for the future.

c. *Referral Service:* It is a guidance service through which pupils that needs special attention or services are directed to relevant institutions or agencies in the society. Primary school teachers are expected to be observant and direct pupils who need special assistance to appropriate organizations for necessary services.

e. *Follow-up Service:* This involves monitoring of pupils' progress even after the completion of primary education. Follow-up provides opportunity for teachers to continually assist their pupils and assess their performance in other areas of life. The performance of a school can be determined through the quality of their products and this is determined through a follow-up study. The service also promotes positive relationship between ex-pupils and school personnel.

In addition to the provision of guidance services, primary school teachers need to acquire skills in the usage of tests. A test is a task, treatment or situation designed to elicit the behaviour or performance of pupils or persons with a view to determining or drawing inferences about specific abilities or other attitudes of pupils (Abiri, 2006). Test can also be described as an instrument used for assessing individual differences in one or more behaviours (Akinpelu, 2004). Kolo (2001) identified six categories of tests that are used in schools. They are:

a. *Achievement Test:* This test assesses the performance of pupils after an exposure to a prescribed content. It measures the extent to which pupils have mastered the subject or content they had been taught. Examples of achievement tests are WAEC Examinations, NECO Examination and Teacher-made-test

b. *Aptitude Test:* This test is designed to measure the potential for success of pupil in a given area of training and learning. Aptitude test predicts potentials and can provide information on the ability or inability of pupils to succeed in a task. The different types of aptitude tests are mechanical aptitude tests, scholastic aptitude tests, clerical aptitude test, and musical aptitude test.

c. *Attitude Test:* The test measures pupils' reactions to events, situations or objects in their environment. Pupils' attitude could be negative or positive. This information is required by primary school teachers in perform their duties.

d. *Mental Ability Test*: Mental ability test is also known as intelligence tests. It is designed to assess the intellectual capability of pupils. The mental ability of any pupil consist of his/her perception, conceptions, memory, Language, reasoning and creative abilities. Examples of mental ability tests are Standard Progressive Matrix and Weschler intelligence Scale.

e. *Interest Inventories:* These are instruments designed to assess pupils' likes and dislikes. Thus, interest inventories are usually based on pupils' education, vocational and social interest. Examples of Interest inventory are Vocational Interest Inventory and Strong Vocational Interest Blank.

f. *Personality Test:* The test is designed to measure human characteristics such as emotions, adjustment, social interaction and motivation. The test assesses an individual's characteristics, temperament and behavioural dispositions. Personality test is broader in scope and measures different dimensions of human behaviours.

Conclusion

The primary school teachers could also use non-test devices to obtain information from pupils. Some of the non-test devices that can be used to complement test data are cumulative record folder, anecdotal record, observation record, socio-metric techniques and case conference. Primary school teachers are not expected to limit themselves to teaching alone, but to also assist in emotional and physical developments of the pupils. Thus, there is need for continuous learning and skill acquisition in different areas of education. These areas of necessity include expertise in guidance and counselling test administration, interpretation and usage.

Observation

Training and support is currently being offered to all childcare providers who are responsible for recruitment and selection for their setting. The training is offered on a one to one basis and will involve the Childcare recruitment Project Co-ordinator coming along to your setting when you have scheduled interviews. The Co-ordinator will assess your current interview style, technique and questions. The support is offered to you in confidence.

The purpose of this type of training is to:

- Observe your interview style.
- The types of questions that you ask.
- Whether those questions are relevant and receive the answers you are looking for.
- How you plan which questions to ask.
- How you short list.
- To give you honest, open and non-judgmental advice on your current style.
- To provide one to one advice and guidance on improvements that can be made.
- Offer different ideas on interview techniques.
- An outsider's point of view.
- A full written report of the findings

The purpose is not to:

- Get involved with the interview.
- Speak to the applicant about the role.
- Pass judgment on the applicant and whether or not they would be suitable.
- Be involved in the recruitment decision in any way.

The aim of this training is:

- To provide support and guidance to each provider on a one to one basis.
- To give individual advice and guidance.
- To provide support and ideas of new ways of interviewing.
- To give an impartial opinion on your current recruitment techniques.

As part of the training each provider will receive:

- A thorough report of the findings and observations.
- The strengths noted.
- The weaknesses noted.
- Improvements I would suggest.
- An action plan.

Please note this is a trial course, which is being offered. It is strictly on a first come first serve basis. Depending on volume of interest and other commitments it may mean that the Co-ordinator may not be able to make an interview. Therefore the more notice given the better. The Co-ordinator will always confirm in writing whether she is able to attend or not.

Observation is often the most reliable way of seeing how well someone performs. It can provide information about the learner's key skills and Skills for Life in action – in addition to their underpinning knowledge – and allows you to make an informed judgement about their current level and learning needs.

Observation can help you to identify when learners are (and are not) using key skills or Skills for Life and to recognise if learners are having problems with a particular skill. It provides a good opportunity to give feedback and encourage learners to practise their skills. It also provides a broader picture of the 'whole' person – how they use a particular key skill in practice and how they integrate the necessary key skill into an activity. **Observation** can suit learners who don't like using paper and pencil or 'test' methods.

Planning the Observation

You can use the **observation** plan to help make yourself clear about what and why you'll be observing.

Decide on the activity (or activities) you will observe. You will find that some activities entail lots of skills and they may not be the best to get a clear view of the specific skills you want to focus on.

Set criteria for each observed activity. In simple terms, these state what it will be like when the activity is done right. It will help you and your learners if all of you are clear on this.

Set a clear brief. The less your learner has to wonder during the activity about what they are supposed to be doing, how it should be done and why you are observing them, the more reliable the **observation** will be! You can go through the plan.

Carrying Out the Observation

When carrying out observations:

Know exactly what you're looking for. Remember that the purpose of the **observation** is to establish current skills levels to help plan learning, not to generate evidence for portfolios.

Be as unobtrusive as possible. You may not even need a clipboard!

Record the results accurately and fully so that they contribute to the learners' overall learning programme. The record sheets in this pack can be adapted to suit your needs.

Be prepared to give learners constructive feedback on their performance. Make it clear when the **observation** has helped identify learning needs and areas of skill that seem pretty solid already.

Try not to cover too much or more than one learner's performance at a time.

Focus on the most relevant areas of the performance. These might be the most crucial skills or they may be the ones that it is most feasible to do something about quickly.

Be flexible enough to take account of the unexpected. If situations crop up which allow you to see aspects of other skills, don't be blinded to them by sticking rigidly to your **observation** plan.

Ensure that people working with learners feed the results of observation into the initial assessment process

in the normal course of their interaction with learners. If you are building the individual's learning plan (ILP), the process is relatively straightforward. If someone else is responsible for the ILP, make sure that your observations are communicated clearly and promptly so that they can be used while they are still fresh and relevant.

Recording the Observation

There are many ways of recording your **observation**. We have included two simple formats, which you can use or adapt to suit your learners and programmes.

Observation record 1 gives an opportunity to record what you observe in terms of the key skills. Don't feel that you have to cover everything, although it can often be really valuable to look at the key skills being used in combination.

Observation record 2 gives an opportunity to record what you observe about each learner in a group context. Don't try to record too much in a single **observation**; getting yourself into a complete muddle will not be helpful! Whatever record you use:

- Assess against criteria.
- Ensure that the learner is engaged. For this, they need to be clear about what they are doing.
- Be prepared to reassess. You don't have to rely on one performance in isolation.
- Support only when necessary. Be conscious of the effect of interventions on the value of the observation.
- Enjoy the observation and remember that it is for planning learning

Cumulative Record

A "Cumulative Record" helps in the understanding of each special needs child academic and behavioral performance in the class. It is important for teachers to have a complete understanding of the learning abilities of every student with special needs in order to maintain his/her cumulative record. It is a helpful current and future guide in charting the progress of a special needs child as it serves as an additional information base for providing vocational and academic guidance for the student, in addition to the student's IEP (Individualized Education Plan).

The record includes the recording of all the activities of a child, special interests, hobbies and personality traits in a systematic order. After continuous observation and comprehensive evaluations, every special needs child can be put into his/her own special grouping in the classroom by interests and abilities according to their special needs and cumulative records.

In the cumulative record, all the different performances, skills, qualities and achievements of each special needs student are identified and the degree of superiority of the aforementioned are recorded for each students' greater learning development. The record further helps teachers to adopt and adapt different teaching methods or strategies according to the measured skill levels of special needs children. It also helps teachers adopt suitable remedial teaching measures and curriculum modifications in addressing student's learning difficulties.

This record also helps to note the behaviors of special needs students in the class. Cumulative records can be helpful for future guidance and counseling in deciding suitable remedial measures to improve the physical or mental health of a special needs child in learning engagements and classroom performance. Special areas of academic or behavioral weaknesses can be identified in the student's cumulative record and the teacher can take steps to include corrective actions to strengthen the defined skill weaknesses.

This record provides tangible evidences of a student's areas of personal and social behavior. A student's records can provide information for the effective execution of behavior modification strategies in a class of special needs children. Cumulative records can contain a wealth of information for teachers and other resource staff to assist them in implementing effective instruction and strategies to assist special needs students in their academic and social development in and beyond the classroom. There are many classroom benefits that be realized from keeping cumulative records on students. The cumulative record of every special needs child can be a path to achieve success in their holistic development and academic growth.

Anecdotal Record

Object of Observation: Observe student's behaviors among return from suspension. According to Mrs. Saner, Scotty is a smart young man who has problems listening and controlling how he behaves. Todays school day was very different from a normal school day because there were several teachers out of their classrooms for a computer workshop and there were several substitutes present throughout the pod. Scotty's appearance was very clean with well-brushed hair, a yellow knit sweater and a nice pair of jeans. In previous months. Scotty had been in trouble with police for placing large rocks into a creek and fire.

Since then, he has had a suspension for an undisclosed behavior problem at school. From the hours I observed. Scotty interacted well with peers. Scotty was observed over the course of regular classroom time as well as time in P.E. and lunch. Scotty's regular classroom consists of twenty one students. During the first class observed. Scotty was told to work on homework that he was behind on due to his suspension from school. During this class. Scotty repeatedly placed his head on his desk so frequency chart data for this behavior was collected. Scotty sat at his desk and tapped his pencil until prompted to work again two minutes later. Scotty was on task from 9:34am-9:38am and completed his worksheet at 9:38am when he got up to tum it in and was told it was incomplete. He finished his worksheet by 9:40am and turned the completed copy once again.

Next in the day was story time discussion. Mrs. Saner discussed a story that the students had been reading and as she addressed the class. Scotty was turned around in his desk looking at classmates. Upon finishing the discussion, Mrs. Saner picked up the story where the students had last stopped reading. Reading began at 9:43am and concluded at 9:52am.

At 9:53am, students were instructed to get out their science books. Scotty got out the correct book, put it back in his desk, and got an incorrect book out. Once his classmates noticed that he had the wrong book, he got out the correct one. After getting out the correct book, Scotty drummed on the book with his hands and tipped backwards in the chair at his desk. Their lesson stopped. and it was time to go to P.E.

During P.E., the teacher put the class into groups at four different basketball hoops. At each hoop, there were five places for the students to rotate. One spot was the shooter, one was the rebounder, one was for jumping rope, and there were two spots for students to sit and keep, count of how many shots the shooter made. The first spot that Scotty was at was the rebounder spot. He rebounded all ten shots without any problems and rotated to the next spot. His next position was one of the counters and, for this, he was seated in an aluminum folding chair. He sat in the chair with his hands to his side and did not speak. By the time the students got through two rotations, their P.E. session was over and they lined up to go back to their pod.

After returning to class at 10:35am. Scotty began working on reading in his science book. The teacher repeatedly asked Scotty to pick his head up off of his desk and read the material. Scotty would raise his head for one minute then resume laying it on his desk and not reading. Scotty was also distracting his neighbors as he talked to his neighbor twice as she was trying to read the assignment. Scotty was once again directed to work on his assignment. The next observation was November 15th.

In math, Scotty was asked a question in which he was unable to answer without **guidance** by the teacher. Three minutes after being asked the question, Scotty placed his head on his desk and stared at the overhead projection slide that the teacher was using for the lesson. When prompted to raise his head once again he began talking to his neighbor and was called on to answer another question. Scotty successfully answered the question and the secretary came to take the class to the cafeteria.

During lunch data was collected every five minutes and information was placed into a profile card format. Scotty was playing with posters while he was waiting in line to get his tray. After five minutes of waiting for his tray he took his seat next to one of his friends. Scotty was cutting and eating his turkey with only a plastic butter knife. He did this for approximately five minutes then began eating his piece of pumpkin pie as if it were a slice of pizza.

After twenty minutes he finished his meal and exited the cafeteria. After leaving the cafeteria he met up with a couple of his friends in the hallway and began fidgeting with some plaques on the wall outside of the front office. Four minutes after leaving the cafeteria. Scotty returned to class.

Case Studies

1. *Identifying and Motivating Underachieving Students:* This case study shows how a school identifies gifted and talented students who are not fulfilling their potential. It looks at how the school motivates them and meets their needs. It also includes examples of enrichment and an alternative programme, methods used in identifying gifted and talented learners, roles and responsibilities of headteachers and addressing inclusion.
2. *Tackling Underachievement*: This case study shows how a community college identified and overcame the barriers to learning facing some of its underachieving gifted and talented students. It also includes methods used to identify gifted and talented learners, teacher support and how provision was arranged for a gifted learner with behavioural problems.
3. *Training on Teaching and Learning Styles*: This case study shows how a school trained its staff to help them stretch gifted and talented students and develop their thinking skills. It also discusses how the training enhanced the students' communications and developed their independent learning skills.

4. *Sharing Training between Schools:* This case study shows how a group of schools worked together as part of the Excellence in Cities project to improve the teaching of 16-to 19-year-old gifted and talented students.
5. *Involving every Department:* This case study shows how an 11-16 school involved every department in tightly targeted work for gifted and talented students. It also discusses issues on curriculum management and timetabling, and support given to teachers.
6. *A Local Authority Programme*: This case study shows how, as part of a 14 to 19 development programme, a local authority is supporting high-quality teaching for gifted and talented students. It also gives examples of enrichment activities, partnerships and support for learners and teachers.
7. *Sixth Formers and Primary Schools*: This case study shows how a school deepened its sixth-form curriculum for gifted and talented students by encouraging links with local primary schools. It gives an example of an alternative programme, an activity that is fun for teachers and learners and describes how learners developed independent learning skills.
8. *Sixth Formers and Younger Pupils:* This case study shows how a school enriched its sixth-form curriculum for gifted and talented students by encouraging them to become partners in the education of younger pupils at the school. It gives an example of an alternative programme, an activity that is fun for teachers and learners and describes how learners developed independent learning skills.
9. *Linking with a University:* This case study shows how a sixth-form centre is aiming to raise the aspirations of gifted and talented students by forming a link with a local university. It gives an example of progression for learners, describes an enrichment programme and a way of easing transition to post 19 education.
10. *Easing the Transition to University*: This case study shows how a school helps able students to make a

successful transition from sixth form to university. It also includes examples on progression for learners, partnerships, celebrating achievement and support for learners and their parents/carers.

11. *Using Mentors from Universities:* This case study shows how a school stretched its gifted and talented students by using tutors from local universities as mentors. It discusses partnerships and support for students and their teachers, and how to motivate underachievers. It also gives an example of an enrichment activity or alternative programme.
12. *An EBP Challenge Event*: This case study shows how an Education Business Partnership (EBP) encourages able students' interest in physics, mathematics and design and technology by running an annual challenge event. It discusses issues of progression. It also provides an example of an enrichment or alternative programme and motivators for student and teacher training.
13. *Offering Extra GCSEs from Year 9*: This case study shows how a school is stretching its gifted students by offering them the opportunity to take an extra GCSE in ICT over years 9, 10 and 11. It also gives an example of an alternative programme, timetabling and support for learners and their teachers.
14. *Curriculum Innovation at GCSE*: This case study shows how a school ensures that fast-tracked GCSE mathematics students make the most of the extra time they have in year 11. It looks at how the school is aiming to stretch gifted English students at key stage 4. It also gives an example of an alternative programme and support for students and their teachers.
15. *Extension Activities for GCSE Mathematics*: This case study shows how a school raised the standards and motivation of its most able GCSE mathematics students. The same approach could also be used in other subjects. It provides an example of an alternative programme, an activity that is fun for learners and teachers and a method of developing independent learning skills.

16. *Stretching Sixth-form Scientists*: This case study shows how a school raised the standards and motivation of its most able scientists at AS and A level by offering extension activities. It also discusses how students developed their independent learning skills and what teachers gained.
17. *Challenging Young Engineers*: This case study shows how a school encourages students' creative and practical talents through activities for young engineers. It also provides an example of an alternative programme, an enjoyable activity for both students and teachers, timetabling and effective partnerships with local industries.
18. *The Advanced Extension Award in English*: This case study shows how a sixth-form college challenges its gifted English students and prepares them for the Advanced Extension Award in English. It also discusses support given to students and their progression.
19. *Preparing to Study English at University*: This case study shows how a sixth-form college challenges its gifted English students and prepares them for studying English at university. It also gives an example of an alternative programme.
20. *Stretching Gifted Linguists*: This case study shows how an 11-16 school aims to stretch its gifted linguists from year 8 onwards. It also gives an example of an alternative programme, an activity that is fun for learners and their teachers, liaison/partnerships with other schools and how to enhance learners' communication skills.
21. *Enrichment Activities for PE*: This case study shows how a school has extended its range of enrichment activities for students who are talented in PE and sport. It also discusses progression for individuals, activities that are enjoyable and motivators and support for learners, and gives an example of an alternative programme.

22. *Support Strategies for Talented Students in PE*: This case study shows how a school has dealt with the increased demands on its students who are most able in PE. It provides an example of arranging activities beyond the institution, an alternative programme that is enjoyable and motivating as well as supportive for learners and their carers/parents.
23. *Extending Opportunities for Musicians*: This case study shows how a school extended the opportunities available to its talented music students. It also provides an example of how students developed their skills and improved their confidence.
24. *Developing Vocational Gifts and Talents*: This case study shows how a school extended and enriched its vocational courses at GCSE and post-16. Its goals were to stretch gifted and talented students and to allow others' hidden abilities to come to the fore. It also provides an example of effective partnerships/liaison with other agencies and how this helped in motivating learners and developing their skills.
25. *John's Story*: This case study gives an interesting insight into the views of one talented student and his parent. It shows how some talented youngsters experience frustration that can lead to issues of behaviour and disaffection.
26. *Jamie's Story*: This case study is a mother's account of her son's (who has Asperger's syndrome) development and experience of school.
27. *Amy's Story:* This hypothetical case study shows how one student might make choices, using her mentors guidance, for the 14 to 19 phase of her education (in light of planned reform 14-19).

Autobiography

You might have read a number of autobiographies of great personalities, some of the common are: 'My Experiments with Truth' by Mahatma Gandhi, autobiography of an unknown Indian by Nirad C. Chaudhary: An autobiography is a description of an individual in his own words. As a **guidance** technique for studying the individual, it gives valuable information about the individual's interests, abilities, personal history, hopes, ambitions, likes, dislikes, etc. In **guidance**, structured autobiographics items are given to the individual and he is asked to write them out. The autobiographical material thus obtained is verified by various other means. Since feelings, values and attitude cannot be measured by any other technique, autobiography appears to be the one technique for appraising these characteristics.

Rating Scales

In this technique presence or absence of a particular type of behaviour or trait in a person is rated in terms of quantity and quality. You might be rating your students' performance, handwriting, habits and many other aspects in your day-today teaching. For example, Ashok has done better than Meena in Maths but Meena scored the highest in Hindi. Ram is taller than Shyam but Shyam is taller than Nitesh. The word 'rate' means judging somebody or estimating the value of something. The rater, who has observed the individual in a number of situations, gives his judgements. In a rating scheme each student is judged on the same general traits and judgements are exptessed in the form of a scale on which **are** marked 'very poor-poor-average – good-very gaod'. For cbntrast and convenience these ratings are shown graphically on profiles.

Sociometry

The term sociometry relates to its Latin etymology, *socius* meaning companion, and *metrum* meaning measure. Jacob Moreno defined sociometry as "the inquiry into the evolution and organization of groups and the position of individuals within them." He goes on to write "As the ...science of group organization-it attacks the problem not from the outer structure of the group, the group surface, but from the inner structure. "Sociometric explorations reveal the hidden structures that give a group its form: the alliances, the subgroups, the hidden beliefs, the forbidden agenda's, the ideological agreements, the 'stars' of the show".

He developed sociometry within the new sciences, although its ultimate purpose is transcendence and not science. 'By making choices based on criteria, overt and energetic, Moreno hoped that individuals would be more spontaneous, and organisations and groups structures would become fresh, clear and lively'.

One of Moreno's innovations in sociometry was the development of the **sociogram**, a systematic method for graphically representing individuals as points/nodes and the relationships between them as lines/arcs. Moreno, who wrote extensively of his thinking, applications and findings, also founded a journal entitled *Sociometry*.

Within sociology, sociometry has two main branches: research sociometry, and applied sociometry. Research sociometry is action research with groups exploring the socio-emotional networks of relationships using specified criteria e.g. Who in this group do you want to sit beside you at work? Who in the group do you go to for advice on a work problem? Who in the group do you see providing satisfying leadership in the pending project? Sometimes called network explorations, research sociometry is concerned with relational patterns in small (individual and small group) and larger populations, such as organizations and neighborhoods. Applied sociometrists utilize a range of methods to assist people and groups review, expand and develop their existing psycho-social networks of relationships. Both fields of sociometry exist to produce through their application, greater spontaneity and creativity of both individuals and groups.

Moreno's Criteria for Sociometric Tests

In "Sociometry, Experimental Method and the Science of Society. An Approach to a New Political Orientation." Moreno describes the depth to which a group needs to go for the method to be "sociometric". The term for him had a qualitative meaning and did not apply unless some group process criteria were met. One of these is that there is acknowledgment of the difference between process dynamics and the manifest content. To quote Moreno: "there is a deep discrepancy between the official and the secret behavior of members". Moreno advocates that before any "social programme" can be proposed, the sociometrist has to "take into account the actual constitution of the group."

Other criteria are: the Rule of adequate motivation: "Every participant should feel about the experiment that it is in his (or her) own cause. .. that it is an opportunity for him (or her) to become an active agent in matters concerning his (or her) life situation." and the Rule of "gradual" inclusion of all extraneous criteria. Moreno speaks here of "the slow dialectic process of the sociometric experiment".

Moreno, J. L., 1951, Sociometry, Experimental Method and the Science of Society. An Approach to a New Political Orientation. Beacon House, Beacon, New York.

Other Approaches and Software

Other approaches were developed in last decades, such as Social Network Analysis, or Sociomapping. Freeware as well as commercial software was developed for analysis of groups and their structure, such as Pajek or InFlow. All these approaches share lot of their basic principles with Sociometry.

UNIT-VIII

Testing Devices in Guidance

Testing Devices in Guidance—Meaning, Definition, Measurement

Background

- Radon is a naturally occurring radioactive gas that can cause lung cancer. It comes from the natural breakdown of uranium which is found in soil and rock all over the United States. Radon travels through soil and enters buildings through cracks and other holes in the foundation.
- Radon is colorless, odorless, and tasteless. Therefore, the only way to know whether an elevated level of radon is present in any room of a school is to test.
- EPA's investigations of radon in schools were initiated in 1988 with a study of schools in Fairfax County, Virginia. As the result of a nationwide survey of radon levels in schools, it is estimated that nearly one in five U.S. schools have at least one ground contact room with short-term radon levels above 4 pCi/L; the level at which the EPA suggests mitigation.
- It is recommended that all schools nationwide be tested for radon. EPA estimates that more than 70,000 schoolrooms in use today have high short-term radon levels.
- According to Connecticut General Statute Section 10-220 (d), *prior to January 1, 2008, and every five years*

thereafter, every school building that is constructed, extended, renovated, or replaced on or after January 1, 2003... shall be inspected and evaluated for radon levels in air and water... Initial Approach Meet with the school's facility manager to obtain a small floorplan of the building and to discuss school structure and dynamics. Ask if school is under renovation currently or renovations are planned for the near future. Also, meet with school's principle or superintendent to discuss EPA protocols regarding communication with students, parents, and staff.

Conduct a walk through inspection to determine **testing** areas and record the information on the floorplan of the building. The school administration shall conduct an informational meeting with representatives of parent and teacher organizations to provide an overview of the scheduled radon **testing**. The individual responsible for radon **testing** should attend to address any questions/concerns.

Two weeks prior to the scheduled radon **testing**, the school administration shall notify parents of students and staff with a letter (See Attachment A template) informing them of the scheduled radon **testing** accompanied by appropriate radon educational materials (See Attachment B pamphlet). *Radon in Schools* pamphlets can be obtained by calling the DPH Radon in advance. An electronic version can be emailed for distribution to staff and hard copies are available for distribution to parents

Use of Psychological Tests

Identifying potential employees that will fulfill position requirements and fit within your organizational culture, however, is a complex process. The "test and tell" approach is inadequate...and, in some cases, unethical. Here are six important factors to consider when incorporating psychological testing into your recruitment and selection strategy.

1. Begin with proper test selection. Tests are developed for specific purposes, so it is essential to begin with the end in mind. Identify a specific assessment outcome (e.g., stress tolerance, personal style/personality type,

leadership potential, values, or skills) and select a test that is designed to measure that characteristic.

2. Assess the quality of the test. Don't be wooed by a slick marketing campaign. Read independent test reviews (e.g., Buros Institute of Mental Measurements at http://buros.unl.edu/buros/jsp/search.jsp). Specifically consider validity (Does the test measure what it says it does?), reliability (Are assessment results trustworthy and consistent?), and appropriateness for your client group (Was all of the research conducted on first year psychology students from a different country?).
3. Identify the potential for results to be manipulated. Some assessments are fairly transparent (i.e., it's easy to figure out what a specific question is measuring). If candidates have a good idea about the characteristics that you are looking for, they may be tempted to tell you what they think you want to hear. More sophisticated assessment tools have built in "lie detectors" that can identify potentially skewed results – particularly if the candidate's response pattern appears to be overly socially desirable or positive.
4. Calculate costs and benefits to ensure a solid Return on Investment (ROI). This is another place to begin with the end in mind. HR professionals know that recruiting is expensive, and that inappropriate hires can be costly mistakes to rectify. However, expensive tests do not necessarily offer the best ROI – in fact, test prices can more closely related to perception of what the market will bear than to the value of the tool. On the other hand, inexpensive tests may not save money in the long run, if they don't accurately measure what you need to assess.
5. Clarify how the results will be used and who will "own" them. Most assessment results are more accurate and meaningful if interpreted with input from the candidate. However, when used for recruiting and selection purposes, test results are often not shared with the test-taker – hiring decisions are made without verifying

the results and the assessment summary may form part of an employee's permanent file. Ethical use of assessments requires clarity about who will have access to the results and how those results will be used.

6. Ensure that tests are being administered and interpreted by qualified professionals. Many psychological tests are only available for purchase by professionals with specialized training to administer, score, and interpret the results. This responsibility extends beyond the "testing day." If assessment results form part of employee files, it is essential to ensure that only those qualified to interpret those results have access to them. There are several training options available to HR professionals – many are designed to qualify individuals to use specific tests (e.g., the Myers-Briggs Type Indicator, Bar on Emotional Quotient Inventory, Leadership Skills Profile). Some Masters level programmes qualify individuals to purchase a range of "B Level" tools.

Psychological testing can be a valuable tool for many organizations. Beyond using it within a recruitment and selection strategy, assessments can support teambuilding, leadership development, career development, and work-life balance initiatives. The challenge is to ensure that selected tests are effective and used appropriately. HR professionals have an ethical responsibility to identify and recommend appropriate tests and to oversee the administration of those tests and the interpretation of their results.

Intellegence Tests

IQ tests are measures of intelligence, while achievement tests are measures of the use and level of development of use of the ability. IQ (or cognitive) tests and achievement tests are common norm-referenced tests. In these types of tests, a series of tasks is presented to the person being evaluated, and the person's responses are graded according to carefully prescribed guidelines. After the test is completed, the results can be compiled and compared to the responses of a norm group, usually comprised of people at the same age or grade level as the person being evaluated. IQ tests which contain a series of tasks typically divide the tasks into verbal (relying on the use of language) and performance, or non-verbal (relying on eye-hand types of tasks, or use of symbols or objects). Examples of verbal IQ test tasks are vocabulary and information (answering general knowledge questions). Non-verbal examples are timed completion of puzzles (object assembly), making designs out of coloured blocks (block design).

IQ tests (e.g., WAIS-III, WISC-IV, Cattell Culture Fair III and academic achievement tests (e.g. WIAT, WRAT) are designed to be administered to either an individual (by a trained evaluator) or to a group of people (paper and pencil tests). The individually-administered tests tend to be more comprehensive, more reliable, more valid and generally to have better psychometric characteristics than group-administered tests. However, individually-administered tests are more expensive to administer because of the need for a trained administrator (psychologist, school psychologist, or psychometrician) and because of the limitation of working with just one client at a time.

Are you a logical thinker? A numerical whiz? A verbal genius? Or are you spatially inclined? Are you looking for intellectual stimulation? Find out how smart you are (and increase your IQ) with the Classical Intelligence Test.

This IQ test measures several factors of intelligence, namely logical reasoning, math skills, language abilities, spatial relations skills, knowledge retained and the ability to solve novel problems. (Please note that it doesn't take into consideration emotional intelligence).

This test is supposed to assess your intellectual potential, not your performance under stress. Therefore, there is no time limit. Nonetheless, this test is usually completed in less than one hour. You may use a calculator, a piece of paper and a pencil. Do not use software to solve the problems, even if you programmed it yourself. And, of course, you will have to work alone. Before you start, make sure that you have about an hour of free time during which nobody will disturb you.

Carefully read every question and select your answer. You will need to select an answer for every question. Some questions are designed to be very difficult. If you cannot figure out the answer, simply select *I don't know* and move on.

After finishing the test, you will receive a Snapshot Report with an introduction and a personalized interpretation for one of your test scores. You will then have the option to purchase the full results.

Aptitude Test

An **aptitude** is an innate, acquired or learned or developed component of a competency (*being the others: knowledge, understanding and attitude*) to do a certain kind of work at a certain level. Aptitudes may be physical or mental. The innate nature of aptitude is in contrast to achievement, which represents knowledge or ability that is gained.

Aptitude and intelligence quotient are related, and in some ways opposite, views of human mental ability. Whereas intelligence quotient sees intelligence as being a single measurable characteristic affecting all mental ability, aptitude breaks mental ability down into many different characteristics which are supposed to be more or less independent of each other.

On the contrary, casual analysis with any group of test scores will nearly always show them to be highly correlated. The U.S. Department of Labor's General Learning Ability, for instance, is determined by combining Verbal, Numerical and Spatial aptitude subtests. In a given person some may be relatively low and others relatively high. In the context of an aptitude test the "high" and "low" scores are usually not far apart, because all ability test scores tend to be correlated. Aptitude is better applied intra-individually to determine what tasks a given individual is relatively more skilled at performing. Inter-individual aptitude differences are typically not very significant due to IQ differences. Of course this assumes individuals have not already been pre-screened for IQ through some other process such as SAT scores, GRE scores, finishing medical school, etc.

Personality Inventories

A **personality test** aims to describe aspects of a person's character that remain stable throughout that person's lifetime, the individual's character pattern of behavior, thoughts, and feelings. An early model of personality was posited by Greek philosopher/physician Hippocrates. The 20th century heralded a new interest in defining and identifying separate personality types, in close correlation with the emergence of the field of psychology. As such, several distinct tests emerged; some attempt to identify specific characteristics, while others attempt to identify personality as a whole.

Overview

There are many different types of personality tests. Common personality tests consist of a large number of items, where respondents must rate the applicability of each item to themselves. Projective tests, such as the TAT and Ink Blots are another form of personality test which attempt to assess personality indirectly.

Scoring

Personality tests can be scored using a dimensional (normative) or a typological (ipsative) approach. Dimensional approaches such as the Big 5 describe personality as a set of continuous dimensions on which individuals differ.

Typological approaches such as the Myers-Briggs Type Indicator (r) describe opposing categories of functioning where individuals differ. Normative responses for each category can be graphed as bell curves (normal curves), implying that some aspects of personality are better than others. Ipsative test responses offer two equally "good" responses between which an individual must choose. Such responses (e.g., on the MBTI) would result in bi-modal graphs for each category, rather than bell curves. Personality tests such as the Strength Deployment Inventory (r), which assesses motivation, or purpose, of behavior, rather than the behavior itself, combine a dimensional and typological approach as described here. Three continuums of motivation are combined to yield 7 distinct types.

Many, but by no means all, psychological researchers believe that the dimensional approach is more accurate, although as judged by the popularity of the Myers-Briggs tool, typological approaches have substantial appeal as a self-development tool.

Few personality tests accurately predict behavior in a specific context. For example, with some of the five factor model tests, only one of the five factors is significantly correlated with job performance.

Emotive tests can become prey to unreliable results as most people strive to pick the answer they feel the best fitting of an ideal character and therefore not their personal response.

Norms

The meaning of personality test scores are difficult to interpret in a direct sense. For this reason substantial effort is made by producers of personality tests to produce norms to provide a comparative basis for interpreting a respondent's test scores. Common formats for these norms include percentile ranks, z scores, sten scores, and other forms of standardised scores.

Test Development

A substantial amount of research and thinking has gone into the topic of personality test development. Development of personality tests tends to be an iterative process whereby a test is progressively refined. Test development can proceed on theoretical or statistical grounds. Theoretical strategies can involve taking psychological or other theory to define the content domain and then developing test items that should in principle measure the domain of interest.

This can then be accompanied by assessment by experts of the developed items to the defined construct. Statistical strategies are varied. Common strategies involve the use of exploratory factor analysis and confirmatory factor analysis to verify that items that are proposed to group together into factors actually do group together empirically. Reliability analysis and Item Response Theory are additional complimentary approaches.

Test Evaluation

There are several criteria for evaluating a personality test. Fundamentally, a personality test is expected to demonstrate reliability and validity.

Criticism and Controversy

Biased Test Taker Interpretation: One problem of a personality test is that the users of the test could only find it accurate because of the subjective validation involved. This is where the person only acknowledges the information that applies to them. This is related to what is called in psychology as the Forer effect.

Application to Non-clinical Samples

Critics have raised issues about the ethics of administering personality tests, especially for non-clinical uses. By the 1960s, tests like the MMPI were being given by companies to employees and applicants as often as to psychiatric patients. Sociologist William H. Whyte was among those who saw the tests as helping to create and perpetuate the oppressive groupthink of the "organization man" mid-20th century corporate capitalistic mentality.

Personality versus Social Factors

In the 60s and 70s some psychologists dismissed the whole idea of personality, considering much behaviour to be content specific. This idea was supported by the fact that personality often does not predict behaviour in specific contexts. However, more extensive research has showed than when behaviour is aggregated across contexts, that personality can be a modest to good predictor of behaviour. Almost all psychologists now acknowledge that both social and individual difference factors (i.e., personality) influence behaviour. The debate is currently more around the relative importance of each of these factors and how these factors interact.

Respondent Faking

One problem with self-report measures of personality is that respondents are often able to distort their responses. This is particularly problematic in employment contexts and other contexts where important decisions are being made and there is an incentive to present oneself in a favourable manner.

Work in experimental settings (e.g., Viswesvaran & Ones, 1999; Martin, Bowen & Hunt, 2002) has clearly shown that when student samples have been asked to deliberately fake on a personality test, they clearly demonstrated that they are capable of doing so.

Several strategies have been adopted for reducing respondent faking. One strategy involves providing a warning on the test that methods exist for detecting faking and that detection will result in negative consequences for the respondent (e.g., not being considered for the job). Forced choice item formats (ipsative testing) have been adopted which require respondents to choose between alternatives of equal social desirability.

Social desirability and lie scales are often included which detect certain patterns of responses, although these are often confounded by true variability in social desirability. More recently, Item Response Theory approaches have been adopted with some success in identifying item response profiles that flag fakers. Other researchers are looking at the timing of responses on electronically administered tests to assess faking.

Psychological Research

Personality testing is frequently used in psychological research to test various theories of personality.

Research published by David Dunning of Cornell University, Chip Heath of Stanford University and Jerry M. Suls of the University of Iowa reveals that observers who are not involved in any type of relationship with an individual are better judges of the individual's relationships and abilities. These workers have studied a large body of investigations into self-evaluation, indicating that individuals may have flawed views about themselves and their social relationships, sometimes leading to decisions that can impact negatively on other persons' lives and/or their own.

Additional Applications

A study by American Management Association reveals that 39 percent of companies surveyed use personality testing as part of their hiring process. However, ipsative personality tests are often misused in recruitment and selection, where they are mistakenly treated as if they are normative measures. More people are using personality testing to evaluate their business partners, their dates and their spouses.

Salespeople are using personality testing to better understand the needs of their customers and to gain a competitive edge in the closing of deals. College students have started to use personality testing to evaluate their roommates. Lawyers are beginning to use personality testing for criminal behavior analysis, litigation profiling, witness examination and jury selection.

Dangers of Such Practices

It is easy for personality test participants to become complacent about their own personal uniqueness and instead become dependent on the decription associated with them. This can be potentially dangerous with persons who are already suffering from a form of identity disorder or may be a catalyst to instigate particular behaviours in a person who was previously believed to be of sound mental health. The severity of the damage that individuals can sustain to their personal identity was made clear during the case Wilson v Johnson & Johnson in which the plaintiff (Wilson) sued his former employer (Johnson&Johnson) for irreperable damages that resulted from the over abundance of personality tests being administered in the workspace. Wilson argued that repeated questioning and scrutiny of his personality was a cause of strain and eventually breakdown.

In this historic case, Wilson was awarded $4.7 million after jurors agreed that excessive testing caused strain and led to unnecessary scrutiny resulting in personal grief. Similar cases have been tried since and won, but none with such a magnitude as this first monumental case that won mental health rights for employees.

Examples of Personality Tests

- The first modern personality test was the Woodworth Personal data sheet, which was first used in 1919. It was designed to help the United States Army screen out recruits who might be susceptible to shell shock.
- The Rorschach inkblot test was introduced in 1921 as a way to determine personality by the interpretation of abstract inkblots.
- The Thematic Apperception Test was commissioned by the Office of Strategic Services (O.S.S.) in the 1930s to identify personalities that might be susceptible to being turned by enemy intelligence.
- The Minnesota Multiphasic Personality Inventory was published in 1942 as a way to aid in assessing psychopathology in a clinical setting.
- Myers-Briggs Type Indicator is a 16-type indicator based on Carl Jung's *Psychological Types*, developed during World War II by Isabel Myers and Katherine Briggs.
- Keirsey Temperament Sorter developed by David Keirsey is influenced by Isabel Myers sixteen types and Ernest Kretschmer's four types.
- The 16PF Questionnaire (16PF) was developed by Raymond Cattell and his colleagues in the 1940's and 1950's in a search to try to discover the basic traits of human personality using scientific methodology. The test was first published in 1949, and is now in its 5th edition, published in 1994. It is used in a wide variety of settings for individual and marital counseling, career counseling and employee development, in educational settings, and for basic research.
- The EQSQ Test developed by Professor Simon Baron-Cohen, Sally Wheelwright, and their team at the University of Cambridge, England, centers on the Empathizing-Systemizing theory of the male versus the female brain types.
- The Personal Style Indicator (PSI) is a self administered, self scoring assessment, it is not a test that can be

passed or failed. The PSI classifies four aspects of innate behavior by testing a person's preferences in word associations.

- The Strength Deployment Inventory, developed by Elias Porter, Ph.D. in 1971 and is based on his theory of Relationship Awareness. Porter was the first known psychometrician to use colors (Red, Green and Blue) as shortcuts to communicate the results of a personality test.
- Other personality tests include the NEO PI-R, Millon Clinical Multiaxial Inventory, Eysenck Personality Questionnaire, and Swedish Universities Scales of Personality.

Attitude Scales

In an effort to study students' attitudes towards math, Elizabeth Fennema and Julia A. Sherman constructed the following attitude scale in the early 1970's. The scale consists of four subscales: a confidence scale, a usefulness scale, a scale that measures mathematics as a male domain and a teacher perception scale. Each of these scales consists of 12 items. Six of them measure a positive attitude and six measure a negative attitude.

This scale could give a teacher and an individual student useful information about that particular student's attitude(s) towards math. Because this scale was originally written twenty years ago and the subtle meanings and connotations of words have changed in that time period, it is important that this scale not be used for research.

We also adapted the scale to provide tools to examine a student's attitude towards science. Following the scales is the scoring key.

Introductory Note (for use with these scales)

Fennema-Sherman Mathematics Attitude Scales: Using this scale will help you and I find out how you feel about yourself and mathematics.

On the following pages is a series of sentences. You are to mark your answer sheets by telling how you feel about them. Suppose a statement says:

Example 1: I like mathematics: As you read the sentence, you will know whether you agree or disagree. If you strongly agree, circle A next to Number 1. If you agree, but not so strongly, or you only "sort of" agree, circle B. If you disagree with the sentence very much, circle E for strongly disagree. If you disagree, but not so strongly, circle D. If you are not sure about a question or you can't answer it, circle C. Now, mark your sheet, then go on and do Example 2.

Do not spend much time with any statement, *but be sure to answer every statement.*

Work fast, but carefully.

There are no "right" or "wrong" answers. The only correct responses are those that are true *for you*. Whenever possible, let the things that have happened to you help you make a choice.

A Modified Fennema-Sherman Mathematics Attitude Scale

1.	I am sure that I can learn math.	A	B	C	D	E
2.	My teachers have been interested in my progress in math.	A	B	C	D	E
3.	Knowing mathematics will help me earn a living.	A	B	C	D	E
4.	I don't think I could do advanced math.	A	B	C	D	E
5.	Math will not be important to me in my life's work.	A	B	C	D	E
6.	Males are not naturally better than females in math.	A	B	C	D	E
7.	Getting a teacher to take me seriously in math is a problem.	A	B	C	D	E
8.	Math is hard for me.	A	B	C	D	E
9.	It's hard to believe a female could be a genius in mathematics.	A	B	C	D	E
10.	I'll need mathematics for my future work.	A	B	C	D	E
11.	When a woman has to solve a math problem, she should ask a man for help.	A	B	C	D	E
12.	I am sure of myself when I do math.	A	B	C	D	E
13.	I don't expect to use much math when I get out of school.	A	B	C	D	E
14.	I would talk to my math teachers about a career that uses math.	A	B	C	D	E
15.	Women can do just as well as men in math.	A	B	C	D	E
16.	It's hard to get math teachers to respect me.	A	B	C	D	E
17.	Math is a worthwhile, necessary subject.	A	B	C	D	E
18.	I would have more faith in the answer for a math problem solved by a man than a woman.	A	B	C	D	E
19.	I'm not the type to do well in math.	A	B	C	D	E
20.	My teachers have encouraged me to study more math.	A	B	C	D	E
21.	Taking math is a waste of time.	A	B	C	D	E
22.	I have a hard time getting teachers to talk seriously with me about math.	A	B	C	D	E
23.	Math has been my worst subject.	A	B	C	D	E
24.	Women who enjoy studying math are a little strange.	A	B	C	D	E
25.	I think I could handle more difficult math.	A	B	C	D	E
26.	My teachers think advanced math will be a waste of time for me.	A	B	C	D	E
27.	I will use mathematics in many ways as an adult.	A	B	C	D	E
28.	Females are as good as males in geometry.	A	B	C	D	E

29.	I see mathematics as something I won't use very often when I get out of high school.	A	B	C	D	E
30.	I feel that math teachers ignore me when I try to talk about something serious.	A	B	C	D	E
31.	Women certainly are smart enough to do well in math.	A	B	C	D	E
32.	Most subjects I can handle OK, but I just can't do a good job with math.	A	B	C	D	E
33.	I can get good grades in math.	A	B	C	D	E
34.	I'll need a good understanding of math for my future work.	A	B	C	D	E
35.	My teachers want me to take all the math I can.	A	B	C	D	E
36.	I would expect a woman mathematician to be a forceful type of person.	A	B	C	D	E
37.	I know I can do well in math.	A	B	C	D	E
38.	Studying math is just as good for women as for men.	A	B	C	D	E
39.	Doing well in math is not important for my future.	A	B	C	D	E
40.	My teachers would not take me seriously if I told them I was interested in a career in science and mathematics.	A	B	C	D	E
41.	I am sure I could do advanced work in math.	A	B	C	D	E
42.	Math is not important for my life.	A	B	C	D	E
43.	I'm no good in math.	A	B	C	D	E
44.	I study math because I know how useful it is.	A	B	C	D	E
45.	Math teachers have made me feel I have the ability to go on in mathematics.	A	B	C	D	E
46.	I would trust a female just as much as I would trust a male to solve important math problems.	A	B	C	D	E
47.	My teachers think I'm the kind of person who could do well in math.	A	B	C	D	E

Science Attitude Scale as Modified from the Fennema-Sherman Attitude Scale

1.	I am sure that I can learn science.	A	B	C	D	E
2.	My teachers have been interested in my progress in science.	A	B	C	D	E
3.	Knowing science will help me earn a living.	A	B	C	D	E
4.	I don't think I could do advanced science.	A	B	C	D	E
5.	Science will not be important to me in my life's work.	A	B	C	D	E
6.	Males are not naturally better than females in science.	A	B	C	D	E
7.	Getting a teacher to take me seriously in science is a problem.	A	B	C	D	E
8.	Science is hard for me.	A	B	C	D	E
9.	It's hard to believe a female could be a genius in science.	A	B	C	D	E
10.	I'll need science for my future work.	A	B	C	D	E
11.	When a woman has to solve a science problem, she should ask a man for help.	A	B	C	D	E
12.	I am sure of myself when I do science.	A	B	C	D	E
13.	I don't expect to use much science when I get out of school.	A	B	C	D	E
14.	I would talk to my science teachers about a career which uses math.	A	B	C	D	E
15.	Women can do just as well as men in science.	A	B	C	D	E
16.	It's hard to get science teachers to respect me.	A	B	C	D	E
17.	Science is a worthwhile, necessary subject.	A	B	C	D	E
18.	I would have more faith in the answer for a science problem solved by a man than a woman.	A	B	C	D	E
19.	I'm not the type to do well in science.	A	B	C	D	E
20.	My teachers have encouraged me to study more science.	A	B	C	D	E
21.	Taking science is a waste of time.	A	B	C	D	E
22.	I have a hard time getting teachers to talk seriously with me about science.	A	B	C	D	E
23.	Science has been my worst subject.	A	B	C	D	E
24.	Women who enjoy studying science are a little strange.	A	B	C	D	E
25.	I think I could handle more difficult science.	A	B	C	D	E
26.	My teachers think advanced science will be a waste of time for me.	A	B	C	D	E
27.	I will use science in many ways as an adult.	A	B	C	D	E
28.	Females are as good as males in science.	A	B	C	D	E
29.	I see science as something I won't use very often when I get out of high school.	A	B	C	D	E
30.	I feel that science teachers ignore me when I try to talk about something serious.	A	B	C	D	E
31.	Women certainly are smart enough to do well in science.	A	B	C	D	E
32.	Most subjects I can handle OK, but I just can't do a good job with science.	A	B	C	D	E
33.	I can get good grades in science.	A	B	C	D	E

34.	I'll need a good understanding of science for my future work.	A	B	C	D	E
35.	My teachers want me to take all the science I can.	A	B	C	D	E
36.	I would expect a woman scientist to be a forceful type of person.	A	B	C	D	E
37.	I know I can do well in science.	A	B	C	D	E
38.	Studying science is just as good for women as for men.	A	B	C	D	E
39.	Doing well in science is not important for my future.	A	B	C	D	E
40.	My teachers would not take me seriously if I told them I was interested in a career in science and mathematics.	A	B	C	D	E
41.	I am sure I could do advanced work in science.	A	B	C	D	E
42.	Science is not important for my life.	A	B	C	D	E
43.	I'm no good in science.	A	B	C	D	E
44.	I study science because I know how useful it is.	A	B	C	D	E
45.	Science teachers have made me feel I have the ability to go on in science.	A	B	C	D	E
46.	I would trust a female just as much as I would trust a male to solve important science problems.	A	B	C	D	E
47.	My teachers think I'm the kind of person who could do well in science.	A	B	C	D	E

Key to Modified Fennema-Sherman Scale for Math and Science

Key:

C = Personal confidence about the subject matter

U = Usefulness of the subject's content

M = Subject is perceived as a male domain

T = Perception of teacher's attitudes

+ = Question reflects positive attitude

– = Question reflects negative attitude

Question #	Category of Question	Attitude
1	C	+
2	T	+
3	U	+
4	C	-
5	U	-
6	M	+
7	T	-
8	C	-
9	M	-
10	U	+
11	M	-
12	C	+
13	U	-
14	T	+
15	M	+
16	T	-
17	U	+
18	M	-
19	C	-
20	T	+
21	U	-

22	T	-
23	C	-
24	M	-
25	C	+
26	T	-
27	U	+
28	M	+
29	U	-
30	T	-
31	M	+
32	C	-
33	C	+
34	U	+
35	T	+
36	M	-
37	C	+
38	M	+
39	U	-
40	T	-
41	C	+
42	U	-
43	C	-
44	U	+
45	T	+
46	M	+
47	T	+

Scoring Directions

Each positive item receives the score based on points

A = 5	B = 4	C = 3	D = 2	E = 1

The scoring for each negative item should be reversed

A = 1	B = 2	C = 3	D = 4	E = 5

Add the scores for each group, T, C, U, M, to get a total for that attitude.

The highest possible score for each group of statements is 60 points.

Measurement of Attitude

Attitudinal behavior is a certain set of observable behavior which is preparatory to and indicative of the subsequent actual behavior. For the purpose of measuring attitudes only the overt symbolic type of acts are taken into account because such acts alone can be observed. Examples of such acts are speaking; writing and gesturing etc.Attitude indicate a tendency which can be helpful in predicting the subsequent behaviour. Herein lies the importance of measuring attitudes. Measurement of attitudes is useful in various aspects of day to day life. For example it helps in predicting consumer behavior in making demand forecasts in providing an insight into the public response to various welfare measured indicated by the Government in maintaining peace and social order and in social research.

The sources of information regarding the attitude of a person are:

- Life history documents including biographies, autobiographies, diaries, letters and memories.
- Oral interviews: opinions of the respondent may be elicited by personally asking them various questions.
- Questionnaires and polls: Sometimes in place of persons contact mailed questionnaire is also used for the purpose of getting opinions. Similarly public opinion polls are conducted to know peoples opinion on various issue.

In order to measure the degree of intensity of the attitude various kinds of scales have been devised.

These scales may be divided into the following categories:

- Point scales
- Ranking scales
- Rating of intensity scales etc.

Other scales for the measurement of attitudes are social distance, scale of Bogardus Thurston Scale, Likert scale and socio-metric scale by Moreno. However standard scales with universal application are yet to be devised.

Likert Scale

The Likert technique presents a set of attitude statements. Subjects are asked to express agreement or disagreement of a five-point scale. Each degree of agreement is given a numerical value from one to five. Thus a total numerical value can be calculated from all the responses.

Analysis and Interpretation of Data

The purpose of assembling data is to present some theoretical analysis or interpretation of it. But the processes of observation and analysis are rarely independent of one another. The problems become redefined as the research proceeds and this means changing accounts of observations made. In the social survey the pilot stage is very important since the sociologist derives preliminary information from it which he then uses to test existing hypotheses in a crude way. He may then have to modify both the hypothesis and in consequence the techniques for example he may change the schedule that he is using.

Unstructured interview techniques and observations are particularly suitable where the questions must be changed when an analysis begins to throw up new problems which demand new information in order to answer them. Analysis of data involves seeking through observations with object of determination in what circumstances they do not or to check that if sociologist can support one interpretation rather then another. At this stage it is necessary to point out two difficulties in the use of sociological information for analytical or interpretative purposes.

The first of these is called the reliability of data. This refers to the extent to which investigation are repeatable that is if the same procedures of data collection the same object categories and the same rules for establishing the veracity are used on the same subject by different observers or by the same observers on different occasions, no relevant changes have taken place on the main attempt results comparable with earlier studies can be obtained. If different answer emerged from the enquiries which should yield the same response then the date may not be used to represent and establish underlying regularity. The measures that sociologist can take to overcome unreliability in response will depend upon what procedures are used to collect the information and what type of analysis is to be made.

The second difficulty is that of the validity of data. Validity refers to the extent to which sociologist interpretation of underlying characteristics he wishes to reflect is in fact the faithful representation of the characteristics. The sociologists working with a positivistic framework may wish to represent some abstract notion such as Alienation by a set of relatively easily identified indicators. He may attempt to combine these into a single indicator of characteristics he wants to represent. Having done this however how can he be sure that his indicator reflects the characteristics of alienation effectively.

The usual way to ascertain the suitability of indicators is to test them empirically on samples of subjects which are known from other evidence to be alienated or not alienated. Given however that the sociologist is reasonable satisfied with both the reliability and validity of data how does the analysis or interpretation proceed? This depends upon the framework within which the sociologist is working. Within a positivistic framework the sociologist will be interested in some hypothesis which he has derived from theory by examining the connection in his data between some specified dependent variable which he suspects have some causal influence.

This implies that the initial stages of analysis which may be going on while the data are being assembled must be concerned with identifying the variables and in deciding what criteria may be reasonably used to represent these variables. Only after the positivist sociologist has satisfactorily defined and operationalised the variables he wants to test the casual proposition he is postulating can be proceed to test this.

Achievement Tests

To test or not to test...that is the question!

You might wonder, what about you, Beverly...what do you do?

- Do you test? No
- Have you tested? Yes
- Will you test again? Good question
- Are you against achievement tests? No

Testing is not required here in California. But achievement tests were required of certain age students in the homeschool support group I used to be involved with. So, I tested. What did I learn by these tests? I learned that I'm not good at giving tests to my own children. I learned that my daughter needed to learn maps, charts and graphs. I learned that overall my kids were doing great. Did it help in our homeschooling? I really don't think so. Does that piece of paper sitting in my files that nobody has ever seen do anybody any good? No. Do I regret testing? No. Like everything else in life, it was a good learning experience for our children.

That said, consider this. Achievement tests will give you an overall picture of how your kids are doing. They will help you to see their strengths and weaknesses. They will help you to track their progress over the years. They can also provide practice and confidence for other tests, like college entrance exams and placement tests.

Sometimes just hearing that your kids are tested every year is the key to smoothing over the problems and doubts your friends and relatives might have with you homeschooling.

Testing at Home versus Testing in a Group: I've done both. In my opinion, testing the children at home, especially when they are younger is a better measurement of where they are, because they are in their natural learning environment. It is difficult for a young child to be thrown in a group all of a sudden to do testing when they are used to doing everything in their own home without the distraction of other kids. Older students should probably start testing in a group to prepare for future testing environments.

To prepare for testing, make sure your children get a good night sleep, eat a good breakfast and have a comfortable, well-lit testing area. If testing at home, it might be a good idea to turn the ringer off on the phone. The distraction of even the answering machine can interrupt the train of thought and cause the mind to wander. If you have younger children, you might want to take them to grandma or make other arrangements to keep the noise level down.

Try Not to be Anxious about the Testing: Let your children know that there are questions on the test that are too easy for them, some at their level and some they aren't expected to know. Provide a piece of scratch paper. Make sure you have a good working timer. Tell them to do their best, but don't spend too much time on each question. If they can't get an answer, take their best guess and move on. They can mark down the questions they were unsure of and go back and try again, time permitting.

Here are some other articles around the net on the pros and cons of testing and links to resources that provide testing materials.

Creativity Tests

Creativity tests, mostly devised during the past 30 years, are aimed at assessing the qualities and abilities that constitute creativity. These tests evaluate mental abilities in ways that are different from—and even diametrically opposed to—conventional intelligence tests. Because the kinds of abilities measured by creativity tests differ from those measured by intelligence quotient (IQ) tests, persons with the highest scores on creativity tests do not necessarily have the highest IQs. Creative people tend to have IQs that are at least average if not above average, but beyond a score of 120 there is little correlation between performance on intelligence and creativity tests.

Most creativity tests in use today are based at least partially on the theory of creativity evolved by J. P. Guilford in the 1950s. Guilford posited that the ability to envision multiple solutions to a problem lay at the core of creativity. He called this process divergent thinking and its opposite—the tendency to narrow all options to a single solution—convergent thinking. Guilford identified three components of divergent thinking: fluency (the ability to quickly find multiple solutions to a problem); flexibility (being able to simultaneously consider a variety of alternatives); and originality (referring to ideas that differ from those of other people). Early tests designed to assess an individual's aptitude for divergent thinking included the Torrance (1962) and Meeker (1969) tests.

The most extensive work on divergent thinking was done under Guilford's direction at the University of Southern California by the Aptitudes Research Project (ARP), whose findings between the 1950s and 1970s produced a broad structure-of-intellect (SI) model which encompassed all intellectual functions, including divergent thinking. A number of the ARP divergent thinking tests, which were originally devised as research instruments for the study of creativity, have been adapted by a variety of testing companies for use by educators in placing gifted students and evaluating gifted and talented programmes. The ARP tests are divided into verbal and figural categories. Those that measure verbal ability include:

- *Word Fluency* : writing words containing a given letter
- *Ideational Fluency* : naming things that belong to a given class (i.e., fluids that will burn)
- *Associational Fluency* : writing synonyms for a specified word
- *Expressional Fluency* : writing four-word sentences in which each word begins with a specified letter
- *Alternate Uses* : listing as many uses as possible for a given object
- *Plot Titles* : writing titles for short-story plots
- *Consequences* : listing consequences for a hypothetical event ("What if no one needed to sleep?")
- *Possible Jobs* : list all jobs that might be symbolized by a given emblem

The figural ARP tests, which measure spatial aptitude, include the following:

- *Making Objects* : drawing specified objects using only a given set of shapes, such as a circle, square, etc.
- *Sketches* : elaborating on a given figure to produce sketches of recognizable items
- *Match Problems* : removing a specified number of matchsticks from a diagram to produce a specified number of geometric shapes

- *Decorations* : using as many different designs as possible to outline drawings of common objects

Divergent thinking tests are generally evaluated based on the number and variety of answers provided; the originality of the answers; and the amount of detail they contain (a characteristic referred to as elaboration). A number of creativity tests currently in use include sections that measure divergent thinking. The Creativity Assessment Packet (ages 6-18) is composed of Test of Divergent Thinking as well as Divergent Feelings Test that measures traits including imagination, curiosity, risk-taking, and complexity.

A Divergent Production subtest is part of the Screening Assessment for Gifted Elementary Students (SAGES) (ages 7-13), together with a Reasoning subtest that emphasizes the identification of relationships and a multiple-choice School Acquired Information subtest. The goals of the Test of Creative Potential (TCP) (ages 2-adult) are described using the language of divergent thinking theory: fluency, flexibility, and elaboration. Like the ARP tests, it has a figural section (Picture Decoration) to measure nonverbal ability, as well as a verbal section and a symbolic section. Among the oldest of the divergent thinking tests are the Torrance Tests of Creative Thinking (TTCT) (ages 5-adult), which also have both verbal and figural sections and measure fluency and other standard categories.

Rather than ways of thinking, some creativity tests evaluate attitudes (based on the child's answers), behavior (based on descriptions by an observer familiar with the child, usually a parent or teacher), creative perception, or creative activity. The Creativity Attitude Survey (CAS) (grades 4-6), composed of 32 statements for which the child indicates agreement or disagreement, assesses confidence in one's own ideas; appreciation of fantasy; theoretical and aesthetic orientation; openness to impulse expression; and desire for novelty. The Preschool and Kindergarten Interest Descriptor (PRIDE) (ages 3-6) is one of the tests completed by an observer rather than by the person being evaluated. It includes 50 items that assess children's behavior in the following areas: Independence-Perseverance, Imagination-Playfulness, Originality, and Many

Interests. The Scales for Rating the Behavioral Characteristics of Superior Students (SRBCSS) (child and adolescent) include 95 questions by which teachers evaluate students in such areas as motivation, leadership, art, music, dramatics, and both precise and expressive communication. The Creativity Checklist (CCL) (grades K-graduate school) is also filled out by an observer; it measures resourcefulness, constructional skill, ingenuity or productiveness, independence, and positive self-referencing behavior, as well as the more standard fluency, flexibility, and complexity that are common to divergent thinking tests.

Some creativity tests specifically address the problem of assessing creativity in minority populations, who are at a disadvantage in tests that place a strong emphasis on verbal and semantic ability. The SOI-Learning Abilities Test (ages 2-adult) includes such categories as constancy of objects in space; auditory attention; psychomotor readiness; auditory concentration for sequencing; and symbolic problem-solving.

The use of creativity tests such as this can aid in identifying gifted minority students, who, as a group, do not perform as well on standard IQ tests as non-minority students and are thus overlooked in the allocation of resources for talented students. (In one minority-populated school in Florida, only four out of 650 students were labeled as gifted according to aptitude standard tests.)

The Eby Gifted Behavior Index (all ages) reflects the growing view of creativity as specific to different domains. It is divided into six talent fields: verbal, social/leadership, visual/spatial, math/science problem-solving, mechanical/technical, and musical. The Watson-Glaser Critical Thinking Appraisal, for adolescents and adults, is a more analytical assessment of giftedness based on five components of critical thinking: inference, deduction, interpretation, awareness of assumptions, and evaluation of arguments.

Creativity tests have been found reliable in the sense that one person's scores tend to remain similar across a variety of tests. However, their validity has been questioned in terms of their ability to predict the true creative potential of those who take them. In one study, there was little correlation between the scores of both elementary and secondary students on divergent thinking tests and their actual achievements in high school in such creative fields as art, drama, and science. Creativity tests have also been criticized for unclear instructions, lack of suitability for different populations, and excessive narrowness in terms of what they measure. In addition, it may be impossible for any test to measure certain personal traits that are necessary for success in creative endeavors, such as initiative, self-confidence, tolerance of ambiguity, motivation, and perseverance. Tests also tend to create an anxiety-producing situation that may distort the scores of some test takers. Teresa Amabile, a well-known researcher in the field of creativity, has advocated assessing creativity by observing a child's creative activities in a natural setting, such as painting or storytelling.

Critiques of tests that involve divergent thinking have also been based on the conclusion of many researchers that creative accomplishment actually requires both divergent and convergent thinking. Besides being original, the successful solution to a problem must also be appropriate to its purposes, and convergent thinking allows one to evaluate one's ideas and reject them if they cannot withstand further scrutiny.

Mental Health

Mental health is a term used to describe either a level of cognitive or emotional well-being or an absence of a mental disorder. From perspectives of the discipline of positive psychology or holism mental health may include an individual's ability to enjoy life and procure a balance between life activities and efforts to achieve psychological resilience.

The World Health Organization defines mental health as “”a state of well-being in which the individual realizes his or her own abilities, can cope with the normal stresses of life, can work productively and fruitfully, and is able to make a contribution to his or her community.” It was previously stated that there was no one “official” definition of mental health. Cultural differences, subjective assessments, and competing professional theories all affect how “mental health” is defined.

History

In the mid-19th century, William Sweetzer was the first to clearly define the term "mental hygiene", which can be seen as the precurser to contemporary approaches to work on promoting positive mental health. Isaac Ray, one of thirteen founders of the American Psychiatric Association, further defined mental hygiene as an art to preserve the mind against incidents and influences which would inhibit or destroy its energy, quality or development.

At the beginning of the 20th century, Clifford Beers founded the National Committee for Mental Hygiene and opened the first outpatient mental health clinic in the United States.

Perspectives

Mental Wellbeing: Mental health can be seen as a continuum, where an individual's mental health may have many different possible values. Mental wellness is generally viewed as a positive attribute, such that a person can reach enhanced levels of mental health, even if they do not have any diagnosable mental health condition. This definition of mental health highlights emotional well-being, the capacity to live a full and creative life, and the flexibility to deal with life's inevitable challenges. Many therapeutic systems and self-help books offer methods and philosophies espousing strategies and techniques vaunted as effective for further improving the mental wellness of otherwise healthy people. Positive psychology is increasingly prominent in mental health.

A holistic model of mental health generally includes concepts based upon anthropological, educational, psychological, religious and sociological perspectives, as well as theoretical perspectives from personality, social, clinical, health and developmental psychology.

An example of a wellness model includes one developed by Myers, Sweeny and Witmer. It includes five life tasks — essence or spirituality, work and leisure, friendship, love and self-direction—and twelve sub tasks—sense of worth, sense of control, realistic beliefs, emotional awareness and coping, problem solving and creativity, sense of humor, nutrition, exercise, self care, stress management, gender identity, and cultural identity—are identified as characteristics of healthy functioning and a major component of wellness. The components provide a means of responding to the circumstances of life in a manner that promotes healthy functioning. Most of the US Population is not educated on Mental Health.

Lack of a Mental Disorder

Mental health can also be defined as an absence of a major mental health condition (for example, one of the diagnoses in the Diagnostic and Statistical Manual, IV) though recent evidence stemming from positive psychology (see above) suggests mental health is more than the mere absence of a mental disorder or illness. Therefore the impact of social, cultural, physical and education can all affect someone's mental health.

Cultural and Religious Considerations

Mental health can be socially constructed and socially defined; that is, different professions, communities, societies and cultures have very different ways of conceptualizing its nature and causes, determining what is mentally healthy, and deciding what interventions are appropriate. Thus, different professionals will have different cultural and religious backgrounds and experiences, which may impact the methodology applied during treatment.

Many mental health professionals are beginning to, or already understand, the importance of competency in religious diversity and spirituality. The American Psychological Association explicitly states that religion must be respected. Education in spiritual and religious matters is also required by the American Psychiatric Association.

Frustration

Frustration is an emotional response to circumstances where one is obstructed from arriving at a personal goal. The more important the goal, the greater the frustration. It is comparable to anger and disappointment. Sources of frustration may be *internal* or *external*. Internal sources of frustration involve personal deficiencies such as a lack of confidence or fear of social situations that prevent one from reaching a goal. Conflict can also be an internal source of frustration when one has competing goals that interfere with one another.

External causes of frustration involve conditions outside the person such as a blocked road; or conditions linked to the person's actions but not directly such as lack of money, or lack of sexual activity. In psychology, passive-aggressive behavior is a method of dealing with frustration. According to N.E. Miller "frustration produces instigation to a number of different types of response, one of which is an instigation to some form of aggression."

Causes

To the individual experiencing frustration, the emotion may more times than not be attributed to external factors which are beyond their control. Although mild frustration due to internal factors (e.g. laziness, lack of effort) is often a positive force (inspiring motivation), it is more often than not a perceived *uncontrolled* problem that instigates more severe, and perhaps pathological, frustration. An individual suffering from pathological frustration will often feel powerless to change the situation they are in, leading to frustration and, if left uncontrolled, further anger.

Frustration can be a result of blocking motivated behavior. An individual may react in several different ways. He may respond with rational problem-solving methods to overcome the barrier. Failing in this, he may become frustrated and behave irrationally. An example of blockage of motivational energy would be the case of the worker who wants time off to go fishing but is denied permission by his supervisor. Another example would be the executive who wants a promotion but finds he lacks certain qualifications.

If, in these cases, an appeal to reason does not succeed in reducing the barrier or in developing some reasonable alternative approach, the frustrated individual may resort to less adaptive methods of trying to reach his goal. He may, for example, attack the barrier physically or verbally or both.

Symptoms

Frustration can be considered a problem-response behaviour, and can have a number of effects, depending on the mental health of the individual. In positive cases, this frustration will build until a level that is too great for the individual to contend with, and thus produce action directed at solving the inherent problem. In negative cases, however, the individual may perceive the source of frustration to be outside of their control, and thus the frustration will continue to build, leading eventually to further problematic behaviour (e.g. violent reaction).

Stubborn refusal to respond to new conditions affecting the goal, such as removal or modification of the barrier, sometimes occurs. As pointed out by Brown, severe punishment may cause individuals to continue nonadaptive behavior blindly: "Either it may have an effect opposite to that of reward and as such, discourage the repetition of the act, or, by functioning as a frustrating agent, it may lead to fixation and the other symptoms of frustration as well. It follows that punishment is a dangerous tool, since it often has effects which are entirely the opposite of those desired".

Examples

The worker who is refused time off to go fishing may "cuss out" his supervisor to his face or behind his back. If he is sufficiently aroused, he may strike out at him with his fists or with the nearest weapon. If the supervisor is not present or the worker's fear of the consequences of direct attack is stronger than his desire to attack, he may transfer his aggression to someone or something else. Taking his frustration out on his family or on some object like his car or his equipment are typical ways of transferring aggression. Another "solution" to frustration is regressive behavior—becoming childish or reverting to earlier and more primitive ways of coping with the goal barrier. Throwing a temper tantrum, bursting into tears, or sulking are examples of regression. Wearing a long face and a worried look are other signs of this method of dealing with frustration.

James Joyce's novel Dubliners depicts very accurately the dimensions of frustration and how it affects people. The adult characters in the book experience all stages of the emotion and the resulting "paralysis", the inability to actively change the situation. Joyce's characters are exemplary of how people usually deal with frustration.

Handling It

Several people have started using the web as a medium to just let out all the frustrations online. Sites such as SoFrustrating.com have become popular places for people to anonymously let out issues. A quick view of the top 10 frustrations on there, shows how the world is thinking.

Conflict

Conflict is actual or perceived opposition of needs, values and interests. A conflict can be internal (within oneself) or external (between two or more individuals). Conflict as a concept can help explain many aspects of social life such as social disagreement, conflicts of interests, and fights between individuals, groups, or organizations. In political terms, "conflict" can refer to wars, revolutions or other struggles, which may involve the use of force as in the term armed conflict. Without proper social arrangement or resolution, conflicts in social settings can result in stress or tensions among stakeholders. When an interpersonal conflict does occur, its effect is often broader than two individuals involved, and can affect many associate individuals and relationships, in more or less adverse, and sometimes even humorous way.

Conflict as taught for graduate and professional work in conflict resolution (which can be win-win, where both parties get what they want, win-lose where one party gets what they want, or lose-lose where both parties don't get what they want) commonly has the definition: "when two or more parties, with perceived incompatible goals, seek to undermine each other's goal-seeking capability".

One should not confuse the distinction between the presence and absence of conflict with the difference between competition and co-operation. In competitive situations, the two or more individuals or parties each have mutually inconsistent goals, either party tries to reach their goal it will undermine the attempts of the other to reach theirs. Therefore, competitive situations will, by their nature, cause conflict but if you have good sportsmanship or are just fair it won't cause undesirable conflict. However, conflict can also occur in cooperative situations, in which two or more individuals or parties have consistent goals, because the manner in which one party tries to reach their goal can still undermine the other individual or party.

A clash of interests, values, actions or directions often sparks a conflict. Conflicts refer to the existence of that clash. Psychologically, a conflict exists when the reduction of one motivating stimulus involves an increase in another, so that a new adjustment is demanded. The word is applicable from the instant that the clash occurs. Even when we say that there is a potential conflict we are implying that there is already a conflict of direction even though a clash may not yet have occurred.

Types of Conflict

A conceptual conflict can escalate into a verbal exchange and/or result in fighting.

Conflict can exist at a variety of levels of analysis:

- community conflict
- diplomatic conflict
- economic conflict
- emotional conflict
- environmental resources conflict
- group conflict
- ideological conflict
- international conflict
- interpersonal conflict
- intersocietal conflict
- intrastate conflict (for example: civil wars, election campaigns)

- intrapersonal conflict (though this usually just gets delegated out to psychology)
- organizational conflict
- intra-societal conflict
- military conflict
- religious-based conflict (for example: Center For Reduction of Religious-Based Conflict).
- workplace conflict
- data conflict
- relationship conflict
- racial conflict

Conflicts in these levels may appear "nested" in conflicts residing at larger levels of analysis. For example, conflict within a work team may play out the dynamics of a broader conflict in the organization as a whole. (See Marie Dugan's article on Nested Conflict. John Paul Lederach has also written on this.) Theorists have claimed that parties can conceptualize responses to conflict according to a two-dimensional scheme; concern for one's own outcomes and concern for the outcomes of the other party. This scheme leads to the following hypotheses:

- High concern for both one's own and the other party's outcomes leads to attempts to find mutually beneficial solutions.
- High concern for one's own outcomes only leads to attempts to "win" the conflict.
- High concern for the other party's outcomes only leads to allowing the other to "win" the conflict.
- No concern for either side's outcomes leads to attempts to avoid the conflict.

In Western society, practitioners usually suggest that attempts to find mutually beneficial solutions lead to the most satisfactory outcomes, but this may not hold true for many Asian societies. Several theorists detect successive phases in the development of conflicts.

Often a group finds itself in conflict over facts, goals, methods or values. It is critical that it properly identify the type of conflict it is experiencing if it hopes to manage the conflict through to resolution. For example, a group will often treat an assumption as a fact.

The more difficult type of conflict is when values are the root cause. It is more likely that a conflict over facts, or assumptions, will be resolved than one over values. It is extremely difficult to "prove" that a value is "right" or "correct".

In some instances, a group will benefit from the use of a facilitator or process consultant to help identify the specific type of conflict. Practitioners of nonviolence have developed many practices to solve social and political conflicts without resorting to violence or coercion.

Conflict can arise between several characters and there can be more than one in a story or plot line. The little plot lines usually enhance the main conflict.

Conflict also defines as natural disagreement resulting from individuals or groups that differ in beliefs, attitudes, values or needs. It can also originate from past rivalries and personality differences. Other causes of conflict include trying to negotiate before the timing is right or before needed information is available. The following are the causes of conflict:

- communication failure
- personality conflict
- value differences
- goal differences
- methodological differences
- substandard performance
- lack of cooperation
- differences regarding authority
- differences regarding responsibility
- competition over resources
- non-compliance with rules (LO)

A definition of a conflict can be the subject of legal action has three invariants :

- legal
- technical
- emotional

Causes

Structural Factors (How the conflict is set up)

- Authority Relationships (The boss and employees beneath them)
- Common Resources (Sharing the same secretary)
- Goal Differences (One person wants production to rise and others want communication to rise)
- Interdependence (A company as a whole can't operate w/o other departments)
- Jurisdictional Ambiguities (Who can discipline whom)
- Specialization (The experts in fields)
- Status inconsistencies
- Need of land, water and food (whole country)

Personal Factors

- Communication barriers
- Conflict management style
- Cultural differences
- Emotions
- Perception
- Personalities
- Skills and abilities
- Values and Ethics

The assertion that "the conflict is emotionally defined and driven," and "does not exist in the absence of emotion" is challenged by Economics. In this context, scarcity means that available resources are insufficient to satisfy all wants and needs. The subject of conflict as a purely rational, strategic decision is specifically addressed by Game Theory, a branch of Economics.

Where applicable, there are many components to the emotions that are intertwined with conflict. There is a behavioral, physiological, cognitive component.

- *Behavioral:* The way emotional experience gets expressed which can be verbal or non-verbal and intentional or un-intentional.
- *Physiological:* The bodily experience of emotion. The way emotions make us feel in comparison to our identity.
- *Cognitive:* The idea that we "assess or appraise" an event to reveal its relevancy to ourselves.

These three components collectively advise that "the meanings of emotional experience and expression are determined by cultural values, beliefs, and practices."

- Cultural values-culture tells people who are a part of it, "Which emotions ought to be expressed in particular situations" and "what emotions are to be felt."
- Physical-This escalation results from "anger or frustration."
- Verbal-This escalation results from "negative perceptions of the annoyer's character."

There are several principles of conflict and emotion.

1. Conflict is emotionally defined-conflict involves emotion because something "triggers" it. The conflict is with the parties involved and how they decide to resolve it—"events that trigger conflict are events that elicit emotion."
2. Conflict is emotionally valence—emotion levels during conflict can be intense or less intense. The "intensity" levels "may be indicative of the importance and meaning of the conflict issues for each" party.
3. Conflict Invokes a moral stance—when an event occurs it can be interpreted as moral or immoral. The judging of this morality "influences one's orientation to the conflict, relationship to the parties involved, and the conflict issues".
4. Conflict is identity based—Emotions and Identity are a part of conflict. When a person knows their values, beliefs, and morals they are able to determine whether the conflict is personal, relevant, and moral. "Identity

related conflicts are potentially more destructive."

5. Conflict is relational—"conflict is relational in the sense that emotional communication conveys relational definitions that impact conflict." "Key relational elements are power and social status."

Emotions are acceptable in the workplace as long as they can be controlled and utilized for productive organizational outcomes and are used at the approiate timing.

Ways of Addressing Conflict

Five basic ways of addressing conflict were identified by Thomas and Kilman in 1976:

- Accommodation – surrender one's own needs and wishes to accommodate the other party.
- Avoidance–avoid or postpone conflict by ignoring it, changing the subject, etc. Avoidance can be useful as a temporary measure to buy time or as an expedient means of dealing with very minor, non-recurring conflicts. In more severe cases, conflict avoidance can involve severing a relationship or leaving a group.
- Collaboration–work together to find a mutually beneficial solution. While the Thomas Kilman grid views collaboration as the only win-win solution to conflict, collaboration can also be time-intensive and inappropriate when there is not enough trust, respect or communication among participants for collaboration to occur.
- Compromise–find a middle ground in which each party is partially satisfied.
- Competition–assert one's viewpoint at the potential expense of another. It can be useful when achieving one's objectives outweighs one's concern for the relationship.

The Thomas Kilman Instrument can be used to assess one's dominant style for addressing conflict.

Ongoing Conflicts

Many NGOs and independent groups attempt to monitor the situation of ongoing conflicts. Unfortunately, the definitions of war, conflict, armed struggle, revolution and all these words which describe violent opposition between States or armed organised groups, are not precise enough to distinguish one from another.

For example, the word *terrorism* is used indifferently by many governments to delegitimate every kind of armed revolt and, at the same time, by many rebel groups to delegitimate the armed repression of sovereign governments.

UNIT-IX

Guidance Services in Schools

Guidance Services at Different School Levels-Meaning, Significance, Types

Guidance Counsellors deliver a vital service in schools, playing a central role in providing educational and career guidance, alongside increasingly important personal and social support to young people.

The presence of more and more diversified users, carrying diversified **guidance** needs, requiring diversified **guidance** answers, makes the situation "diverse" and shows the strong need of coordination.

Attention of policymakers is now focused on national coordination, harmonisation and promotion of the existing initiatives, innovative projects and best practices.

The Ministries decided to enlarge the **services** offered and the groups of users served. One of the main new **services** offered has been career **guidance**.

Class teachers are the key players in the provision of **guidance services** at general **school** level, but they are supported also by external counsellors and **guidance** staff.

The common **guidance** policy of Italian Universities has been settled within the framework of the recent Italian reform of higher education. However, the **different** Faculties may still organize autonomously specific **guidance** initiatives.

Territorial Permanent Centres have been created with the aim to strengthening the policies of the training offer, addressed to adult population, through the valorisation of the formal and the non-formal education opportunities.

Within these Centres **guidance** becomes a service that accompanies people during their lifespan, providing them information and facilitating their choices.

The standards-focused middle level school or programme is purposeful. It has two basic goals:

The intellectual development and academic achievement of all students, and the personal and social development of each student.

In a standards-focused middle-level school or programme these two goals are not in conflict or competition; rather, they are compatible, complementary, mutually supportive, and inextricably linked.

The seven essential elements of standards-focused middle-level school programmes are:

- A philosophy and mission that reflect the intellectual and developmental needs and characteristics of young adolescents.
- An educational programme that is comprehensive, challenging, purposeful, integrated, and standards-based.
- An organization and structure that support both academic excellence and personal development.
- Classroom instruction appropriate to the needs and characteristics of young adolescents provided by skilled and knowledgeable teachers.
- Strong educational leadership and a building administration that encourages, facilitates, and sustains involvement, participation, and partnerships.
- A network of academic and personal support available for students.
- Professional training and staff development that are ongoing, planned, purposeful, and collaboratively developed.

Essential Element 1: Philosophy and Mission

A philosophy and mission that reflect the intellectual and developmental needs and characteristics of young adolescents.

The middle-level educational programme has a purpose beyond linking the elementary grades and the high school. Its basic aims are to educate and nurture. It has a culture of collective and shared responsibility.

To be successful, it must attend to both the intellectual development and the personal needs of young adolescents. The philosophy and mission of a standards-focused middle-level school or programme must reflect a set of shared beliefs.

The school and staff within the school must commit to:

- Developing the whole child, intellectually and academically, personally and socially, and physically and emotionally.
- Working together to ensure that all students achieve at high levels and develop as individuals.
- Accepting - individually and collectively - responsibility for the educational and personal development of each and every student.
- Connecting each young adolescent in positive ways with the school and with caring adults within the school.
- Providing each student with a variety of learning experiences in order for each of them to make informed life decisions (both educational and personal).
- Establishing partnerships with the home and the community.

Essential Element 2: Educational Programme

An educational programme that is comprehensive, challenging, purposeful, integrated, and standards-based.

A standards-focused middle-level educational programme:

- Emphasizes not only intellectual development but also personal/social development.
- Is challenging, rigorous, and purposeful.

- Is comprehensive and inclusive, embracing and encompassing all of the State's 28 learning standards. (See New York State's Learning Standards, page 15.)
- Reflects interdependence, emphasizes cross-programme connections, and promotes shared responsibility.
- Is articulated vertically and horizontally, within and across the various curricular areas, learning standards, and grade levels.
- Has a set of learning skills (e.g., how to read for understanding, how to take notes, etc.) that are common across all grades and subject area and taught and reinforced in each grade and subject area.
- Has performance expectations that are common across all grades and subject areas (e.g., students must write in complete sentences).
- Is articulated with the elementary feeder schools and with the secondary receiving schools.
- Has up-to-date written curricula (that are based on the State's learning standards) for all subject areas.
- Includes diagnostic assessments (similar in design to the State's assessments) that regularly and routinely monitor the learning of each student relative to the State' standards.
- Engages and involves the family, local community, and the world outside school in the education and personal development of young adolescents.

Essential Element 3: Organization and Structure

An organization and structure that support both academic excellence and personal development. Standards-focused schools with middle-level grades are organized to promote academic excellence and to establish within staff and students a feeling of belonging and a sense of personal identification with the school and its purposes. A standards-focused school that enrolls young adolescents should:

- Have teacher teams sharing responsibility for the education and personal development of a common group of students.

- Have common planning time for those teachers and teacher teams sharing responsibility for a common group of students.
- Have schedules with flexible time assignments within blocks of time to encourage interdisciplinary programmes and the creative use of time.
- Contain at least three grade levels.
- Have comparatively small enrollments so that every student is viewed as an individual and receives personal attention. When the student population is large, have "houses" within schools or schools-within-schools to promote a sense of family and to reduce the feeling of anonymity and isolation among students.
- Be structured to create close, sustained relationships between students and teachers.
- Provide, for those students needing additional help to meet the State's standards, opportunities for additional time, instruction, and personal support (e.g., after school, before school, summer school, reduced class size, tutoring, pupil personnel services, etc.).
- Provide a variety of co-curricular and extra-curricular activities.
- Provide opportunities for students to participate in youth service, community service and/or service learning activities.
- Encourage active parent involvement through a variety of activities.
- Establish ties with the school community that strengthen connections between school/education and career opportunities.
- Promote and encourage appropriate participation of pupils with disabilities in all curricular, co-curricular, and extra-curricular activities.
- Have students with disabilities or other special needs, as well as their programmes and services, integrated throughout the school building rather than clustered in a separate area.

- Provide support services such as guidance, counseling, and health-related services to all students.
- Integrate technology into the educational programme so that it supports student learning in a purposeful way.
- Provide a gradual transition from the more self-contained classrooms of the elementary school to the more departmentalized structure of the high school.

Essential Element 4: Classroom Instruction

Classroom instruction appropriate to the needs and characteristics of young adolescents provided by skilled and knowledgeable teachers.

Teachers in middle-level classrooms understand and appreciate the emotional, intellectual, physical, psychological, and social changes that are occurring within their students and recognize the behaviors manifested by these changes. They use instructional techniques and processes that capitalize on the unique developmental characteristics and individual needs of early adolescents.

Successful middle-level teachers in a standards-focused school:

- Provide instruction that is challenging, rigorous, and purposeful.
- Know and understand the needs and developmental characteristics of young adolescents.
- Have a deep understanding of their subject matter, of different approaches to student learning, and of diverse teaching techniques.
- Know and understand each of the State's 28 learning standards and - when and where appropriate - reinforce them routinely during regular classroom instruction.
- Use a range of successful, research-based teaching strategies that are developmentally and cognitively appropriate, matching instruction to the students' varied learning styles and different intelligences.
- Involve students in their learning, encouraging them

to contribute to their learning experiences, to make choices, to explore, to question, to experience, to learn, to grow.

- Vary activities to maintain student interest.
- Use technology purposefully to support and enhance learning.
- Focus instruction on thinking, reasoning, and problem solving and, at the same time ensure that students acquire necessary content and subject matter.
- Use interdisciplinary approaches to help students integrate their studies and meet learning standards.
- Use flexible grouping based upon student needs and interests to help each student achieve the learning standards, with students changing groups often, depending on individual needs and programme purposes.
- Use classroom assessments that reflect the State's learning standards and are aligned with State assessments.
- Use classroom assessments that are instructionally useful indicators of individual student growth and performance not only to monitor each student's progress in meeting the State's learning standards but also to plan instruction.
- Use cooperative learning groups and peer-tutoring opportunities to develop social and interpersonal skills in addition to academic proficiency.
- Consult with each other and with other school personnel. Teachers with regular education assignments and those assigned to programmes for students with special needs work closely together.
- Inform and involve parents of middle-level students in their children's education by helping them understand the learning standards their children must meet, the instructional programme, their children's progress, and how to help their children at home with schoolwork,

school decisions, and successful development through adolescence.

- Are themselves learners who are constantly engaged in professional and intellectual growth activities.
- Recognize that they must work together cooperatively and collaboratively - rather than individually and in isolation - to ensure that all their students achieve at high levels and meet all the State's learning standards.

Essential Element 5: Educational Leadership

Strong educational leadership and a building administration that encourages, facilitates, and sustains involvement, participation, and partnerships.

Standards-focused middle-level schools and programmes need leadership if they are to develop and prosper.

Those in positions of leadership must:

- Know and understand the needs and developmental characteristics of young adolescents.
- Know and understand the essential elements of a standards-focused, high performing middle-level school or middle-level programme.
- Know and understand each of the 28 learning standards and how they interrelate.
- Know and understand the State's assessment system.
- Have an understanding of the subject matter in the middle grades and its interconnections, of different approaches to student learning, and of diverse teaching strategies.
- Create, promote, and sustain a school culture of mutual support and collective responsibility for the educational and personal development of each and every young adolescent.
- Articulate and maintain high standards for classroom instruction and student performance.
- Have high expectations for students and staff.
- Know a range of successful, research-based teaching techniques that are developmentally and cognitively

appropriate, matching instruction to the students' varied learning styles and different intelligences.

- Involve staff and others in the operation of the school or programme, empowering and encouraging them to contribute and to make decisions that benefit students.
- Support and encourage teachers to take risks, to explore, to question, to try new instructional approaches, to continue as learners, and to grow.
- Promote and facilitate inter-school cooperation, collaboration, and communication with feeder elementary schools and receiving high schools.
- Inform and involve parents of middle-level students in their children's education by helping them understand the needs and developmental characteristics of young adolescents, the learning standards their children must meet, the instructional programme, their children' progress, and how to help their children at home with schoolwork, school decisions, and successful development through adolescence.
- Promote school/community partnerships and involve members of the community in school activities and initiatives, empowering and encouraging them to contribute and make decisions that benefit students.

Essential Element 6: A Network of Academic and Personal Support

A network of academic and personal support available for students.

Middle-level students need academic and personal support as they experience the changes associated with the transition from childhood to adolescence and from elementary school to high school.

Academic and personal support includes:

- Adults and older youths to provide positive role models and constant affirmation and recognition.
- Respect and caring to engender a feeling of self-worth, self-confidence, and personal efficacy.
- Opportunities to examine, explore, discuss, and

understand the changes associated with early adolescence.

- Counseling and guidance services to assist students in making life, career, and educational choices.
- A network of trained professionals, special programmes, and community resources available to assist those who have extraordinary needs and require additional services to cope with the changes of early adolescence and/or the academic demands of middle-level education. Schools need to collaborate and cooperative with other human service agencies in the community.
- An adult mentor in addition to a guidance counselor, either formally through a teacher/student, advisor/ advisee programme or informally through a school culture of caring in which teachers or other adults assume responsibility for individual students.

Essential Element 7: Professional Training and Staff Development

Professional training and staff development that are ongoing, planned, purposeful, and collaboratively developed.

Teachers, administrators, and other school staff in a standards-focused middle-level school or programme need regular, planned opportunities for professional and intellectual growth.

Teachers, administrators, and staff need to:

- Know the needs and characteristics of students in the middle grades and the instructional strategies and techniques that work best for these students.
- Understand the philosophy and mission of the standards-driven middle-level school.
- Have high expectations for all students.
- Be familiar with each of the State's 28 learning standards and incorporate in their own classrooms and work spaces educational experiences that help all students achieve all the standards - including those that are outside their own area of content expertise.

- Know and understand their subject matter and course curriculum thoroughly.
- Know and understand the State's assessment system.
- Collaborate and cooperate in planning and providing professional training and staff development opportunities.
- Routinely and systematically monitor and evaluate student learning to assess and improve instructional effectiveness.

Conclusion

The middle grades play a critical role in the educational continuum. Schools with middle-level grades that are standards-focused attend to the twin purposes of academic preparation and individual self-development for all young adolescents. They do this by:

- Accepting collective responsibility for ensuring that all students are successful and learning at high levels.
- Creating small communities for learning and providing comprehensive guidance and support services.
- Establishing and maintaining a climate for learning that is respectful, purposeful, physically and psychologically safe, and personalized to ensure close, sustained relationships between students and teachers.
- Providing a comprehensive educational programme that is standards-based - reflecting the State's 28 learning standards - challenging, integrative, and exploratory.
- Using flexible organizational structures and creative use of time.
- Using a variety of research-based, instructional strategies that are cognitively and developmentally appropriate and that respect individual experiences, learning styles, and learning needs.
- Employing knowledgeable and qualified personnel who are committed to the education of young adolescents.
- Fostering each student's personal development, health, wellness, and safety.

- Engaging families in the education of young adolescents.
- Connecting schools with the larger community.

A high-performing, standards-focused middle-level school or programme that successfully addresses both the intellectual and personal needs of young adolescents is profoundly different from many middle-level schools today. To create schools that are true standards-focused, middle-level schools will necessitate systemic change that will not be easy to accomplish. It will require leadership, persistence, additional resources, time, and a strong will to succeed. The task is challenging and daunting. However, it is necessary, and it can be done.

Organization of Guidance Services in Schools

Guidance in Second Level Schools

Guidance in schools refers to a range of learning experiences provided in a developmental sequence, that assist students to develop self-management skills which will lead to effective choices and decisions about their lives. It encompasses the three separate, but interlinked, areas of personal and social development, educational guidance and career guidance.

Counselling in Second Level Schools

Counselling is a key part of the school guidance programme, offered on an individual or group basis as part of a developmental learning process and at moments of personal crisis. Counselling has as its objective the empowerment of students so that they can make decisions, solve problems, address behavioural issues, develop coping strategies and resolve difficulties they may be experiencing. Counselling in schools may include personal counselling, educational counselling, career counselling or combinations of these.

The Aims of Guidance and Counselling

The guidance and counselling process aims to help students to develop an awareness and acceptance of their talents and abilities; to explore possibilities and opportunities; to grow in independence and to take responsibility for themselves; to make informed choices about their lives and to follow through on those choices. In this document, the word *guidance* is used to describe the activities provided by the *guidance and counselling* services identified under *support services* in paragraph 2 of the Education Act 1998.

The Importance of Guidance and Counselling

Significant changes are taking place in economic and social structures in this country which have important implications for the education system and for the students who are its principal focus. The value of guidance and counselling in responding to these challenges is widely recognised in Government policy statements and by other national and international bodies:

- The National Development Plan (NDP) 2000-2006 states that the provision of guidance and counselling in second level schools is vital to enable each pupil to gain the maximum benefit from the education system. The NDP identifies the school guidance service as a social inclusion measure within the education sector. The New Deal 1998 also supports this theme, it states that guidance plays a *major preventative role in helping young people at risk to stay within the formal education system.*
- The importance of lifelong guidance is emphasised by the White Paper *Learning for Life - 2000,* which lists it as a key support *necessary for successful access and learning*.
- The Commission on the Points System states that *good quality, comprehensive guidance can contribute significantly to broadening the views of second-level students and their parents on diverse pathways to careers. The Commission supports the need for an effective and comprehensive guidance and counselling service in schools and considers that the provision of such a service should be viewed in terms of the right of a student to access to an appropriate level of such services.*
- The Organisation for Economic Co-operation and Development (OECD), which carried out a comparative

review of national policies for career information, guidance and counselling services in 14 OECD countries, including Ireland, describes guidance within education systems as having an important role to play in laying the foundations for lifelong career development, *including knowledge and competencies regarding self-awareness, the world of work, and making decisions and transitions. It defines guidance services as services that assist individuals, of any age and at any point throughout their lives, to make educational, training and occupational choices and to manage their careers.* It stresses that effective advice and guidance on educational and training options and on links between these options and later occupational destinations *can help better match individuals' learning choices to their interests, talents and intended destinations.* In the OECD's view, this can help to reduce early school leaving, improve flows between different levels of education and improve transitions from education to the labour market. It states that *these outcomes help to make better use of educational resources, and to increase both individual and social returns to investments in education.* A report of the review was published by the OECD in 2004.

- European Union Presidency Conclusions on the importance of guidance throughout life in supporting and furthering the Lisbon Agenda10, issued after the informal meeting of the European Ministers for Education and the Commission of the European Union in Dublin on 28/29 April 2004, stress the importance of all European citizens having access to guidance services at school level and at all later life stages, as appropriate and reflecting local circumstances. The need for particular attention to be paid to early intervention with individuals and groups at risk of not completing their schooling and at risk of alienation from society is highlighted as well as the need for provision for persons with special educational needs.

- In May 2004, a Resolution1 was adopted by the Council of Ministers of the European Union on Strengthening Policies, Systems and Practices in the field of Guidance throughout life in Europe. The Resolution highlights the need for guidance provision within the education system, especially in schools. Guidance has an *essential role to play in ensuring that individuals' educational and career decisions are firmly based, and in assisting them to develop effective self-management of their learning and career paths*. The Resolution stresses the role of guidance services in:
    - o the prevention of early school leaving
    - o the empowerment of individuals to manage their own learning and careers
    - o the re-integration of early school leavers into appropriate education and training programmes.

Planning Guidance Provision in Schools

Guidance as a Whole School Responsibility

The development and implementation of the school's guidance plan is a whole school responsibility. It should involve the guidance counsellor/s in the first instance, as well as all other relevant members of management and staff of the school. Parents and students must be seen as an essential part of this process and representatives of the local community, especially local business, NEPS and other relevant agencies should also be consulted and actively involved as appropriate.

The Role of Other Members of Staff

While the guidance counsellor/s has/have primary responsibility for the delivery of the school's guidance and counselling programme, other members of staff have important and worthwhile contributions to make to the planning NAMEand delivery of many aspects of the programme.

These activities begin with the induction of incoming students into second level education. Some students may experience this transition as a traumatic time in their young lives and may need continuing support well into the first term. The more familiar incoming students are with the second level school, the easier will be their induction into the new system. Activities such as exploratory visits to the second level school, taster classes for students and information sessions for parents can contribute to dispelling doubts and uncertainties as well as helping the development of the confidence of the incoming students.

It is important that students and their parents are clear about the role and functions of the various members of staff concerned with aspects of student support, such as the guidance counsellor/s, chaplain, class tutors/year heads, Home School Community Liaison (HSCL) co-ordinator etc (some of these titles may vary between schools). It can help if the names and the different roles of support team members are explained to incoming first year students and their parents. This contributes to the elimination of confusion and helps to ensure that both students and their parents know who to approach for information, support or help when needs arise. The principal and /or deputy principal and teachers of first year students together with the guidance counsellor should endeavour to participate as far as possible in contacts between the school and the primary schools from which their students come.

Every effort should be made by schools to draw on the knowledge, experience and contacts of all staff members in providing the best possible guidance programme for students, for example:

- subject teachers are best placed to provide students with information and expertise on both the content and demands of their particular subject(s) syllabus
- subject teachers have a key role to play when students are choosing subjects and levels for the Junior and Leaving Certificate examinations
- subject teachers may also be in a position to indicate to senior cycle students the content and study commitments of particular subjects in further and higher education courses

- te expertise of the subject teachers, learning support teacher and/or resource teacher, guidance counsellor/s and programme co-ordinators can combine to assist students in choosing the most appropriate, for them, of the educational programmes offered by the school
- teachers with special ICT skills and responsibilities may have opportunities to collaborate with the guidance counsellor/s in assisting students to use QualifaX and other guidance software packages and in enabling them to access the most up-to-date career information via the Internet
- teachers may have close links with community agencies and local businesses and, therefore, may be well placed to help individual students benefit from contact with these bodies for activities such as work experience or working with their local communities, as part of their guidance programme.

Guidance in Second Level Schools

The Importance of School Guidance Planning in Identifying Student Needs: The school, through the planning process, makes decisions regarding the provision of guidance using the professional expertise of management, guidance counsellor/s and other members of staff and taking into account the views of students, parents and other partners. It is important that the school guidance plan should balance the needs of all junior and senior cycle students in a sequential, developmental and comprehensive way, including those with special educational needs, those from minority ethnic groups, members of the Traveller community, those at risk of early school leaving, Post Leaving Certificate (PLC) students and those on Vocational Training Opportunities Schemes (VTOS).

Choosing Educational Programmes

Schools should ensure that students and their parents are informed of the benefits to be gained from the programme options available. In addition to the Junior Certificate (JC) and Leaving Certificate (Established) (LC), such options are likely to be:

- Junior Certificate School Programme (JCSP)
- Transition Year Programme (TYP)
- Leaving Certificate Applied (LCA)
- Leaving Certificate Vocational Programme (LCVP)
- Post Leaving Certificate (PLC) courses.

Students also need to be made aware of how the choice of programme can have a bearing on future career options.

Appropriate Guidance

Following on from the identification of student needs in the planning process (see *Planning the School Guidance Programme* Chapter 4), schools will be in a position to define the principal activities to be included in the guidance programme. These will include providing students with:

- clear information concerning subject choices. This includes information about the consequences of subject choice and level taken for future educational, training and career options
- opportunities to explore their interests and subject choices and how these link to further education, training and career areas
- an awareness of the content and the syllabus demands of particular subjects
- assistance in the choice of educational programmes offered by the school
- assistance in identifying their own most effective learning styles and in developing effective study and note-taking skills, examination techniques and time management skills
- objective assessments of their aptitudes and achievements and feedback on these assessments
- guidance on the educational, vocational and career options available, including career progression routes and lifelong learning opportunities
- encouragement to explore a wide range of educational and career choices, including non-traditional careers

- the integration, as far as is practicable, of career themes and information into relevant aspects of the curriculum
- oportunities to develop information-seeking skills, including the use of ICT, with particular reference to career exploration and planning
- guidance in developing individual career plans based on the individual's achievements, ambitions, interests and personal circumstances.

The most up-to-date course and career information is to be found on the Internet. The planned connection of all schools to broadband will provide schools with greater access to multimedia applications and will facilitate more efficient use of the Internet to obtain up-to-date information on educational and training courses. In view of this, schools should work towards ensuring that students have regular and adequate access, for guidance purposes, to web-based information sources.

Given the nature of some aspects of the work of the guidance counsellor, schools should be cognisant of the need to ensure that adequate physical facilities are available for guidance purposes. Individual work with students requires appropriate surroundings and equally, work with small groups and classes requires suitable facilities. Space for the storage and display of guidance materials should also be provided to the extent possible.

Personal and Social Education

It is recommended that staff members involved in Social Personal and Health Education (SPHE) and Religious Education (RE) as well as HSCL co-ordinators should work together with guidance counsellors and others involved in guidance provision, since they share the objective of promoting the students' personal development and growth.

The particular contribution of guidance to SPHE is in facilitating students to:

- recognise their own talents and achievements and to identify their strengths and weaknesses
- develop coping strategies to deal with stress, personal

and social issues and the challenges posed by adolescence and adulthood

- cope with the demands of school programmes, study and examinations
- organise the management of time for school, study, sporting and leisure activities
- develop interpersonal skills and awareness of the needs of others
- establish good patterns of decision-making and to learn how to make informed choices
- make successful transitions from primary to second level and from second level to further or higher education, training or directly into employment.

Where young people have serious learning, personal and social difficulties, these may need to be addressed by the relevant professional/s, such as the learning support teacher, guidance counsellor and/or NEPS psychologist or health services personnel, before the student can begin to make educational and career choices. Such young people may require ongoing learning and guidance support in order to enable them to participate fully in the education process.

Counselling: Individual and Group

Counselling should be available when necessary, on an individual and/or group basis, to assist students in their personal and social, educational and career development. Guidance counsellors are qualified to provide counselling support to students.

The demands for counselling will vary among schools, and within any particular school from year to year, in response to student needs. Schools, therefore, require flexibility in determining the allocation of time for the guidance counsellor/s to engage in counselling.

However, schools need to balance the time available to the guidance counsellor/s for individual counselling against their responsibilities to the full student body in the school. It is recommended, therefore, that in cases where students require personal counselling over a protracted period of time, guidance counsellors should refer such cases to relevant outside agencies.

Referrals

In cases where a student requires specialist support, the guidance counsellor should become involved in assessing his/her needs and where necessary, arrange a referral to an appropriate outside agency. Procedures for the referral of students to the guidance counsellor and for referral to outside agencies should be included in the School Plan. NEPS psychologists provide a source of advice to guidance counsellors on appropriate referral pathways.

The Role of Guidance in Promoting Educational and Social Inclusion

Education plays a key role in the promotion of a more inclusive society. Educational qualifications, or the lack of them, are significant in determining the life chances of most people. Now, more than ever, underachievement at school tends to result in social difficulties that can lead to a life of uncertainty, marginalisation and dependence on the structures of social assistance. Equally, a lack of formal qualifications can prevent an individual progressing into further education, training or stable employment.

Addressing Educational Disadvantage

To address disadvantage adequately, schools should endeavour to streamline and formalise their policies and practices so that all students have access to the fullest possible range of educational services and supports. The Education Act 1998 defines educational disadvantage as *...the impediments to education arising from social or economic disadvantage which prevent students from deriving appropriate benefit from education in schools* [Paragraph 32(9)].

Students whose families have little or no tradition of progressing to further or higher education or training require access to a guidance programme that allows them to explore the full range of learning and career opportunities available. In such cases, schools should endeavour to give every assistance to those students and their parents to become aware of the benefits to be gained from continuing in school, obtaining qualifications and progressing to further study and/or training. Students should be given the opportunity and encouragement to study subjects at the highest possible level in accordance with their individual needs and ambitions. Therefore, it is important that all incoming students and their parents be informed of the importance of making appropriate subject choices and the possible implications of these choices and levels at senior cycle, e.g. that the study of a subject at foundation level for JC does not easily transfer to the study of that subject at a higher level in senior cycle.

Early School Leaving

Early school leaving and low educational attainment can be attributed to a number of factors which may be related to the individual, home, community or school.

A key objective of the NDP is the prevention of early school leaving and it identifies the school guidance service as playing a major preventative role in helping young people at risk to remain in the formal education system.

One of the strands under which additional guidance resources were allocated to schools as part of the Guidance Enhancement Initiative (GEI) was to increase retention rates/combat early school leaving. Schools included in the School Completion Programme (SCP) can use some of the resources available through the programme to provide additional guidance for students at risk of leaving school before obtaining any formal qualifications. Schools with discretionary posts e.g. posts under the designated disadvantaged scheme, also can use some of these hours to provide additional guidance to students at risk of leaving school early.

Disability and Special Educational Needs

The Education for Persons with Special Educational Needs Act 2004, provides for the rights of people with special educational needs to avail of and benefit from an appropriate education which should take place, wherever possible, in an inclusive environment. Such students' particular needs should be addressed within the school's guidance programme. They should also be assisted to leave school and progress into adulthood with the skills necessary to participate, to the level of their capacity and in an inclusive way, in the social and economic activities of society and to live independent and fulfilled lives.

For those with a specific learning, intellectual or physical disability, guidance should be planned and delivered in formats and using methodologies, appropriate to individual needs. Parents and students need to be fully informed of all third level access programmes, of particular FÁS (and other agency) schemes and other initiatives designed to give special support to those wishing to avail of reserved places in third level and further education colleges and on training programmes. While in school, students with specific disabilities should be empowered to explore the fullest range of options available and to acquire the skills necessary to reach individual goals.

Students with special educational needs may require particular support to achieve their full potential and to become aware of the range of career and other options available to them. The school's guidance plan should take cognisance of the available support services and include provision for an appropriate range of interventions, information formats and delivery methodologies to meet the special needs of these students.

This should include provision for liaison between the school and the Special Education Support Service, FÁS and other relevant agencies in relation to planning for the long-term educational and training needs of such students. NEPS also has a role to play in the identification and support of students with special needs, in accordance with the procedures outlined in the NEPS Model of Service.

Non-national Students

In recent years the number of non-national students, including those whose first language may not be English, residing in Ireland has risen. Learners from ethnic minority groups may not have access to the same information about available education and training opportunities as their national counterparts. As well as being unfamiliar with the Irish education system, non-national students and/or their parents/ guardians may not have the confidence or the language skills to approach the appropriate sources.

In allocating guidance and counselling resources, managements of schools with significant numbers of non-national students need to be aware of the time and other supports that guidance counsellors may require when working with students whose cultural background and language ability may be radically different to that of the majority of the school population.

Adult Students

Where a school's population includes adult students participating in, for example, VTOS, PLC and other adult education courses, the guidance programme should reflect their particular needs. Adults may need guidance and support on an individual basis to assess their abilities and skills, to discuss and explore their life, work and educational experiences and to discuss their interests, course selection and progression routes. In turn, drawing on the life experiences of adult learners may significantly enhance the guidance programme in the school for younger students.

Promoting Inclusion

The school's guidance programme can support the operation of a proactive inclusive school policy by promoting:

- strategies for building motivation and self-esteem
- the identification and support of students with special educational needs
- an awareness and understanding of racial, ethnic and intellectual differences
- early identification and support (through counselling and other measures) of students at risk of early school leaving
- guidance support for school attendance strategies

- awareness among students of the consequences of early school leaving
- knowledge among those who decide to leave early, of the options available to them after they leave school in the areas of further education, training and employment.

Elements of the School Guidance Programme

Guidance in Junior Cycle

The early years of second level education are critically important ones for young people. There are transitions to be undertaken and many choices and decisions to be made by the student. The school guidance programme can facilitate this decision-making process, and make it an exciting and positive experience. The main challenges and choices for junior cycle students are likely to relate to:

- the transition from primary to second level school
- the choice of JC or JCSP (where available)
- choice of subjects
- the levels at which JC examination subjects are to be taken
- participation in TYP
- which Leaving Certificate programme to pursue (LC (Established), LCA or LCVP, as available)
- subject choice for senior cycle.

Making the Transition from Primary to Second Level Education

Most students need time and support in order to adjust to the second level school environment, involving as it does a variety of teachers, new subjects and teaching methods as well as a changed social context. Some students may need individual help, and possibly counselling, in order to complete this transition successfully.

Links between Primary and Second Level Schools

In order to facilitate the smooth transition of students to second level school, it is recommended that there should be a formal communication structure established between second level schools and their main feeder schools. This should include structures to support students with special educational needs. The guidance counsellor/s should participate in the development of links with schools from which their students come and, in co-operation with other relevant members of staff, should develop a guidance programme for incoming students and their parents. This programme should include information about subject choices available, levels of study, the choice of programmes at junior cycle and support services provision.

It is recommended that schools consider formalising their support activities for the transition from primary to second level education into a defined set of measures within the school plan. Such activities could include orientation days, information sessions for parents and meetings with principals from feeder schools. These measures should start before students enter the school and extend at least until the end of the first term of the school year. In order for transition programmes to facilitate the students' successful transition to second level, the co-operation and input of the primary schools are essential.

Support Services within the School

Students and their parents/guardians are entitled to be informed of the support services available in the school. It is recommended that first year students be given a clear outline of the roles of the personnel involved in the support structures e.g. guidance counsellor, chaplain, HSCL co-ordinator, learning support teachers, care team, year heads, class tutors and others as appropriate. In the context of the school guidance programme, each first year student should have access to individual support from a member of this staff team, in order to assist with his/her integration into the school.

Progressing through the Junior Cycle

Students in junior cycle must prepare for State examinations for the first time. They are also faced with making subject and programme choices that will have implications for their career choice. In addition to the activities outlined in the section of this document on Guidance in Second Level Schools, the guidance programme should aim to give junior cycle students the opportunity to acquire the following:

- understanding of their strengths and weaknesses
- study skills, including time management
- examination techniques (in 3rd year)
- awareness of the implications of subject selection and levels therein for career choice
- awareness of the need to consider all subject options including non-traditional subjects
- knowledge of the potential benefits of TYP (where it is available)
- knowledge of senior cycle options - LCA, LCVP and the LC (Established), as applicable.

The school guidance programme throughout junior cycle should enable students to begin their exploration of career options. The programme should encourage consideration of a wide range of educational, training and career choices, not bounded by traditional considerations of gender or social stereotyping.

The guidance programme should begin the process of linking students' aptitudes, achievements and interests to career options. Activities to support this could include:

- the encouragement of students in first and second year to explore a range of educational and career areas including non-traditional careers
- project work and team work as a means towards group discussion on career opportunities
- information on the competencies and skills required for the working world, including employability skills
- objective assessment of students' aptitudes and consideration of their achievements, interests and subject choices and how these link to career paths.

During the junior cycle, students and their parents need to be assisted to understand the implications of choices of specific subjects and levels taken, on the range of further study and career options available to them in the future. Ideally, such information should be incorporated into the teaching of these subjects. Where the level of provision by the school of certain subjects or timetable constraints limit a student's options, it is essential that parents and students should be informed of the possible implications as early as possible. For example, under current conditions students should know that:

- higher level Gaeilge is a requirement for entry to the colleges of education for primary teaching
- higher level mathematics is a requirement for most honours degree courses in engineering
- a laboratory science subject is a requirement for all medical and most paramedical courses and higher level chemistry is a requirement for some specific medical and paramedical courses in a number of third level institutions.

Students not wishing to progress to senior cycle or to TYP should be provided with opportunities (with their parents) to meet with the guidance counsellor to discuss possible progression routes and training options, such as Youthreach. This vocational programme offers education and training opportunities for 16-21 year olds in local community settings. Those wishing to enter the labour force should be encouraged to contact FÁS and access local employment support agencies to secure viable employment opportunities.

Guidance in Senior Cycle

The Transition Year Programme: Students in TY often sample the full range of subject options available at senior cycle and gain vocational skills and competencies by undertaking work experience and/or work shadowing. In TY, students are encouraged to develop their full range of intelligences through a greater variety of activities than is available in the other years of second level education. Students undertake a variety of new roles and responsibilities and they engage in new means of personal development, e.g. work experience or mini-companies. These features are an integral part of the TYP.

As part of the TY guidance programme, students should be facilitated in developing and progressing their career plans.

Through ongoing exploration and feedback they should develop a growing understanding of their skills, aptitudes and achievements. The work experience/ shadowing module should provide each student with the opportunity to participate in a structured work experience/shadowing programme, and in structured and detailed debriefing sessions.

Leaving Certificate Programmes

Currently, there are three programmes available at senior cycle: the LC (Established), LCA and LCVP. The guidance programme at senior cycle aims to assist the full development of each student's potential, to help the student grow in self-knowledge and self-esteem and to prepare him/her for higher or further education, training and/or employment. In addition to the guidance activities outlined in the section of this document on Guidance in Second Level Schools students have additional guidance requirements in senior cycle. The guidance programme should endeavour to provide students with opportunities to:

- prepare to manage their successful transition from second level to further or higher education, training or employment
- identify their own key motivating factors
- prepare for successful transition into adulthood
- learn about job search and job retention skills
- develop research and ICT skills so that they can be self-directed in their career exploration and development
- learn about the world of work, including employment rights and responsibilities
- develop awareness of the need for lifelong learning
- develop skills to become independent and self-motivated learners.

Successful guidance at this level requires an environment that facilitates students in developing an understanding of themselves, their values and their future adult roles. The guidance programme at senior cycle should assist students to continue to develop a range of self-management skills, including the ability to access information concerning further study and career options. To enable students to gain the maximum benefits from the guidance programme in the senior cycle, it is recommended that the following should be included:

- the provision of access to information prepared by public agencies and employers regarding career opportunities
- the provision of information about further and higher education and training courses, including entry requirements, course content, workload and progression routes
- the establishment and development of linkages with further and higher education institutions and training organisations to facilitate students' decision-making concerning course and institution choice
- the provision of opportunities for students to attend events such as college open days, career exhibitions, visits to employers. Such activities require careful planning, management and follow-up, in order to ensure that students get maximum benefit from them
- meetings with relevant role-models such as former students and parents to discuss their chosen career paths
- the organisation of mock interview sessions.

The LCVP and the LCA each includes a guidance module designed to help students become more aware of their interests, aptitudes and skills with regard to the world of work. These modules are designed to complement, but not replace, individual career planning interviews between the guidance counsellor and individual students.

The LCA course has developed a module on Job Search Skills from which every senior cycle student could benefit and which, consequently, could form part of the general guidance programme in senior cycle. By linking the LC subjects into vocational groupings, the LCVP strengthens their vocational dimensions. The two link modules -*Preparation for the World of Work* and *Enterprise Education* - sharpen the vocational focus of the LC subjects. Students of the LCVP have the opportunities to identify personal aptitudes and interests, to complete a career investigation, to develop job-seeking skills and interview techniques and to integrate their learning across the LC subjects they are studying.

The aims of the guidance elements of both the LCA and LCVP are directly related and complementary to the general aims of the guidance and counselling activities in senior cycle.

Progression from Second Level Education

The transfer from senior cycle to higher/further education, to training or to employment is the last major transition for the second level student. While it is an exciting period in a young person's life, it can also be a time of anxiety and challenge for both students and parents. Although a decreasing number of students completing the senior cycle now progress directly to employment, it is important for schools to recognise that for those young people who decide to do so, this may well be their last experience of fulltime education. In this context, it is essential that students be prepared for entry to working life and that their needs and expectations are identified. Knowledge of second-chance educational and training opportunities available may be of particular importance to these students so that they may be encouraged to resume their education at a later date.

Three programmes—TYP, LCA and LCVP - are designed to offer students the opportunity to experience the world of work either through work experience or shadowing. Some schools also provide a work experience module for students in their first year of the two year Leaving Certificate programme. As a result, a high proportion of senior cycle students gain some knowledge of the work place. This practical experience, coupled with the modules studied in LCA or LCVP, can form a solid basis upon which students can confirm career and/or course choice.

The transition from second level to third level or to the world of work requires significant levels of adjustment for most young people. As a result, schools need to prepare students for a lifestyle change and the increase in personal responsibility that accompanies adulthood. Self-confidence and self-esteem are especially important at this point and young people need to have been prepared for independence from school and from home. They need to be aware of how the adult world they are entering operates and what supports are available to them should they experience difficulties or need personal support.

Higher and Further Education

Since the early 1980s, the percentage of senior cycle students progressing to further or higher education has increased significantly, with approximately 90% of school leavers now going on to some form of higher or further study or training (including apprenticeship training). The number of institutions and courses in the Central Applications Office (CAO) system increased from 9 institutions and 95 courses in 1982 to 43 institutions and 895 courses in 2004. With the current level of choice, students need to carry out accurate and thorough research on their options and choices.

It is not uncommon for students progressing to further and higher education to experience difficulty during the first year of their course. A recent study of students at Institutes of Technology suggests that efforts to improve completion rates should begin long before students arrive in the college and that students need to build independent learning skills prior to entry to the colleges.

Colleges of higher and further education provide careers and appointments services as well as a range of student supports. College open days are an ideal time for students to become acquainted with all of these services so that they can avail of the relevant supports, if required, at an early stage in their third level education. The more structured contact there is between the school and third level institutions the better prepared students are for the reality of life in these institutions.

PLC and Adult Education Programmes

In schools offering a wide range of education options, the school guidance plan should include a programme designed to meet the educational, personal and vocational needs of those choosing PLC and adult education courses. The majority of PLC courses are of 1-2 years duration. On successful completion of the course students are awarded a Further Education and Training Awards Council (FETAC) certificate and may seek employment or continue to third level education. Adults returning to education, to VTOS for example, also need access to support and guidance to choose educational courses and to make worthwhile transitions into further or higher education, training or employment.

Student Feedback and Support for Guidance Programme

Students in the final year of senior cycle are well placed to provide valuable feedback to the school on the content and delivery of its guidance programme.

Through the Student Council, students should be able to provide useful feedback related to the guidance programme. This also should be a channel through which students can communicate constructive suggestions for changes that they, based on their experience, consider would enhance aspects of the programme for particular year group/s.

Past students also are well positioned to offer valuable insights on their experience of the school's guidance programme. It is recommended that schools avail of this type of information as part of their evaluation of guidance provision. In addition, past students can be a rich resource to the school by offering role-model support for students as they prepare to progress into further and higher education, training or the world of work.

A comprehensive school guidance and counseling programme is developmental and systematic in nature, sequential, clearly defined, and accountable. It is jointly founded upon developmental psychology, educational philosophy, and counseling methodology.

The school guidance and counseling programme is integral to the K-12 educational experience. A school counseling programme based upon student needs necessitates the involvement of the entire school community to integrate educational, career, and personal/social development of students into the mission of each school. School counselors work with all students, school staff, families, and members of the community. The programme is proactive and preventative in its focus. It assists students in acquiring and using life-long learning skills. More specifically, the school guidance and counseling programme employs strategies to enhance academics, provide career awareness, develop employment readiness, encourage self-awareness, foster interpersonal communication skills, and impart life success skills for all students.

The guaranteed services listed in this programme guide have four components:

1. Identified Needs
2. Services Provided That Respond To Identified Needs
3. Expected Outcomes
4. Programme Evaluation

While it is important to understand the needs being addressed by the various services and to know the expected outcomes produced by those services, only the delivery of the services is guaranteed.

While the services listed will often be delivered by counselors there are many instances in which counselors will serve in a leadership/coordinating role and the services may be provided by other staff members, peer helpers, or other individuals. Frequently, the delivery of services may be initiated at the request of a student, parent, or staff member.

Many vehicles for providing services exist; student advisement, peer helpers, tutoring programmes, career planning, classroom guidance sessions, individual and group counseling, in-services, and a variety of other forms of communication. While the mode of delivery may vary widely, it is intended that the service would be consistently and uniformly delivered throughout the district.

The guaranteed services are best delivered under the following conditions:

1. The students are in regular attendance.
2. The schools maintain adequate counseling staffs.
3. The counselors are aware of students' need for services.
4. The counselors are provided adequate clerical assistance.

5. Necessary resources are readily available.
6. A cooperative partnership exists between school and home.

School Counselor Roles, School Counseling Programme Framework, and Ethics

Professional School Counselors ideally implement a data-driven, evidence-based (Dimmitt, Carey, & Hatch, 2007) comprehensive school counseling programme that promotes and enhances student achievement, career and college readiness, and personal and social competencies at the elementary, middle, and high school levels (ASCA, 2005). A fully-implemented school counseling programme ideally delivers academic, career, college readiness, and personal/social competencies to every student K-12—just as the district's mathematics programme is for 100% of the students. Professional School Counselors, in most U.S. states, usually have a Master's degree in school counseling from a Counselor Education graduate programme.

They are employed in elementary, middle, and high schools and in district supervisory, counselor education faculty positions (usually with an earned Ph.D. in Counselor Education) and post-secondary settings doing academic, career, college readiness, and personal/social counseling, consultation, and programme coordination. Their work is varied, with attention focused on developmental stages of student growth, including the needs, tasks, and student interests related to those stages (Schmidt, 2003).

Professional School Counselors meet the needs of student in three basic domains: academic development, career development, and personal/social development (Dahir & Campbell, 1997; ASCA, 2005) with an increasing emphasis on college readiness (Carey et al., 2008). Knowledge, understanding and skill in these domains are developed through classroom instruction, appraisal, consultation, counseling, coordination, and collaboration. For example, in appraisal, school counselors may use a variety of personality and career assessment methods (such as the Self-Directed Search (SDS) or Career Key (based on the Holland Codes) to help students explore career and college needs and interests.

Delivery methods include academic, career, college and personal/social planning for every student; developmental classroom lessons for all students; and individual and group counseling for some students who need more intensive assistance beyond classroom lessons or planning/advising sessions. Classroom lessons and the school counseling curriculum are designed to be preventive in nature and include academic, career, college, and personal/social skills and competencies including self-management and self-monitoring skills (Stone & Dahir, 2006).

The Responsive Services component of the Professional School Counselor's role provides individual and/or small group counseling for students. For example, if a student's behavior is interfering with his or her achievement, the Professional school counselor will observe that student in a class, provide consultation to teachers and other personnel to develop (with the student) a plan to address the behavioral issue(s), and then work together (collaboration) to implement the plan. They also help by providing consultation services to family members such as college readiness, career development, parenting skills, study skills, child and adolescent development, and help with school-home transitions.

Additionally, professional school counselors may lead classroom lessons on a variety of topics within the three domains such as personal/social issues relative to student needs, or establish groups to address common issues among students, such as divorce or death. The topics of character education, diversity and multiculturalism (Portman, 2009), and school safety are important areas of focus for school counselors. Often counselors will coordinate outside groups that wish to help with student needs such as academics, or coordinate a state programme that teaches about child abuse or drugs, through on-stage drama (Schmidt, 2003)

The ASCA National Model (2005) operationalizes much of the above into four main areas of focus: Foundation (a written school counseling programme mission statement, a beliefs and philosophy statement, and a focus on the ASCA standards and competencies and how they are implemented for every student;

Delivery System (how lessons and individual and group counseling are delivered); Management System (use of calendars, time, building leader-school counselor role agreements, creation of action plans); and Accountability System (use of a SC programme audit, results reports, and School Counselor Evaluations based on 13 key competencies. The model is implemented using key skills from the Education Trust's Transforming School Counseling Initiative: Advocacy, Leadership, Teaming and Collaboration, and Systemic Change.

School Counselors are also expected to follow a professional code of ethics in many countries. In the United States, they are primarily the American School Counselor Association Code of Ethics (www.schoolcounselor.org) and the American Counseling Association Code of Ethics.

Elementary School Counseling

Elementary professional school counselors following best practices provide developmental school counseling curriculum lessons (Stone & Dahir, 2006) on academic, career, college readiness, and personal and social competencies, advising and academic/career/college readiness planning to all students, and individual and group counseling for some students and their families to meet the developmental needs of young children K-6 (ASCA, 2005). Increased emphasis is starting to be placed on college readiness counseling at the elementary school level as more school counseling programmes move to evidence-based work with data and specific results (Dimmitt, Carey, & Hatch, 2007). Research has shown that school counseling programmes help to close achievement and opportunity gaps in terms of which students have access to school counseling programmes and early college readiness activities and which students do not (Bryan, Holcomb-McCoy, Moore-Thomas, & Day-Vines, 2009; College Board, 2008; Holcomb-McCoy, 2007;).

To facilitate the school counseling process, school counselors use a variety of theories and techniques including developmental, cognitive-behavioral, person-centered (Rogerian) listening and influencing skills, systemic, family, multicultural

(Holcomb-McCoy & Chen-Hayes, 2007; Portman, 2009), narrative, and play therapy. Sink & Stroh (2003) released a research study showing the effectiveness of elementary school counseling programmes in Washington state.

Middle School Counseling

In middle school counseling, professional school counselors following best practices provide developmental school counseling curriculum lessons (Stone & Dahir, 2006) on academic, career, college readiness, and personal and social competencies, advising and academic/career/college readiness planning to all students and individual and group counseling for some students and their families to meet the developmental needs of late childhood and early adolescence according to sources such as the ASCA National Model (ASCA, 2005). Increasing emphasis has been placed on college readiness counseling at the middle school level as more school counseling programmes move to evidenced-base work with data and specific results (Dimmitt, Carey, & Hatch, 2007) that show how school counseling programmes help to close achievement and opportunity gaps in terms of which students have access to school counseling programmes and early college readiness activities and which students do not (Bryan, Holcomb-McCoy, Moore-Thomas, & Day-Vines, 2009; College Board, 2008; Holcomb-McCoy, 2007).

Middle School College Readiness curricula have been developed by The College Board that can be used to assist students and their families in this process. To facilitate the school counseling process, school counselors use a variety of theories and techniques including developmental, cognitive-behavioral, person-centered (Rogerian) listening and influencing skills, systemic, family, multicultural (Holcomb-McCoy & Chen-Hayes, 2007; Portman, 2009), narrative, and play therapy. Transitional issues to ensure successful transitions to high school are a key area including career exploration and assessment with seventh and eighth grade students. Sink, Akos, Turnbull, & Mvududu released a study in 2008 confirming the effectiveness of middle school comprehensive school counseling programmes in Washington state (Sink, Akos, Turnbull, & Mvududu, 2008).

High School Counseling

In high school, professional school counselors following best practices provide developmental school counseling curriculum lessons (Stone & Dahir, 2006) on academic, career, college readiness, and personal and social competencies, advising and academic/career/college readiness planning to all students and individual and group counseling for some students to meet the developmental needs of adolescents according to sources such as the ASCA National Model (ASCA, 2005).

Increasing emphasis is being placed on college readiness counseling at the early high school level as more school counseling programmes move to evidence-based work with data and specific results (Dimmitt, Carey, & Hatch, 2007) that show how school counseling programmes help to close achievement and opportunity gaps ensuring all students have access to school counseling programmes and early college readiness activities (Bryan, Holcomb-McCoy, Moore-Thomas, & Day-Vines, 2009; Carey et al., 2008; Holcomb-McCoy, 2007). High School College Readiness curricula have been developed by The College Board to assist this process.

To facilitate school counseling, school counselors use varied theories and techniques including developmental, cognitive-behavioral, person-centered (Rogerian) listening and influencing skills, systemic, family, multicultural (Holcomb-McCoy & Chen-Hayes, 2007; Portman, 2009), narrative, and play therapy. Transitional issues to ensure successful transitions to college, other post-secondary educational options, and careers are a key area. The high school counselor helps students and their families prepare for rigorous post-secondary education and/or training options (e.g. college, trade school) by engaging students and their families in finding accurate and meaningful information on entrance requirements, financial aid, recommendation letters, test-preparation and so forth. Professional School Counselors at the high school level spend much of their time helping students and their families monitor their progress toward graduation and being adequately prepared for post-secondary options including college. Some students now turn to private college admissions counselors specialized in college admissions but the ethics of so doing is open to great debate in terms of who has access to this funding and there is little research-based evidence of effectiveness on the part of these outside parties.

The fees for these college admissions counselors can be as high as $30,000.

A framework for Professional School Counselor responsibilities and roles is outlined in the ASCA (American School Counselor Association) National Model (2005). Lapan, Gysbers, & Sun's (1997) study showed correlational evidence of the effectiveness of fully implemented school counseling programmes on high school students' academic success. Carey et al.'s 2008 study showed specific best practices from school counselors raising college-going rates within a strong college-going environment in multiple USA-based high schools with large numbers of students of nondominant cultural identities.

Education and National/international Certification/ credentialing of School Counselors

The education of school counselors (school counsellors) around the world varies greatly based on the laws and cultures of specific countries and the historical influences of their respective educational and credentialing systems and professional identities related to who delivers academic, career, college readiness, and personal/social information, advising, curriculum, and counseling and related services..

In the United States, a professional School Counselor is a certified educator with a master's degree in school counseling (usually housed in a Counselor Education graduate programme) with specific school counseling graduate training including unique qualifications and skills to address all students' academic, career, college readiness and personal/social needs through the use of school counseling programmes that deliver specific measurable competencies.

About half of all Counselor Education programmes that offer school counseling are accredited by the Council on the Accreditation of Counseling and Related Educational

Programmes (CACREP) and all but one are currently in the United States with one in Canada and one programme under accreditation review in Mexico as of 2008 and maintains a current list of accredited programmes and programmes in the accreditation process on their website (www.cacrep.org). CACREP has identified in 2008 an interest in accrediting more programmes outside of the United States (www.cacrep.org).

According to CACREP, an accredited school counseling programme offers specific coursework in Professional Identity and Ethics, Human Development, Counseling Theories, Group Work, Career Counseling, Multicultural/Diversity Counseling, Assessment, Research and Programme Evaluation, and Clinical Coursework in a 100-hour practicum under the supervision of both a school counseling faculty member and a certified school counselor site supervisor (master's degree in school counseling or higher, and appropriate certification) and a 600-hour internship under the supervision of both a school counseling faculty member and a certified school counselor site supervisor (master's degree in school counseling or higher, and appropriate certification) (CACREP, 2001).

CACREP released the revision of the Standards for 2009 in 2008, and made a major change moving toward performance-based accreditation including evidence of school counselor candidate learning. In addition, in the 2009 standards, CACREP greatly tightened and enhanced the school counseling standards with specific evidence needed of how school counseling students receive education in foundations; counseling prevention and intervention; diversity and advocacy; assessment; research and evaluation; academic development; collaboration and consultation; and leadership in K-12 school counseling contexts. (CACREP, 2009).

Certification practices for school counselors vary around the world. School Counselors in the United States may opt for national certification through two different boards. The National Board for Professional Teaching Standards (NBPTS) requires a two-to-three year process of performance based assessment, and demonstrate (in writing) content knowledge in human growth/development, diverse populations, school counseling programmes, theories, data, and change and collaboration. As of February, 2005, 30 states offer financial incentives for this certification.

Also based in the USA, The National Board for Certified Counselors (NBCC) requires passing the National Certified School Counselor Examination (NCSC), which includes 40 multiple choice questions and seven simulated cases which assess school counselors' abilities to make critical decisions on the spot. Additionally, a master's degree and three years of supervised experience are required. NBPTS also requires three years of experience, however a master's degree is not required, but only state certification (41 of 50 require a master's degree). At least four states offer financial incentives for the NCSC certification (McLeod, 2005). Both certifications have benefits and costs that a school counselor would want to consider for national certification. NBCC has credentials counselors in the United States and internationally. For more information, see external links.

Job Growth and Earnings for School Counselors in the United States and Internationally

The rate of job growth and earnings for school counselors depends greatly on the country that one is employed in and whether the school is funded publicly or privately. School Counselors working in international schools or "American" schools around the world may find similar work environments and expectations to current best practices in the United States. Outside of those schools, expectations (and pay) vary greatly based on the level of school counselor or school counselor roles, identity, expectations, and legal and certification requirements and expectations.

In the United States, according to the United States Occupational Outlook Handbook (OOH) the median salary for school counselors in the United States in May 2006 was $53,750. Also, school counselors can earn additional money working summer months in school or agency counseling positions. Among all counseling specialty areas, public elementary, middle and high school counselors are currently (2009) paid the highest salary on average of all counselors in the United States. Overall employment for counselors is average, especially in rural and urban areas. Budget cuts, however, are looming, and stimulus monies may be deployed in public school districts to keep school counseling positions in place. In the United States, rural areas and urban areas traditionally have been under-served by school counselors in public schools due to both funding shortages and often a lack of best practice models. With the advent of No Child Left Behind legislation in the USA and a mandate for school counselors to be working with data and showing evidence-based practice, school counselors able to show and share results in assisting to close gaps are in the best position to argue for increased school counseling resources and positions for their programmes (ASCA, 2005).

Role of Guidance Personnel

Good information and **guidance** during the transition phase become more important as education and training pathways become more varied and more flexible, and as occupational requirements change and tend to become less clearly defined. As young people face both more choices and increasingly complex choices, the tasks of information and **guidance** providers become increasingly demanding, both at the upper secondary level and within tertiary education, and the target group for these services becomes wider.

In addition, information and **guidance** services are increasingly being called upon to assist those young people who are at risk of getting lost in the process of transition from school to work: those who have left school early without achieving a qualification for work or further study; those who are unemployed; and those who are on welfare benefits. For these young people information and **guidance** services are increasingly being integrated with labour market and social benefit services. Rather than specialised services for the few, career information and **guidance** need to be seen as essential transition services for all: important for the efficient functioning of complex education systems and labour markets as well as for the satisfaction of the individual young person's needs.

Information and **guidance** services must provide accurate information on future educational options; develop young people's understanding and realistic knowledge of the world of work; and assist them to make satisfying job choices. Some young people can make confident educational and job choices with little assistance, but others need more intensive and often individual assistance. Some young people also require assistance with study and personal difficulties during the transition phase in order to benefit from career **guidance** and information services, and others need help in the process of job search. These tasks further complicate the demands made upon information and **guidance** services, raising difficult questions about the organisation and delivery of information and **guidance**, about roles and responsibilities, and about qualifications and training.

Nevertheless setting policy frameworks for and resourcing information and **guidance** services is often a low priority of central governments. Where decisions on educational resourcing are decentralised and resources are tight, individual **schools** often place a higher priority upon direct teaching than upon information and **guidance**. Staff are often given too little time to meet all of the demands upon them. Where a priority is allocated to information and **guidance**, it can be within a narrow area of young people's transition needs: for example within public employment offices rather than within educational institutions.

"What have countries undertaken, or what do they plan to undertake, in order to improve access to career information and **guidance** services for all young people? In which countries is career education a compulsory element of the curriculum? Do central policies exist on staffing levels for information and **guidance personnel** in **schools** and other educational institutions? What provision is made for information and **guidance** services within national public employment services?

"Within national policies for information and **guidance**, which groups of young people receive the most attention and the best services?

"Have information and **guidance** been made essential elements of national policies to meet the needs of those at risk in the transition: both those at risk of leaving school early; and those who have left school and not found a secure place in work or further study?

No country appears to have been able to develop fully satisfactory provision of information and **guidance** services for all young people, despite the many examples of good practice that can be found across countries, and despite the seriousness with which information and **guidance** services are treated in a small number of countries. Part of the reason is a failure to allocate a high priority to the development and provision of career information and **guidance** services. Part of it is due to a failure to provide an appropriate balance of services, able to meet the full range of needs. The following are some of the problems highlighted by the Thematic Review:

"The training provided to information and **guidance personnel** is often brief and limited. Full pre-service qualifications are often neither available to nor required of information and **guidance personnel**, and in-service opportunities to update knowledge and skills are often limited.

"Where the **guidance** function is well resourced, greater emphasis is often given to educational and personal **guidance** than to information and **guidance** for career choice.

"Often those aiming for tertiary study receive a higher priority and more detailed services than those bound directly for jobs.

"Career information and **guidance** are often peripheral to **schools'** main educational purposes, are often not clearly integrated into the curriculum, and are often not supported by quality curriculum materials.

"The information available to young people about the career choices that they face can be limited, out of date, in formats that are not appealing, and difficult to gain access to. It is not always easy for young people to relate this information to what they know about their talents, achievements and interests.

"Services provided within **schools** and tertiary institutions are often not well integrated with services provided by labour market authorities. The **role** of the private sector in providing an increasing range and variety of information and **guidance** materials in print and electronic forms is often not well integrated with the **role** of the public sector.

Issues for Discussion

"What qualifications are required of information and **guidance personnel**? Need all be fully "professional"? Is there a **role** for people such as normal classroom teachers or employment office staff without special training?

"What have countries undertaken, or what do they plan to undertake, in order to improve the training and qualifications of **guidance personnel**?

"How do information and **guidance** policy frameworks help to tailor services to differing individual needs? How are those in need of more intensive individual help identified? How are specialised services such as educational counselling and job placement integrated with careers **guidance**?

"How can an appropriate balance be assured in the provision of information and **guidance** services, so that the needs of the job-bound receive as much attention as the needs of those bound for tertiary study?

"How can an appropriate balance be assured, in the provision of information and **guidance** services, between information and **guidance** directed at career choice, and counselling for personal and educational problems?

Whatever the qualifications and training of the **personnel** involved, information and **guidance** services have traditionally been provided in one of two principal ways: by classroom teachers during normal lesson time; and through one-to-one, face-to-face assistance. The classroom model allows a wide range of young people to gain access to services that can provide a generalised form of orientation and assistance, but by itself cannot provide more individualised assistance to those who need it. The face-to-face model allows more intensive individual assistance, but can be very costly as a way of providing high quality assistance to large numbers, as well as wasteful if provided to many for whom less intensive assistance is sufficient. Both delivery models need to find cost-efficient ways to provide information, about both courses and jobs, that is up-to-date and relevant to young people's needs.

Guidance personnel have available to them a range of methods to both make information and **guidance** more cost-effective, and to allow it to meet a wider range of needs. Both classroom-based and face-to-face **guidance personnel** have normally had available to them a range of print, and increasingly electronic (both CD-ROM and on-line), information about courses and jobs. More and more examples exist of computerised job and course information systems that allow young people to undertake a self-analysis of their aptitudes and interests, and to integrate this with information about appropriate jobs and courses. Other methods used to raise quality, tailor services to needs and reduce costs include careers fairs, periods of work experience and job shadowing, small group rather than individual **guidance**, student projects, and the involvement of community members such as employers and alumni in careers programmes.

The Thematic Review has suggested that high quality and yet affordable information and **guidance** services should be built around a number of key elements. Among these are:

"The availability in several formats—electronic as well as print-based—of high quality information on education and training pathways, jobs and working life, produced by specialist organisations;

"The use by students of self-directed techniques of personal assessment and job and course exploration;

"The inclusion of mandatory career education and orientation in the school curriculum;

"Opportunities for all students to undertake periods of experience in real work settings; and

"Systematic and organised involvement of community members such as employers, trade unions, alumni and parents.

Issues for Discussion

"What criteria do countries use to assess the quality of information and **guidance** services?

What techniques have they found to be most effective in raising the quality of information and **guidance** services?

"What methods are used to make sure that information about jobs and courses is up-to-date?

"What roles are played by employer groups, trade unions and private publishers in providing young people with career information in different countries? What examples can be given of the integration of their efforts with the public sector's **role**?

"Do national policies for information and **guidance** services allocate a special priority to ways of providing services apart from classroom teaching and face-to-face assistance: for example group **guidance**, careers fairs, work experience, or computer based methods?

"How are the roles of the various actors — **schools**, labour offices, social welfare services, municipal services — distributed in different countries in serving different groups of young people? Could they be more complementary, either by each developing their special contribution, or through an increased integration of their services?

"What examples can be given of information and **guidance** policies requiring community members such as employers, alumni and parents to be systematically involved in careers programmes?

Career and Occupational Information—Sources, Gathering, Filling, Dissemination, Career Corner—Career Conference

College and career guidance and counseling programmes aim to help students make more informed and better educational and career choices. Among other things, programmes offer information on high school course offerings, career options, the type of academic and occupational training needed to succeed in the workplace, and postsecondary opportunities that are associated with their field of interest. Programmes also often provide teachers, administrators, and parents with information they can use to support students' career exploration and postsecondary educational opportunities.

Activities associated with career guidance and counseling programmes typically include:

- Advising students and parents on high school programmes and academic curriculum, preparing them for college application and admission.
- Arranging dual/concurrent enrollment and Advanced Placement credits to prepare students for the rigour of postsecondary education.
- Planning and preparation for college admissions tests, SAT and ACT.
- Informing students about postsecondary financing that can be used to support advanced education and training.
- Developing career portfolios, which include test and grades results, examples of student work, and resumes and cover letters to prospective employers.
- Arranging job shadowing, work placements, and community-based learning programmes to allow students to directly experience workplace situations.
- Sponsoring workshops, classes, focus groups, and special presentations that focus on job skills and personal development.
- Providing specialized counseling and intervention services to provide students with individualized attention.
- Well planned and well organised **career guidance** services are increasingly important. Countries in the OECD and the European Union are implementing lifelong learning strategies, as well as policies to encourage the development of their citizens' employability. To be successfully implemented, such strategies and policies require citizens to have the skills to manage their own education and employment.

- They require all citizens to have access to high quality information and advice about education, training and work. Yet often the gap between how **career guidance** services are delivered and the goals of public policy is wide. The aim of this handbook is to help policy makers within OECD countries and the European Union to develop effective policies for **career guidance**: in education, training and employment. It has been developed by the European Commission and the OECD in response to on-going changes in education, training and employment policies. In Europe these changes are expressed in the Lisbon (2000) goals of making Europe the most competitive knowledge-based economy and society in the world by 2010, marked by social cohesion. The handbook is based on international reviews of policies for **career guidance** undertaken by the OECD, by the European Centre for the Development of Vocational Training, by the European Training Foundation, and by the World Bank. In clear and simple language it sets out for policy makers in education, training and employment settings:
- Challenges that they face in making sure that **career guidance** services can meet public policy goals;
- Questions that they need to ask themselves in responding to these challenges;
- Some of the options that are open to them for the delivery of **career guidance** within a lifelong learning and active employability framework; and
- Some examples of effective responses, drawn from OECD and European Union countries.
- The handbook covers four broad policy themes: Improving **career guidance** for young people; Improving **career guidance** for adults; Improving access to **career guidance**; and Improving the systems that support **career guidance**.

Improving Career Guidance for Young People:

- To improve **career guidance** for young people, policy makers must address challenges in compulsory schooling, in upper secondary schooling, in tertiary education, and for young people at risk. There are challenges in meeting gaps in access, and in improving the nature, level and quality of services. In schools, the principal challenges are: to provide sufficient human and capital resources of the right type, both within the **school** and within its surrounding community; to ensure that these resources are dedicated to **career guidance**; and to make the best use of the resources that are available. Gaps in access are particularly evident in primary schools and in the vocational tracks of upper secondary **school**. Policy options include formally strengthening collaboration between all relevant stakeholders, making the acquisition of **career** management skills by students the focus of **career** education programmes, and improved accountability mechanisms.

- A significant number of young people leave **school** early, without qualifications. They need programmes in the community to help them make transitions to the working world and to re-engage with further learning, and **career guidance** needs to be part of such programmes. **Career guidance** also needs to be a stronger part of programmes within the **school** designed to prevent early leaving.
- There is generally a lack of **career guidance** provision for students in tertiary education, despite the significant cost of such studies to both participants and taxpayers. The range of **career** services that are offered within tertiary education needs to be broadened. Policy levers to ensure that a broader range of services is provided need to be strengthened. Options available to policy makers include the specification of goals for tertiary **career** services, and more explicitly linking public funding arrangements for tertiary education to the level and quality of **career** services.

Improving Career Guidance for Adults:

- The heterogeneous nature of the adult population presents a range of challenges to policymakers who are trying to improve **career guidance** services. Few easily accessible services are available for employed adults; few enterprises cater for the **career** development needs of their employees; fee-for-service provision that people can purchase privately is very limited; employers and trade unions have shown limited interest to date in providing **career guidance** even though they often recognise in principle the need for workforce development in order to improve competitiveness and equity. Despite these problems, new partnerships between employer organisations, education and training institutions, public employment services and other relevant organisations can lead to workplace and workforce **career guidance** provision, and **career guidance** should be an integral part of adult learning programmes.

- **Career guidance** is seen as having a key role in preventing inflows into unemployment, particularly long-term unemployment. Public employment services (PES) in most countries have a lead role in such prevention. Yet **career guidance** services within the PES are undeveloped. Strong collaboration strategies, between the PES and private and community-based **guidance** services, and with local education and training institutions, can enable unemployed persons to make transitions to employment and to re-engage with learning.
- Ageing populations and pension funding problems in many countries will require both later retirement ages and more flexible transitions to retirement. To date policymakers have been slow to mobilise **career guidance** services to support active ageing. Employers and worker representatives can promote and take initiatives in service delivery of third age **guidance**, using combinations of public and private partnerships.

Improving Access to Career Guidance Services:

- The demand for **career guidance** services exceeds its supply. More flexible delivery methods, including the use of ICT and of call centres, have great potential for extending access. If all citizens are to have access to **career guidance**, there is often a need to target **career guidance** services to at-risk groups.

- Actively involving vulnerable groups in designing, planning, implementing and monitoring **career guidance** policies and services for them greatly enhances the development of services that are relevant to their needs.
- Improving the quality and relevance of **career** information materials to support universal access is an on- going challenge. There is often a lack of collaboration between different government ministries, agencies, and between national and regional levels of government in providing and sharing **career** information. Materials developed by the private sector are not subject to any agreed standards. In order to develop a coherent policy and strategy for the delivery of quality **career** information to citizens, national, regional and local mapping exercises of **career guidance** information provided through a range of media (such as newspapers and television) to a range of target groups (youth, employed, unemployed) is an essential starting point.

UNIT-X

Guidence for Exceptional Children

Guidance for Exceptional Children—Meaning and Types

The Development of Education for Exceptional Children

The education for exceptional children, or special education as it is often called, appears to be an interesting new field of professional activity to the student who explores it for the first time. So much has happened recently that even those who have been engaged in work with exceptional children and youth for some time frequently fail to realize the long history which this phase of education has had. While it is undoubtedly true that greater strides have been made since 1940 than in any comparable previous period, this does not negate the remarkable developments of many earlier periods and the significant contributions of dozens of professional and lay people prior to 1940. In this chapter an analysis of the foundations of special education as it is now known will be made. First, however, it will be well to ascertain the scope of interest of those who participate in the education of exceptional children and youth.

The Definition of the Problem

The exceptional child is difficult to define, for the term represents many different medical and psychological groupings of children. Essentially, an exceptional child is one who deviates intellectually, physically socially, or emotionally so markedly from what is considered to be normal growth and development that he cannot receive maximum benefit from a regular school programme and requires a special class or supplementary instruction and services. This is a loose definition, but it is essentially accurate. A decision as to what is *normal* is crucial and is always relative.

However, for the purpose of this discussion it is assumed that there is a general understanding of normal and normative growth processes. Entire chapters will be devoted to the various clinical groups of exceptional children later in this volume, so that only sufficient mention to orient the student will be made here to the discussions which follow.

The Intellectually Exceptional Child

The phrase *intellectually exceptional child* encompasses two large groups, each of which presents significant challenges to educators and each of which has essentially different characteristics. In statistical terms, these two groups contain those children beyond two and one-half to three standard deviations from the mean in the typical normal distribution. At one extreme are children who are characterized by *high mental ability*; at the other extreme are children who may be referred to as *slow learning*, and *mentally handicapped*, and *mentally deficient*.

The Gifted Child

Dunlap, in his chapter in the present volume, refers to children of high mental ability as being *superior*, *gifted*, and *extremely gifted*. Essentially he is referring to a group of children whose minimum measured intelligence exceeds an intelligence quotient of 125 or 130, but often these children will have I.Q.'s of 150, 170, 180, or above. Such children constitute about 2 to 7 per cent of the average population, a much larger group than is usually realized. They present a unique challenge to teachers and administrators who must plan a realistic programme geared to meet the special needs of the gifted pupil and at the same time insure that society will benefit to the maximum from the unusual abilities and leadership qualities which the children and youth with high mental ability possess.

The Mentally Handicapped

The *mentally handicapped* children are those with intelligence quotients between 55 or 60 and 80. In New York this group is referred to as "children with retarded mental development."

Types of Exceptional School Children

The accompanying tabular classification of children may be helpful to the reader if it is not allowed to convey the impression that individuals fall into rigid psychological compartments. The classification is intended to call attention to the wide ranges of mental variation and deviation which may be found in a large group of unselected children. With only a few exceptions, representatives of every type included in the classification will be found in any large school system.

The individual differences in general intelligence are particularly constant; probably because they are native or constitutional. At any rate we now expect to find them just as certainly as we do differences in height and weight. The range of intelligence differences, however, is, if anything, more striking than that for stature. For example, in one of the schools of New Haven there is a little girl, Mary, age nine, with an intelligence quotient* of only 22 ; her mental status is idiocy ; she cannot count two. In a neighboring school there is another girl, Jane, age seven, with an intelligence rating of 180. Her mentality bears the symptoms of great intellectual distinction, if not of genius. She has the ability to do fifth grade work at an age when many children have just entered school. Assuming that our units of measurement are sound in principle we may be permitted to say that Jane's mental caliber is nine times that of Mary and almost twice that of an average child.

The gamut of variation in any school district is not, of course, ordinarily as wide as that represented by these two extremes. And yet among an unselected group of 100 primary pupils one is likely to find at least one child who is definitely feeble-minded (unable to benefit from ordinary instruction) ; another who is extremely bright (ardent, resourceful, sociable) ; another who is correspondingly dull, without being actually defective ; another who is over-sensitive and nervous (with an exaggerated dependency upon others or abnormal emotional tendencies) ; still another child with a more or less serious speech defect, possibly stuttering ; and another who is physically so handicapped by malnutrition, or otherwise, as to constitute both a hygienic and educational problem.

Individually these educationally exceptional children make a strong appeal to our active sympathies. In the aggregate they place a considerable responsibility upon the public school. If a census or survey should prove that as many as five or six school children out of a hundred are definitely exceptional in mental or educational status, it would mean that the problem is one of administrative and legislative importance.

Certainly there should be a consistent public school policy undertaken at least with reference to those children who are mentally so subnormal that they cannot as adults succeed independently of external safeguard and support. Was not Graham Wallas probably right in his recent statement that an educational system should be based upon the differences rather than upon the likenesses between children? The survey of the New Haven schools reveals some of the most significant of these mental differences which prevail among children.

Guidance for Gifted, Backward, Mentally retarded, Orthopaedically Handicapped, Visually Impaired, Deaf and Dumb, Juvenile Delinquents

Many parents of gifted children wonder if their local school will be able to provide an appropriate education for their children. Should they stick with the local school? Look for a private school? Quite often a parent will assume that a private school is better than a public school. However, that is not necessarily true. Gifted children need a special environment, as does any special needs child, and it's important for parents to understand what to look for in a school, whether it's private or public.

Whether your child is already in school or about to start, you will want to evaluate what it has to offer. In order to do that, you need criteria. The elements described here are the elements of a good gifted programme. Use them as criteria for evaluating any school you are considering for your child.

- *Philosophy and Goals:* What is the philosophy and what are the goals of the programme? Are the goals similar or different for different ages? If they are different, what are the differences and why are they different? Gifted children are gifted for life. They start out gifted and end up gifted. As a result, they have similar academic needs throughout their school years. Any differences in goals should be based on age-appropriate differences in instruction, but those differences should be based on what is appropriate for gifted children.
- *Acceleration and Enrichment:* Acceleration refers to the speeding up of instruction. Gifted children are fast learners and require little repetition of information. Enrichment refers to the increased depth of study of a particular topic. It extends the regular curriculum. Both are needed in some form.
- *Multiple Options:* Is the programme a "one size fits all" programme or are there various options for the different needs of the different types of gifted children? A profoundly gifted child has significantly different educational needs than does a mildly gifted child, for example. In addition, a child may be exceptionally gifted in math, but not in language arts. Multiple options are essential.
- *Student Learning Expectations:* What are the students expected to learn by the end of the programme session? Learning outcomes must be clear. The students may have fun, but they must also learn something new. Any child could participate in fun activities, but a gifted programme should be one that is designed specifically for gifted children.
- *Challenging Curriculum:* Gifted children need a stimulating curriculum. Without it, they can "tune out,"

losing interest in school. A curriculum for gifted children should require them to stretch their minds.

- *Flexibility:* Flexibility is needed in order to respond to the needs of individual gifted children. Rigid adherence to the system often prevents some gifted children from appropriate challenges. For example, a gifted 3rd grader may have mastered 6th grade level math. That child does not need to complete third grade math assignments. A school needs to be flexible enough to consider options for that child's math instruction. Another possibility is a gifted child musician. A junior high student with exceptional talent playing the violin could be allowed time off from school to take advantage of opportunities to study with exceptional violinists or take part in special musical programmes.
- *Sound Identification Process:* Multiple assessment procedures should be used to determine which children would benefit from placement in a gifted programme. Every effort should be made to include children who are frequently overlooked. These children include LD gifted, underachievers, and children from under-represented groups, like economically deprived and minority children. Too often schools rely on one test, usually a group test, or simply teacher recommendations for identification.
- *Staff Development Plan:* Teachers who have been trained to work with gifted children are much more effective than those who have not. Do the teachers who work in the gifted programme or teach the gifted children have gifted endorsements? Does the school have regular in-service sessions about gifted children?
- *Guidance Component:* Gifted children often feel isolated or "different." They sometimes don't feel like they fit in socially with the other children. They also can be very sensitive and have a harder time than other children dealing with the day-to-day stress of school or growing up. The guidance can be individual or group guidance.

- *Honoring Academic Talent:* Schools must honor all talent areas in the same way athletic talent is honored. For example, pep rallies can be held for academics and artistic talent as well as for sports. Groups of students often participate in the Science Olympiad or local and state band competitions, and pep rallies could be held for these. Names of achievers can be listed or announced in the same way sports heroes are listed and announced.

The Backward Child

The special arrangements in behalf of the numerous group of academically backward children are perhaps more complete than those of any American city of similar size. Some thirty-five special teachers are attached to as many buildings giving individual instruction to pupils who are in academic arrears. This tutorial instruction in the aggregate must accomplish considerable salvage. What is probably most needed in the future development of this work is an increasing emphasis upon the actual measurement and interpretation of the mental factors which are at the basis of the academic backwardness. These factors are so diverse and variable that they often need special psychological investigation before they can be evaluated. A supervisory assistant competent to conduct such elementary psychological inquiry could be of real service to the group of special teachers in the interpretation and management of their backward pupils.

The Superior Child

The superior child is more in danger of retardation than the dullard. Whether the provisions for the superior child should be of the same extent and of the same character as those enjoyed by the backward pupil is a question. Although mental measurements show that superior children are just about as numerous as subaverage and deficient children, it is unsafe at present to make sweeping generalizations. It is certain, however, that the superior child should be more definitely recognized by teachers and school authorities. It is very significant, in our mental survey, that while the elementary teachers suspected 725 children as being mentally deficient; these same teachers regarded only 45 children as being superior. One child in 33 reported as possibly deficient and only one child in 527 reported as superior ! Whatever else this may mean, it proves that superior children are in need of more general recognition. In a democracy which is so constantly demanding numerous leaders a greater premium must be placed in the public school upon mental ability. This great social problem of picking and training leaders begins in the elementary school.

Many superior children are of the rapid promotion type, and the local summer school provisions for doubling a grade, are a definite benefit to this type when systematic hygienic safeguards are not neglected. For other children of superior intelligence and distinctive talent the problem is one of providing more abundant opportunities for expression and assimilation. For them the educational diet is far too limited and needs a generous addition of growth protein. Modified school schedules and special supplementary programmes for selected pupils are needed to meet the situation. Regular teachers could do more to make such rearrangements, but they need guidance and detailed suggestions which a special supervisory assistant in this field of auxiliary education could organize. There are group methods which need consideration; but the problem of the superior child will to no small extent remain one of individualization under expert guidance.

Mental Retardation

Mental retardation is a generalized disorder, characterized by subaverage cognitive functioning and deficits in two or more adaptive behaviors with onset before the age of 18. Once focused almost entirely on cognition, the definition now includes both a component relating to mental functioning and one relating to the individual's functional skills in their environment.

Alternative Terms

The term "mental retardation" is a diagnostic term designed to capture and standardize a group of disconnected categories of mental functioning such as "idiot", "imbecile", and "moron" derived from early IQ tests, which acquired pejorative connotations in popular discourse over time. The term "mental retardation" has itself now acquired some pejorative and shameful connotations over the last few decades due to the use of "retarded" as an insult. This may in turn have contributed to its replacement with expressions such as "mentally challenged" or "intellectual disability". While "developmental disability" may be considered to subsume other disorders (see below), "developmental disability" or "developmental delay" (for children under age 18), are generally considered more acceptable terms than "mental retardation" among members of the disability community.

- In North America mental retardation is subsumed into the broader term **developmental disability**, which also includes epilepsy, autism, cerebral palsy and other disorders that develop during the developmental period (birth to age 18.) Because service provision is tied to the designation developmental disability, it is used by many parents, direct support professional, and physicians. However, in school-based settings, the more specific term mental retardation is still typically used, and is one of 13 categories of disability under which children may be identified for special education services under Public Law 108-446.
- The phrase **intellectual disability** is increasingly being used as a synonym for people with significantly below-average cognitive ability. These terms are sometimes used as a means of separating general intellectual limitations from specific, limited deficits as well as indicating that it is not an emotional or psychological disability. Intellectual disability may also used to describe the outcome of traumatic brain injury or lead poisoning or dementing conditions such as Alzheimer's disease. It is not specific to congenital disorders such as Down syndrome.

The American Association on Mental Retardation continued to use the term *mental retardation* until 2006. In June 2006 its members voted to change the name of the organization to the "American Association on Intellectual and Developmental

Disabilities," rejecting the options to become the AAID or AADD. Part of the rationale for the double name was that many members worked with people with pervasive developmental disorders, most of whom are not mentally retarded.

In the UK, "mental handicap" had become the common medical term, replacing "mental subnormality" in Scotland and "mental deficiency" in England and Wales, until Stephen Dorrell, Secretary of State for Health for the United Kingdom from 1995-7, changed the NHS's designation to "learning disability." The new term is not yet widely understood, and is often taken to refer to problems affecting schoolwork (the American usage): which are known in the UK as "learning difficulties." British social workers may use "learning difficulty" to refer to both people with MR and those with conditions such as dyslexia.

In England and Wales between 1983 and 2008 the Mental Health Act 1983 defined "mental impairment" and "severe mental impairment" as "a state of arrested or incomplete development of mind which includes significant/severe impairment of intelligence and social functioning and is associated with abnormally aggressive or seriously irresponsible conduct on the part of the person concerned." As behavior was involved, these were not necessarily permanent conditions: they were defined for the purpose of authorising detention in hospital or guardianship. The term Mental Impairment was removed from the Act in November 2008, but the grounds for detention remained. However, English statute law uses "mental impairment" elsewhere in a less well-defined manner—*e.g.* to allow exemption from taxes—implying that mental retardation without any behavioural problems is what is meant.

Visual Impairment

Visual impairment or **vision impairment** is vision loss (of a person) having reduced vision as to constitute a handicap that constitutes a significant limitation of visual capability resulting from disease, trauma, or a congenital or degenerative condition that cannot be corrected by conventional means, including refractive correction, medication, or surgery. This functional loss of vision is typically defined to manifest with

1. best corrected visual acuity of less than 20/60, or significant central field defect,
2. significant peripheral field defect including homonymous or heteronymous bilateral visual, field defect or generalized contraction or constriction of field, or
3. reduced peak contrast sensitivity either of the above conditions.

In the U.S., the terms partially sighted, low vision, legally blind, and totally blind are used in the educational context to describe students with visual impairments. They are defined as follows:

1. *Partially sighted* indicates some type of visual problem, with a need of person to receive special education in some cases;
2. *Low vision* generally refers to a severe visual impairment, not necessarily limited to distance vision. Low vision applies to all individuals with sight who are unable to read the newspaper at a normal viewing distance, even with the aid of eyeglasses or contact lenses. They use a combination of vision and other senses to learn, although they may require adaptations in lighting or the size of print, and, sometimes, braille;
   1. *Myopic*-unable to see distant objects clearly, commonly called near-sighted or short-sighted
   2. *Hyperopic*-unable to see close objects clearly, commonly called far-sighted or long-sighted
   3. *Legally blind* indicates that a person has less than 20/200 vision in the better eye after best correction (contact lenses or glasses), or a field of vision of less than 20 degrees in the better eye; and
   4. *Totally blind* students learn via braille or other non-visual media.

Visual impairment is the consequence of a functional loss of vision, rather than the eye disorder itself. Eye disorders which can lead to visual impairments can include retinal degeneration, albinism, cataracts, glaucoma, muscular problems that result in visual disturbances, corneal disorders, diabetic retinopathy, congenital disorders, and infection." Visual impairment can also be caused by brain and nerve disorders, in which case it is usually termed cortical visual impairment (CVI).

The American Medical Association's *Guides to the Evaluation of Permanent Impairment* attempts to provide "a standardized, objective approach to evaluating medical impairments." The Visual System chapter "provides criteria for evaluating permanent impairment of the visual system as it affects an individual's ability to perform activities of daily living." The *Guide* has estimated that the loss of one eye equals 25% impairment of the visual system and 24% impairment of the whole person; total loss of vision in both eyes is considered to be 100% visual impairment and 85% impairment of the whole person.

Visual impairments have considerable economic impact on even developed countries.

Visual impairment is one of the potential dangers of ultraviolet germicidal irradiation.

A Day with The Deaf and Dumb

My new year eve celebration was different. I went to a school to attend a cultural programme. Kids danced, performed a skit and did some mono action. The programme commenced with a group of tiny and not so tiny tots paying homage to the nation by enacting A.R. Rahman's immortal composition Vande Mataram. This was followed by a couple of break dance performances to the foot tapping tunes of Hindi film chartbusters. A delightful skit showing the antics of a tough *saas* (mother-in-law) and her docile *bahu* (daughter-in-law) had the audience clapping for an encore. A tribute to Indian mythology was paid by kids as they acted out the legend of Radha and Krishna. The programme ended with a drama where the children presented slices from the life of the cave man.

Now you may well wonder what is so special about children acting and dancing? Well these children are no ordinary kids. They are special, really special. They cannot speak and they cannot hear. They are the students of a small, neglected school in Bhubaneswar : the Sriharsa Mishra Memorial Sisuvidyalaya for the Deaf and Dumb. The school with 183 students is run from five rented buildings since it doesn't have a building of its own. It is managed on a paltry government grant and the little ones struggle for the bare necessities of life.

As I watched them dance in perfect rhythm with the music and act like veteran stage artists even though they cannot hear or speak a syllable, I was amazed at their talent, confidence and commitment. I was told that many of these kids are also terrific at drawing and painting and also do well in academics. Another thing which impressed me was their sense of camaraderie. The pride on their faces as they watched their friends being applauded was, to say the least touching. Many of them came up to me pushing their class mates and through gestures explaining his or her talent. Tell me do you share this kind of bonding, with your friends?

Eleven year old Ankita who too witnessed the show had this to say, " People like us treat them with pity. They don't need that. They need to be treated like equals. In fact we have a lot to learn from them. They are hardworking and confident and most important they don't feel sorry for themselves." Touche!

Juvenile Delinquency

Juvenile delinquency refers to criminal acts performed by juveniles. Most legal systems prescribe specific procedures for dealing with juveniles, such as juvenile detention centers. There are a multitude of different theories on the causes of crime, most if not all of which can be applied to the causes of youth crime. Youth crime is an aspect of crime which receives great attention from the news media and politicians. Crime committed by young people has risen since the mid-twentieth century, as has most types of crime. The level and types of youth crime can be used by commentators as an indicator of the general state of morality and law and order in a country, and consequently youth crime can be the source of 'moral panics' Theories on the causes of youth crime can be viewed as particularly important within criminology. This is firstly because crime is committed disproportionately by those aged between fifteen and twenty-five. Secondly, by definition any theories on the causes of crime will focus on youth crime, as adult criminals will have likely started offending when they were young. A Juvenile Delinquent is one who repeatedly commits crime, however these juvenile delinquents could most likely have mental disorders/behavioral issues such as schizophrenia, post traumatic stress disorder or bipolar disorder.

Theoretical Perspectives on Juvenile Delinquency

Rational Choice Theory: Classical criminology stresses that causes of crime lie within the individual offender, rather than in their external environment. For classicists, offenders are motivated by rational self-interest, and the importance of free will and personal responsibility is emphasised. Rational choice theory is the clearest example of this approach. It states that people weigh the pros and cons of committing a crime, and offend when the former outweigh the latter. A central deficiency of rational choice theory is that while it may explain when and where people commit crime, it can't explain very well why people choose to commit crimes in the first place. Neither can it explain differences between individuals and groups in their propensity to commit crimes. James Q. Wilson said the conscience and self-control of a potential young offender must be taken into account, and that these attributes are formed by parental and societal conditioning. Rational choice does not explain why crime should be committed disproportionately by young people, males, city dwellers, and the poor. (Walklate: 2003 p.2) It also ignores the influence a young choice theory does not take into account the proven correlations between certain social circumstances and individuals' personalities, and the propensity to commit crime.

Social Disorganization Theory

Current positivist approaches generally focus on the Culture, which would produce the breakdown of family relationships and community, competing values, and increasing Individualism.

Studies also show only 16 in every 100 kids will do something bad opposed to adult 26 in 100 will do something bad or illegal.

Strain Theory

Strain Theory is associated mainly with the work of Robert Merton. He felt that there are institutionalized paths to success in society. Strain theory holds that crime is caused by the difficulty those in poverty have in achieving socially valued goals by legitimate means. As those with, for instance, poor educational attainment have difficulty achieving wealth and status by securing well paid employment, they are more likely to use criminal means to obtain these goals. Merton's suggests five adaptations to this dilemma:

1. *Innovation*: individuals who accept socially approved goals, but not necessarily the socially approved means.
2. *Retreatism*: those who reject socially approved goals and the means for acquiring them.
3. *Ritualism*: those who buy into a system of socially approved means, but lose sight of the goals. Merton believed that drug users are in this category.
4. *Conformity*: those who conform to the system's means and goals.
5. *Rebellion*: people who negate socially approved goals and means by creating a new system of acceptable goals and means.

A difficulty with strain theory is that it does not explore why children of low-income families would have poor educational attainment in the first place. More importantly is the fact that much youth crime does not have an economic motivation. Strain theory fails to explain violent crime, the type of youth crime which causes most anxiety to the public.

Subcultural Theory

Related to strain theory is subcultural theory. The inability of youths to achieve socially valued status and goals results in groups of young people forming deviant or delinquent subcultures, which have their own values and norms. (Eadie & Morley: 2003 p.552) Within these groups criminal behaviour may actually be valued, and increase a youth's status. (Walklate: 2003 p.22) The notion of delinquent subcultures is relevant for crimes that are not economically motivated. Male gang members could be argued to have their own values, such as respect for fighting ability and daring. However it is not clear how different this makes them from 'ordinary' non-lawbreaking young men. Furthermore there is no explanation of why people unable to achieve socially valued goals should necessarily choose criminal substitutes.

Subcultural theories have been criticised for making too sharp a distinction between what is deviant and what is 'normal'. (Brown: 1998 p.23) There are also doubts about whether young people consciously reject mainstream values. (Brown: 1998 p.23)

Differential Association

The theory of Differential association also deals with young people in a group context, and looks at how peer pressure and the existence of gangs could lead them into crime. It suggests young people are motivated to commit crimes by delinquent peers, and learn criminal skills from them. The diminished influence of peers after men marry has also been cited as a factor in desisting from offending. There is strong evidence that young people with criminal friends are more likely to commit crimes themselves. However it may be the case that offenders prefer to associate with one another, rather than delinquent peers causing someone to start offending. Furthermore there is the question of how the delinquent peer group became delinquent initially.

Labeling Theory

Labeling theory states that once young people have been labeled as criminal they are more likely to offend. (Eadie & Morley: 2003 p.552) The idea is that once labelled as deviant a young person may accept that role, and be more likely to associate with others who have been similarly labelled. (Eadie & Morley: 2003 p.552) Labelling theorists say that male children from poor families are more likely to be labelled deviant, and that this may partially explain why there are more lower-class young male offenders. (Walklate: 2003 p. 24)

Juvenile Delinquency as a Male Phenomenon

Youth crime is disproportionately committed by young men. Feminist theorists and others have examined why this is the case. (Eadie & Morley: 2003 p.553) One suggestion is that ideas of masculinity may make young men more likely to offend. Being tough, powerful, aggressive, daring and competitive may be a way of young men expressing their masculinity. (Brown: 1998 p.109) Acting out these ideals may make young men more likely to engage in antisocial and criminal behaviour. (Walklate: 2003 p. 83) Alternatively, rather than young men acting as they do because of societal pressure to conform to masculine ideals; young men may actually be naturally more aggressive, daring etc.

As well as biological or psychological factors, the way young men are treated by their parents may make them more susceptible to offending. (Walklate: 2003 p. 35) According to a study led by Florida State University criminologist Kevin M. Beaver, adolescent males who possess a certain type of variation in a specific gene are more likely to flock to delinquent peers. The study, which appears in the September 2008 issue of the Journal of Genetic Psychology, is the first to establish a statistically significant association between an affinity for antisocial peer groups and a particular variation (called the 10-repeat allele) of the dopamine transporter gene (DAT).

Risk Factors

Individual Risk Factors: Individual psychological or behavioural risk factors that may make offending more likely include intelligence, impulsiveness or the inability to delay gratification, aggression, empathy, and restlessness. (Farrington: 2002) Children with low intelligence are likely to do worse in school. This may increase the chances of offending because low educational attainment, a low attachment to school, and low educational aspirations are all risk factors for offending in themselves. (Walklate: 2003 p. 2) Children who perform poorly at school are also more likely to truant, which is also linked to offending. (Farrington: 2002 p.682) If strain theory or subcultural theory are valid poor educational attainment could lead to crime as children were unable to attain wealth and status legally. However it must be born in mind that defining and measuring intelligence is troublesome. Young males are especially likely to be impulsive which could mean they disregard the long-term consequences of their actions, have a lack of self-control, and are unable to postpone immediate gratification. This may explain why they disproportionately offend. (Farrington: 2002 p.682) (Walklate: 2003 p. 36) Impulsiveness is seen by some as the key aspect of a child's personality that predicts offending. (Farrington: 2002 p.682) However is not clear whether these aspects of personality are a result of "deficits in the executive functions of the brain", (Farrington: 2002 p.667) or a result of parental influences or other social factors. (Graham & Bowling: 1995 p.32)

Family Environment

Family factors which may have an influence on offending include; the level of parental supervision, the way parents discipline a child, parental conflict or separation, criminal parents or siblings, parental abuse or neglect, and the quality of the parent-child relationship (Graham & Bowling: 1995 p.33) Children brought up by lone parents are more likely to start offending than those who live with two natural parents, however once the attachment a child feels towards their parent(s) and the level of parental supervision are taken into account, children in single parent families are no more likely to offend then others. (Graham & Bowling: 1995 p.35) Conflict between a child's parents is also much more closely linked to offending than being raised by a lone parent. (Walklate: 2003 p. 106) If a child has low parental supervision they are much more likely to offend. (Graham & Bowling: 1995) Many studies have found a strong correlation between a lack of supervision and offending, and it appears to be the most important family influence on offending. (Farrington: 2002 p.610) (Graham & Bowling: 1995 p.38) When parents commonly do not know where their children are, what their activities are, or who their friends are, children are more likely to truant from school and have delinquent friends, each of which are linked to offending. (Graham & Bowling: 1995 p.45,46) A lack of supervision is connected to poor relationships between children and parents, as children who are often in conflict with their parents may be less willing to discuss their activities with them. (Graham & Bowling: 1995 p.37) Children with a weak attachment to their parents are more likely to offend. (Graham & Bowling: 1995 p.37)

Delinquency Prevention

Delinquency Prevention is the broad term for all efforts aimed at preventing youth from becoming involved in criminal, or other antisocial, activity. Increasingly, governments are recognizing the importance of allocating resources for the prevention of delinquency. Because it is often difficult for states to provide the fiscal resources necessary for good prevention, organizations, communities, and governments are working more in collaboration with each other to prevent juvenile delinquency.

With the development of delinquency in youth being influenced by numerous factors, prevention efforts are comprehensive in scope. Prevention services include activities such as substance abuse education and treatment, family counseling, youth mentoring, parenting education, educational support, and youth sheltering.

Bibliography

Altbach, Philip G. and Gail Kelly : *New Approaches to Comparative Education,* Chicago, The University of Chicago Press, 1986.

Anthony, K.: *Technology in counseling and psychotherapy: A practitioner's guide,* Houndmills:Palgrave Macmillan, 2003.

Bender, S. J., and G. S. Smith: *Teaching Archaeology in the Twenty-First Century,* Society for American Archaeology, Washington, D.C., 2000.

Bentley, T. : *Learning beyond the Classroom: Education for a Changing World*, London, Routledge. 1998.

Bloom, J. W., & Walz, G. R.: *Cybercounseling and cyberlearning: Strategies and resources for the millennium,* Alexandria, VA: American Counseling Association, 2000.

Boer, P. M.: *Career counseling over the Internet: An emerging model for trusting and responding to online clients,* Mahwah, NJ: Lawrence Erlbaum Associates, 2001.

Carl R. Rogers: *Client-Centered Therapy: Its Current Practice, Implications and Theory*, Boston, Houghton Mifflin, 1965.

Carr, W. & Kemmis, S. : *Becoming Critical: Education, Knowledge and Counselling*, London, Falmer, 1986.

Castelnuovo, G., Gaggioli, A., & Riva, G.: *Towards CyberPsychology: Mind, cognition and society in the Internet age,* Amsterdam: IOS Press, 2004.

Chechele, P. J., & Stofle, G.: *Technology in counseling and psychotherapy: A practitioner's guide*, Houndmills, UK: Palgrave Macmillan, 2004.

Chumbow, B.S. : *The Place of Mother Tongue in the National Policy of Educational Guidance,* Port Harcourt, Nigeria, 1990.

Davis, M. E.: *How Students Understand the Past: From Theory to Practice,* Altamira Press, Walnut Creek, California, 2005.

Donaldson, Gordon A. : *Cultivating Leadership in Schools*, New York, College Press, 2001.

Elliott, J. : *Action Research for Educational Counselling*, Milton Keynes, Open University, 1991.

Evers, C. & Lakomski, G. : *Knowing Educational Guidance*, Oxford, Pergamon, 1991.

Furth, H.G. : *The World of Grown-ups: Children's Conceptions of Society,* New York, Elsevier North Holland, 1980.

Galbraith, M.W. : *Education Through Community Organizations*, San Francisco, Jossey-Bass, 1990.

George Brown & Madeleine Atkins: *Effective Teaching in Higher Education*, London, Routledge, 1991.

George, J.: *Taking issue: Debates in guidance and counselling in learning*, London: Routledge/Open University, 1998.

Gibson, R. : *Critical Theory and Education*, London, Hodder & Stoughton, 1986.

Giroux, H. : *Critical Theory and Educational Practice*, Geelong, Australia, Deakin University, 1983.

Goodlad, John I. : *Educational Renewal: Better Teachers, Better Schools*, San Francisco, Jossey-Bass, 1994.

Grace, G. : *School Leadership: Beyond Educational Management*, London, Falmer, 1995.

Grohol, J. M.: *Psychology and the Internet, intrapersonal, interpersonal, and transpersonal implications,* San Diego: Academic Press, 1998.

Harris-Bowlsbey, J., Riley Dikel, M., & Sampson, J. P., Jr.: *The Internet: A tool for career planning.* Tulsa, OK: National Career Development Association, 2002.

Jameson, J. H. : *Presenting Archaeology to the Public: Digging for Truths,* Altamira Press, Walnut Creek, California, 1997.

Jayasuriya, J.E. *Education in Korea: A Third World Success Story*, Colombo, Associated Educational Publishers, 1980.

Jeffs, T. and Smith, M. : *Using Informal Education*, Milton Keynes, Open University Press, 1990.

Jones, P. W.: *Cybercounseling and cyberlearning: An encore*, Greensboro, NC: CAPS Press, 2004.

Kakar, Sudhir : *The Inner World: A Psychoanalytic Study of Childhood and Society in India*, New Delhi, Oxford University Press, 1978.

Kennedy, K.J. : *Citizenship Education and the Modern State*, Washington, D.C: Falmer Press, 1997.

Koning, K. de and Martin, M. : *Participatory Research in Health: Issues and Experiences*, London, Zed Books, 1996.

Kottack, C. P., J. J. White, R. H. Furlow, and P. C. White: *The Teaching of Anthropology: Problems, Issues, & Decisions*, Mayfield Publishing, Mountain View, California, 1996.

Leone Burton : *Gender and Mathematics: An International Perspective,* Norwich, Cassell Educational Limited, 1990.

McConnell, C. : *Community Education: The Making of an Empowering Profession*, Edinburgh, Scottish Community Education Council, 1996.

McGinn, Noel F. : *Education and Development in Korea*, Cambridge, Harvard University Press, 1980.

McGivney, V. : *Informal Learning in the Community, A Trigger for Change and Development*, Leicester, NIACE, 1999.

Nuna, S.C. : *Education and Development*, NIEPA, New Delhi, 1987.

Nurullah, S. and J.P. Naik : *A Students History of Education in India,* New Delhi, Macmillan, 1974.

Okech, J.G.; Asiachi, A.J. : *Curriculum Development for Schools*, Nairobi, Educational Research Publications, 1992.

Poster, C. and Kruger, A. : *Community Education in the Western World*, London, Routledge, 1990.

Potter D. : *Information Technology and Higher Education: A Twenty Year View*, Unpublished Paper, 1996.

Premi, M.K. : *Educational Planning in India*, New Delhi, Sterling, 1972.

Reimer, E. : *School is Dead, An Essay on Alternatives in Education*, Harmondsworth, Penguin, 1971.

Rosenfield, M.: *Counselling by telephone*, London, Sage, 1997.

Scott, C. : *Social Education*, Boston, Ginn and Co., 1908.

Seth, Michael J. : *Education Fever: Society, Politics, and the Pursuit of Schooling in South Korea*, Honolulu, University of Hawai Press, 2002.

Simkins, T. : *Non-formal Education and Development*, Manchester, Manchester University, 1977.

Smith, M.K. : *Local Education, Community, Conversation, Action*, Buckingham, Open University Press, 1994.

Starratt, R.J. : *Centering Educational Administration: Cultivating Meaning, Community and Responsibility*, Mahwah, Lawrence Earlbaum, 2003.

Stenhouse, L. : *Authority, Education and Emancipation*, London, Heinemann, 1983.

Taylor, C. : *Multiculturalism: Examining the Politics of Recognition*, Princeton, Princeton University Press, 1994.

Thomas, A. : *Educating Children at Home*, London, Cassell, 1998.

Thrupp, J. & Willmott. : *Educational Management in Managerialist Times: Beyond the Textual Apologists*, Maidenhead, UK, 2003.

Tsurumi, E. Patricia : *Colonial Education in Korea and Taiwan*, Princeton, Princeton University Press, 1984.

Walz, G. R.:. *Cybercounseling and cyberlearning: An encore*, Greensboro, NC: CAPS Press, 2004.

Warner D. and Palfreyman D. : *Higher Education Management: The Key Elements*, London, The Society for Research into Higher Education and Open University Press, 1996.

Wiggins, Grant : *Educative Assessment: Designing Assessments to inform and Improve Student Performance*, San Francisco, Jossey-Bass, 1998.

Wootton, R., Yellowlees, P., & McLauren, P.: *Telepsychiatry and e-mental health,* London, Royal Society of Medicine Press, 2003.

Yeaxlee, B. : *Lifelong Education, A Sketch of the Range and Significance of the Adult Education Movement*, London, Cassell and Company, 1929.

Index

A

Achievement, 13, 20, 24, 43, 45, 46, 47, 60, 61, 63, 64, 65, 66, 67, 71, 90, 93, 115, 118, 124, 155, 166, 175, 176, 177, 191, 192, 211, 244, 245, 246, 247, 248.
Administration, 45, 87, 106, 109, 156, 173, 175, 211, 217.
Adolescence, 66, 111, 119, 121, 124, 216, 218, 219, 228, 247.
Approaches, 26, 33, 36, 78, 108, 124, 171, 178, 179, 181, 198, 215, 216, 217, 218, 276.
Aptitude Test, 109, 155, 177.

C

Campaign, 174.
Central Government, 51.
Civic Responsibility, 121.
Commission, 222, 223, 259.
Community, 5, 21, 23, 33, 41, 50, 51, 53, 60, 70, 79, 102, 103, 154, 164, 197, 203, 212, 213, 214, 218, 219, 220, 224, 225, 226, 231, 237, 242, 256, 257, 258, 260, 261, 271, 276.
Conditions, 2, 9, 12, 22, 41, 54, 81, 101, 107, 150, 229, 249, 250, 281.
Conflict Management, 83, 206.
Conflict Resolution, 202.
Constitution, 103, 171.
Contribution, 51, 197, 228, 257.
Culture, 39, 51, 73, 77, 116, 173, 176, 207, 212, 217, 219, 276.

D

Democracy, 270.
Developmental Tasks, 118, 119, 120, 121, 123, 124.
Developments, 59, 127, 156, 263.
Dimensions, 13, 156, 178, 201, 239.
Distance Education, 46.
Distribution, 44, 173, 264.

E

Educational Guidance, 19, 20, 221.
Educational Management, 45.
Educational Planning, 113.
Educational Technology, 45.
Emotional Development, 150.
Emotional Intelligence, 176.
Emotions, 35, 72, 75, 124, 156, 206, 207, 208.

Evaluation, 18, 21, 43, 44, 45, 46, 52, 69, 111, 180, 181, 196, 242, 243, 250, 274.

F

Family Environment, 49, 280.
Freedom, 9, 118.
Frustration, 168, 199, 200, 201, 202, 207.

G

Globalization, 49.
Government, 42, 51, 52, 59, 62, 103, 104, 189, 222, 262, 275.
Group Counselling, 83, 94.
Group Guidance, 83, 85, 86, 87, 90, 257, 268.

H

Health Education, 228.
Human Rights, 73.

I

Information Technology, 17, 30.
Innovation, 18, 19, 54, 166, 277.
Institutions, 20, 41, 61, 95, 121, 123, 155, 237, 239, 241, 253, 255, 261.
Intellegence Tests, 175.
Intelligence, 3, 15, 16, 41, 156, 175, 176, 177, 183, 193, 264, 265, 270, 272, 279, 280.

J

John Dewey, 41.
John Holland, 115.
Justice, 48, 59.
Juvenile Delinquency, 275, 276, 279, 281.

L

Languages, 48.
Laws, 15, 68, 249.
Leadership, 61, 65, 69, 97, 108, 111, 170, 174, 175, 196, 211, 217, 221, 243, 246, 250, 264.
Learning Environment, 18, 192.
Learning Experiences, 18, 212, 215, 221.
Learning Process, 46, 221.

M

Mahatma Gandhi, 168.
Maintenance, 122, 141.
Management, 30, 45, 57, 64, 65, 83, 86, 88, 117, 165, 182, 198, 206, 221, 224, 226, 227, 229, 236, 238, 239, 245, 246, 260.
Management Skills, 221, 227, 238, 260.
Maturation, 5, 47, 118, 149.
Measurement, 172, 188, 189, 192, 265, 269.
Mental Health, 47, 48, 49, 50, 51, 52, 53, 54, 78, 161, 182, 197, 198, 199, 200, 272.
Moral Development, 58, 150.

N

Nonviolence, 205.
Nutrition, 198.

O

Observation, 107, 142, 156, 158, 159, 160, 161, 162, 163, 190.

Occupational Information, 106, 113, 257.
Opportunity, 7, 8, 27, 31, 57, 61, 65, 66, 67, 71, 73, 87, 90, 93, 95, 97, 99, 106, 112, 113, 114, 128, 155, 158, 160, 166, 171, 231, 235, 238, 240, 246, 247, 248.

P

Personal Guidance, 23, 254.
Philosophy, 2, 3, 19, 44, 65, 100, 211, 212, 219, 242, 245, 267.
Planning Guidance, 224.
Preservation, 151.
Primary Education, 54, 56, 153, 155.
Professional Developments, 59.
Projects, 18, 62, 85, 210, 256.
Promotion, 200, 241, 258, 281.
Protection, 51, 80.
Provisions, 42, 269, 270.

R

Relationship, 4, 5, 6, 10, 12, 24, 27, 28, 36, 37, 72, 73, 75, 77, 78, 79, 80, 86, 90, 128, 129, 131, 133, 134, 135, 136, 137, 138, 140, 141, 145, 147, 148, 149, 150, 151, 154, 155, 181, 184, 204, 207, 208, 280.
Religions, 48.
Research, 18, 43, 44, 46, 59, 60, 61, 62, 65, 66, 68, 69, 74, 105, 106, 108, 109, 118, 170, 174, 179, 180, 181, 183, 184, 189, 190, 194, 215, 217, 220, 238, 241, 246, 247, 249, 250.

S

Secondary Education, 20, 54, 67, 248.
Social Development, 63, 161, 211, 212, 221, 242, 244.
Social Justice, 48, 59.
Society, 1, 4, 93, 116, 118, 119, 155, 170, 171, 204, 223, 230, 232, 259, 264, 277.
Sociometry, 169, 170, 171.
Staff Development, 211, 219, 220, 268.
Supervision, 6, 69, 250, 280.

T

Technology, 17, 18, 30, 45, 50, 116, 166, 215, 216.
Terrorism, 209.
Tolerance, 173, 197.
Tradition, 5, 10, 12, 119, 230.

U

University, 29, 34, 43, 44, 45, 46, 60, 61, 88, 102, 165, 166, 167, 181, 183, 194, 279.

V

Violence, 53, 205.
Vocational Guidance, 19, 21, 41, 42, 58, 59.

W

Welfare, 189, 252, 257.

□□□